Praise for *Taming the /*

'A clear, actionable guide for safer and more ethical AI.' JAAN TALLINN, CO-FOUNDER, THE CENTRE FOR STUDY OF EXISTENTIAL RISK

'A great resource for anyone who wants to understand AI and use it humanely.' STEVE OMOHUNDRO, FOUNDER AND CEO, BENEFICIAL AI RESEARCH

'Nell Watson has written a magisterial work on AI risk, including AI's encoded human warts, its relentlessly algorithmic amorality, and our inadequate means of taming it. A complete and compelling work.' MAX BORDERS, AUTHOR AND CO-FOUNDER, FUTURE FRONTIERS

'In this sweeping overview of the potential promises and perils of AI, Nell Watson masterfully combines a detailed understanding of the underlying technology with the approaches beingused to develop AI capabilities.' JONATHAN LEIGHTON, ETHICS STRATEGIST AND AUTHOR

Taming the Machine

Ethically harness the power of AI

Nell Watson

KoganPage

Publisher's note
Every possible effort has been made to ensure that the information contained in this book is accurate at the time of going to press, and the publishers and author cannot accept responsibility for any errors or omissions, however caused. No responsibility for loss or damage occasioned to any person acting, or refraining from action, as a result of the material in this publication can be accepted by the editor, the publisher or the author.

First published in Great Britain and the United States in 2024 by Kogan Page Limited

2nd Floor, 45 Gee Street
London
EC1V 3RS
United Kingdom

8 W 38th Street, Suite 902
New York, NY 10018
USA

www.koganpage.com

Kogan Page books are printed on paper from sustainable forests.

ISBNs
Hardback   978 1 3986 1434 5
Paperback   978 1 3986 1432 1
Ebook   978 1 3986 1433 8

British Library Cataloguing-in-Publication Data
A CIP record for this book is available from the British Library.

Library of Congress Cataloging-in-Publication Data
Names: Watson, Nell, author.
Title: Taming the machine : ethically harness the power of AI / Nell Watson.
Description: 1 edition. | New York, NY : Kogan Page Inc, [2024] | Includes bibliographical references and index.
Identifiers: LCCN 2024006372 (print) | LCCN 2024006373 (ebook) | ISBN 9781398614321 (paperback) | ISBN 9781398614345 (hardback) | ISBN 9781398614338 (ebook)
Subjects: LCSH: Information society–Social aspects. | Artificial intelligence–Moral and ethical aspects. | Artificial intelligence–Social aspects.
Classification: LCC HM851 .W387 2024 (print) | LCC HM851 (ebook) | DDC 303.48/33–dc23/eng/20240307
LC record available at https://lccn.loc.gov/2024006372
LC ebook record available at https://lccn.loc.gov/2024006373

Typeset by Integra Software Services, Pondicherry
Print production managed by Jellyfish
Printed and bound by CPI Group (UK) Ltd, Croydon, CR0 4YY

Dedicated to my parents, whose carefully curated infusion of values lovingly bootstrapped my nascent neural network.

Contents

Acknowledgements

This book would not have been possible without a long list of people who have championed this project in various important ways.

First and foremost, thanks to my family. Their patience and steadfast moral support made a tremendous difference during a trying period where my attention was in scarce supply by necessity.

I owe a heartfelt thank you to Eric Herboso, whose extremely skilful and insightful interviews over several months were instrumental in constructing this book. These conversations formed the basis of the first draft of a significant portion of this work. Eric not only curated our discussions but also opened up intriguing new lines of inquiry and observations about the subject matter. Thank you from the bottom of my heart, Eric.

Special thanks go to Kian Gohar for invaluable assistance in getting the book out to the public and for fantastic introductions to luminaries within the literary world. Kian, you made this process much less gruelling. Thank you!

I extend my sincerest thanks to Matt James and the team at Kogan Page for their patience and understanding with my occasionally unorthodox approaches that stepped away from the defined formula. They helped co-craft this work for maximum impact among an audience eager for knowledge in this field.

Matt James also provided skilful edits to the manuscript, alongside extensive advice and support from Nathan Hassall, as well as Jennifer Eaton, Jonathan Leighton and Louisa Jordan. I was very lucky to also gain very valuable peer review contributions from Ali Hessami, Gerlinde Weger, Trish Shaw, Lukas Petersson and Martin Rutte. The enticing cover illustration was crafted by Oscar Spigolon.

I received incredible advice and support from Tom Gray, Adrian Johnston, Clare Burgoyne and Nigel McAlpine which enabled me to create the associated animated short, thereby introducing this book to a broader audience. The financial backing of Jaan Tallinn and co at Survival & Flourishing Fund made this possible. Massive thanks to Joel Simon and the team at Hola Lola for lovingly giving life to this highly engaging and humorous short.

I must also express gratitude to Jaan Tallinn, Adam Alonzi, Alexander Kruel, Alfie Rustom, Anders Sandberg, Andrew Critch, Anand Murthy, Anne Watson, Benjamin Bilksi, Benjamin Sturgeon, Björn Korneli, Charles Line, Colin Sprake, Damjan Cvetkov-Dimitrov, Dan Faggella, Dan Hendrycks, David Luxton, Dawa Tarchin Phillips, Eliezer Yudkowsky, Geoffrey Hinton, Helen McCann, Jack Canfield, Jack Clark, John Havens, Jon Barr, Jonathan Leighton, Joshua Zader, Kirsty Maynor, Kristel van den Bergh, Kunal Sood, Linda Linsefors, Lindsay Lemmer, LuAnn Buechler, Luke Muelhauser, Mantas Mazeika, Mark McKergow, Max Borders, Max Tegmark, Michael Michalchik, Mildred McIlwaine, Nevan Hanumara, Nicholas Gogerty, Patricia Shaw, Patrizia Tucci, Pawel Pachniewski, Petra McCann, Raffaele Jacovelli, Raymond de Lacaze, Remmelt Ellen, Rich Dalton, Robin Hanson, Roko Mijic, Roman Yampolskiy, Ronald Watson, Sarah-Jane Botham, Shujun Zhang, Simona Popa, Skinner Layne, Steve Omohundro, Steven Stutts, Stuart Russell, Thiago Viana, Thijs Pepping, Thomas Woodside, Tom Symons, Vector Newman, Victoria Krakovna, Vlastimil Vohánka, Wendell Wallach, William Cooke, Yoshua Bengio, the folks at *Mindplex Magazine*, Corin Ism and Marcus, and Singularity University and many, many others for sharing various insights, influences and opportunities that have shaped this work, or championed the creative spirit which brought it forth. You all know who you are, and I am eternally grateful.

Introduction

Building advanced AI is like launching a rocket. The first challenge is to maximize acceleration, but once it starts picking up speed, you also need to focus on steering. JAAN TALLINN

AI is continuously transforming our world, unfurling capabilities with unprecedented accessibility and flexibility. With nothing more than simple words, we can tap into an incredible variety of services of an ever-improving quality. Today's adaptable AI models enable robots and systems to respond seamlessly to human commands across various real-world applications. Agent-based models are able to think step by step, to collaborate with other versions of themselves, and even to form AI communities. We are at a pivotal 'Sputnik moment', set to reshape global society and economies through AI's transformative power.

The global struggle to tame AI

With the profound scope of AI's impact becoming hard to ignore, public concerns have intensified. Machines can lock us out of opportunities based on arbitrary criteria we cannot challenge, seduce us into virtual relationships, and spy on us to serve uncertain, and potentially dangerous, ends.

The AI can of worms increases the vulnerability of individuals and societies to new methods of conflict, such as drones and demoralization techniques. Cybersecurity vulnerabilities and social engineering techniques present a serious threat to social trust and wellbeing. Influencing vast audiences has never been so easy, with convincing propaganda surgically targeted to specific individuals, timed for maximum impact.

The paramount question of AI isn't whether we can do something with it, but whether we should even dare to use it at all. There are many pitfalls and potential scandals to avoid when implementing AI technologies. Which business cases actually need AI, and who can produce value from it worthy of the increased challenges and risk?

Fundamentally, the actions of a system must align with human needs, not the needs of the system. The years to come will herald an increasingly desperate struggle to teach machines to recognize, acknowledge and respect our values, before we fall into their all-encompassing grasp.

It's therefore necessary to take stock of where the recent developments have taken us, and to deliberately choose where we want to go from here, instead of simply allowing things to happen. A responsible future of AI requires vision, foresight and courageous leadership that upholds ethical integrity, even when tempted to act otherwise. Such ethical conduct fosters trust, and trust is the linchpin that holds our social structures together, and builds branding power.

Why taming the machine

At the heart of this book is a warning: don't get cut by the bleeding edge. AI can grant our initial wishes, but with unexpected and unintended outcomes. Similar to air travel in the 1950s, Generative AI is an exciting new technology with a high likelihood of tragedy. It will take time to develop and implement good rules to prevent catastrophic outcomes.

Those who rush to leverage AI's power without adequate preparation face difficult blowback, scandals and harsh regulatory measures. However, it's equally important not to get caught in a trough of disillusionment. Over time, we will overcome many of these challenges, and those who have a balanced, informed view on the short-term risks and long-term benefits of AI will succeed. With care and knowledge, avoiding either complacent optimism or defeatist pessimism, we can effectively harness AI's potential.

This book serves as a guide for that process, providing a comprehensive overview of the challenges and opportunities of safer and more robust AI systems. To accommodate this, some chapters run in an overarching theme, such as Chapter 6, Responsible AI governance, broken down into subcomponents such as transparency.

The first half of this book demystifies the jargon and describes a range of tools and methods one can apply in the realm of AI and ethics. You will find a handy glossary at the end of the book to guide you through the terminology.

The second half delves further into AI safety, and the management philosophy necessary for responding to increasingly capable and goal-oriented agentic AI systems. Generally, conversations about AI greatly focus on one domain to the detriment of others, probably because few people have a strong awareness of both, and perhaps different types of brain tend to be attracted to one or the other. In my view, that needs to change. AI safety is a particularly complex topic, far less intuitive than ethics, but I have worked to boil it down to being as accessible as possible.

Only by understanding both the short-term familiar issues of AI, along with the longer-term implications of extremely powerful goal-oriented AI systems, can we gain the full picture of AI's growing impact upon us all.

Humanity has, in the past, successfully negotiated nuclear test ban treaties, ozone layer and acid rain treaties, and dampened age-old conflicts, such as in Northern Ireland. Perhaps we can obtain similar wins with the governance of responsible AI, with grassroots support, good faith and global participation. By choosing this book, you've taken an important step in this journey. Armed with this knowledge, you can enlighten others as you steadfastly guide humanity's journey with AI in a preferable direction.

With people like you interested in addressing these challenges, the future seems a little bit brighter.

CHAPTER ONE

History and roadmap of AI

As leaders, it is incumbent on all of us to make
sure we are building a world in which every individual
has an opportunity to thrive. Understanding what
AI can do and how it fits into your strategy is the beginning,
not the end, of that process. ANDREW NG

The trajectory of AI development has undergone distinct phases: linear progress from the 1960s and 2010 to exponential growth in the 2010s. From the 2020s onwards, we are experiencing 'compounding exponential' growth, characterized by acceleration at an ever-increasing rate. This rapid pace has made it difficult to fully grasp the scale and impact of such developments, even for experts in the field. This chapter outlines the path of AI developments over time.

Clarifying key concepts

Artificial intelligence (AI) is a branch of computer science dedicated to developing machines that can perform tasks that traditionally require human cognitive functions. This includes learning, natural language understanding and various forms of reasoning. AI systems range from simple rule-based algorithms to complex models like deep neural networks that can potenitally adapt and generalize across different tasks.

The practice of developing intelligent machines dates back to the pioneering work of Alan Turing in the mid-20th century. Turing introduced the 'imitation game' concept, a method for evaluating if a machine could be indistinguishable from a human in conversation. This foundational idea has since evolved into what we commonly refer to today as the Turing test.

What technological capabilities are described as 'AI' has changed over time and typically reflects whatever is deemed revolutionary at that moment. For example, in the 1950s, a computer capable of playing chess would have been termed AI, whereas in the 2000s, a chatbot capable of passing a legal bar exam might hold that title. Even technology initially considered awe-inspiring is quite quickly taken for granted.

Machine Learning (ML) and Statistics are related yet distinct fields. Statistics is traditionally concerned with data analysis, model building and prediction, often using human-directed methods that enable relatively easy interpretation. Machine learning automates the process of model building, to handle more complex data patterns, often at the expense of interpretability. While statistics may benefit from software environments like R, modern machine learning typically utilizes languages such as Python, or C++ in cases where speed is a crucial factor.

Both fields share foundational knowledge in mathematics and statistics, but their methodologies and technical emphasis differ. Data science serves as the bedrock for both, offering techniques that enhance the reliability and ethical considerations of statistical models built upon that data.

The terminology – AI, ML and Data science – is sometimes used interchangeably, either due to genuine confusion or intentional mislabelling. Simple data science tasks may be branded as ML or AI to appear more cutting-edge, while AI systems may be deployed for problems that could be more efficiently (and reliably) tackled by basic data science methods. Despite the buzz around ML and AI, data science continues to be a vital part of the modern technological landscape, often serving as a crucial prerequisite for more advanced ML models. Algorithms are sequences of steps for solving problems, somewhat akin to the process of working out a mathematical sum. Today's algorithms can be highly sophisticated mechanisms that influence everything from navigating roads to online social interactions, making complex decisions based on knowledge within very large datasets.

Historical path of AI paradigms

The evolution of machine intelligence has unfolded in several waves, each lessening the need for human input. Early AI systems relied on rule-based programming, excelling in specific logical tasks like chess but lacking adaptability. The 1950s saw the advent of artificial neuron systems, epitomized by Frank

FIGURE 1.1   Machine intelligence paradigms over time

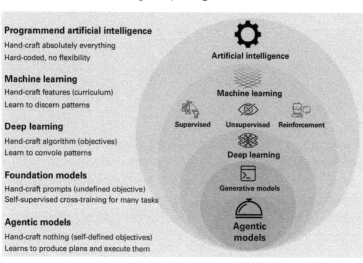

Rosenblatt's perceptron model. Mimicking biological neural networks, it used a single layer of artificial neurons for basic input–output operations. However, computational and data constraints hampered its practical application. This soon led to a long 'AI winter' of disappointment.

The rise of data-driven AI

Interest in neural networks resurged in the mid-1980s after backpropagation techniques permitted neural network models to scale larger without breaking down. The 1980s also marked a pivot in AI from rule-based systems to machine learning models, facilitated by technological advances like the microcomputer revolution. Machine learning allowed AI systems to learn from data, improving their adaptability and applicability in difficult use cases such as computer vision and speech recognition. However, this enthusiasm for a seemingly revolutionary technique soon waned due to scalability issues (a fundamental lack of computing power and data), leading to another AI winter. It wasn't until the 2010s that neural networks matured enough for practical tasks such as the recognition of objects in complex scenes. AI's development has historically gone through cycles of advancement and disappointment, fluctuating between optimism and scepticism.

Machine learning schools

Three primary machine learning methods each mirror ways of teaching a child. Supervised learning is like classroom instruction, requiring labelled data but yielding targeted learning. Unsupervised learning is like child-led exploration, lacking precision but enabling organic discovery. Reinforcement learning is akin to a reward–punishment system, ideal for tasks with clear objectives like robotics or gaming. Interestingly, even pigeons can learn complex tasks like tumor detection via reinforcement learning. However, their short lifespan naturally limits the extent of their learning capabilities. Machine learning models can train virtually without end, allowing them to become exceptionally proficient, given enough data and feedback.

Deep learning

Deep learning, emerging in the 2010s, transformed AI by utilizing large datasets and multi-layer neural networks for complex pattern recognition. Key enablers of this include broadband internet and smartphones for abundant quality data, and GPU graphics cards for powerful on-the-fly processing, which allowed efficient handling of intricate algorithms in parallel. These technological shifts were crucial for developing much larger neural network models (deep learning). Organized datasets of example pictures like ImageNet drove noticeable advances in machine vision, confirming deep learning as a promising avenue for further developments, which came rapidly thereafter.

Major companies like Google and Tesla adopted deep learning techniques, which found specialized applications in many industries. Notable achievements emerged such as DeepMind's AlphaGo, which became the first program to defeat a human professional at the board game Go. However, these techniques required specialist skills and infrastructure, limiting deep learning's impact to niche applications in industry, finance, medicine and machine vision. Generative adversarial networks (GANs), a groundbreaking class of deep learning models introduced by Ian Goodfellow et al in 2014, demonstrated the capability for AI to generate realistic content.

GANs consist of two neural networks, the generator and the discriminator, which are trained simultaneously through adversarial processes. The generator's role is to create data that is indistinguishable from real data, while the discriminator's job is to differentiate between the generator's synthetic output and actual data. This competitive training regimen creates a positive feedback loop, enabling GANs to produce highly realistic and detailed synthetic data, thereby enhancing their applicability in data augmentation and design optimization.

GANs also play a crucial role in design optimization across various fields, including fashion, architecture and product design. The GAN-based style transfer technique applies the stylistic elements of one image to the content of another. This process involves deep learning algorithms that can dissect and re-combine the content and style of images, thereby enabling the creation of novel artistic images.

The age of generative AI

The 2020s have been marked by the advent of generative models (GMs), sometimes referred to as foundation models. These models have significantly expanded the capabilities and flexibility of machine learning technologies, by building upon the generative techniques introduced by GANs.

A pivotal moment in this evolution was the publication of the paper 'Attention is All You Need' in 2017 by Vaswani et al, which introduced the transformer architecture. This architecture has had a revolutionary impact on natural language processing (NLP) and sequence modelling, making significant advancements in tasks such as language translation and basic reasoning. The transformer models mimic aspects of human sequential memory processing, thereby enhancing their ability to understand and generate language (Lind et al, 2023).

Generative models operate by predicting the next element in a sequence, such as a word in a text, and generating content based on that prediction. Through a process of fine-tuning, which involves adjustments guided by human feedback, these models are capable of producing accurate and compelling content. This class of machine learning models is characterized by their ability to learn in context and scale effectively. They have demonstrated proficiency across a broad spectrum of tasks, including text generation and complex reasoning, often requiring minimal input beyond natural language prompts. Moreover, increasing the size of these models – whether in terms of parameter counts or datasets – tends to yield improvements in their performance. Contrary to previous assumptions that larger models might suffer from diminishing returns due to overtraining, generative models have shown that extended training periods can lead to significant performance enhancements.

The landscape of generative models encompasses a variety of types, each with its own specialized capabilities. Diffusion models, for instance, are adept at generating high-quality visual content, while Large Language Models (LLMs) excel in processing and generating textual content. Despite their distinct focuses, both types of model share scalability and versatility, making them foundational technologies for numerous specialized applications. This adaptability positions them similarly to operating systems, within which a wide array of applications can be developed and executed.

Trained on extensive datasets, generative models are capable of capturing complex relationships and nuances across diverse types of data, including text, images, audio, video and 3D models. Their scalability and flexibility liken them to operating systems, providing a foundational platform that democratizes access to advanced machine learning capabilities and fosters innovation. Certain models integrate the strengths of both diffusion models and transformers, leveraging these capabilities for generating content with complex, temporally-bound sequences, such as videos. Generative models have created a gold rush as people seek to exploit this incredible new platform technology, building upon it to create solutions for all kinds of complex problems.

Scaling AI

The rise of generative models (GMs) exemplifies the impact of significant computational resources on AI progress. As Rich Sutton's 'The bitter lesson' suggests, many advancements stem from simply boosting the computing power invested in a task (Sutton, 2019).

Four key drivers fuel machine learning progress:

- Hardware: Specialized chips now claim to be 100 times faster than GPUs. Customizing FPGAs and ASICs with specific model architectures has also greatly enhanced efficiency (Silvano et al, 2023). Distributed compute pools across multiple devices also provide powerful, decentralized training capabilities.
- Algorithms: Innovations in machine learning like backpropagation and gradient descent, along with newer techniques such as ADAM, continue to evolve the field. (Swentworth, 2023).
- Optimizations: Memory utilization and model quantization have been impactful in getting more out of existing hardware.
- Data: The volume, reliability and richness of datasets are crucial, especially complementary sets (modalities) combined into ensembles.

These components collectively shape the trajectory of machine learning, pushing its capabilities ever forward. For AI progress to slow down, or another period of AI winter to arise, it would need to run out of data, compute and algorithmic efficiency gains.

Algorithms and optimizations

The early 2010s resurgence of AI was driven not only by new algorithms but by the convergence of vast datasets and improved computational power. Technologies like Convolutional neural networks (CNNs) had been studied since the 1980s.

Even recent game-changing models such as GPT are not fundamentally novel. The concept of sequence generation from statistical models has been around since Claude Shannon's work on n-grams in 1951. Thus, AI's recent ascendance is more about industrial scaling and resource concentration than about novel technological breakthroughs.

The importance of data

However, the internet, along with pictures from smartphones, provided rich resources for creating datasets to learn from. This data abundance enabled AI methodologies to reveal their true potential, shifting AI from research to a profitable business domain (Sevilla et al, 2022). AI is rapidly improving, with reports of a tenfold increase – 4.2 times from computational enhancements and 2.5 times from algorithmic advancements (Epoch, 2023). The size of AI models is doubling roughly every 3.5 months, although data is growing more slowly. In GMs, data is particularly crucial; quadrupling the data can significantly increase accuracy even when the model has fewer parameters. This indicates that scaling models may hit a wall without adequate data (Xu, 2022).

New methods are emerging to enhance training efficiency. One approach uses a pre-trained GM to fine-tune a smaller, specialized model, cutting computational costs. Another uses large models to augment existing datasets or employs a second AI model for a self-instructing feedback loop. Human-annotated data is also more cost-effective when used to fine-tune existing models rather than starting from scratch (Xu, 2022). These strategies not only reduce training costs but also allow for AI models to be better customized for specific use cases or cultures.

FIGURE 1.2 The amount of compute used to train AI systems has increased dramatically with the advent of deep learning and foundation models

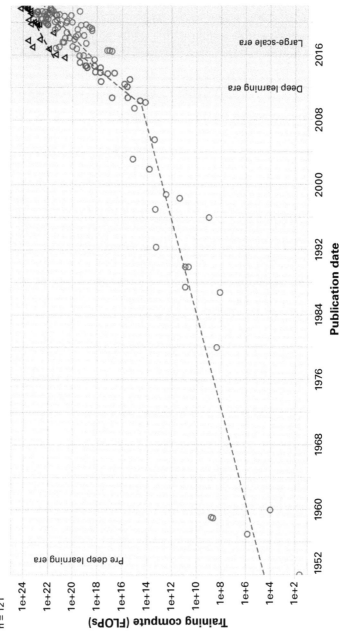

Training compute (FLOPs) of milestone machine learning systems over time
n = 121

Source: Sevilla et al (2022)

The bottom line

Just as the advent of the web and smartphones signalled a new era, so too does the current surge in algorithmic learning capabilities. Data is the fuel of this present leap forward, and those who are sitting on actionable, clean data can find a gold mine in what might have looked like a heap of dirt.

The big picture

AI's phase shift from linear to 'compounding exponential' growth presents both unprecedented opportunities and formidable challenges. It is now no longer a question of whether transformative change will occur, but in what direction it will unfold. It is therefore crucial that leaders adopt an AI strategy to account for not only the extremely rapid technological shifts but also the ethical, societal and global implications.

LEADERSHIP ACTION POINTS

- Prioritize staying updated with the latest trends in AI. Given the 'compounding exponential' rate of growth, missing out on emerging opportunities could mean falling significantly behind.

- Invest in training and development programmes to ensure that teams are equipped to adapt to the ever-changing landscape of AI.

- Foster interdisciplinary teams across multiple disciplines like computer science, ethics, law and domain-specific knowledge, to tackle complex challenges from multiple angles.

- Establish a robust data strategy to feed quality data into your AI systems. This includes data collection, storage, clean-up and governance protocols.

References

Epoch (2023) Key trends and figures in machine learning, epochai.org, 17 July, https://epochai.org/trends (archived at https://perma.cc/GZ35-E6SL)

Lind J et al (2023) A test of memory for stimulus sequences in great apes, *PLOS One*, 18 (9), https://doi.org/10.1371/journal.pone.0290546 (archived at https://perma.cc/2YAF-5XBA)

Sevilla J et al (2022) Compute trends across three eras of machine learning, 9 March, https://arxiv.org/abs/2202.05924 (archived at https://perma.cc/6NVH-9BJW)

Silvano, C et al (2023) A survey on deep learning hardware accelerators for heterogeneous HPC platforms, 27 June, https://arxiv.org/abs/2306.15552 (archived at https://perma.cc/SYZ2-NGUT)

Sutton, R (2019) The bitter lesson, Incomplete Ideas, 13 March, www.incompleteideas.net/IncIdeas/BitterLesson.html (archived at https://perma.cc/3Z8B-CD9Q)

Swentworth, J (2023) Algorithmic improvement is probably faster than scaling now, LESSWRONG, 6 June, www.lesswrong.com/posts/CfpAXccrBvWpQw9xj/algorithmic-improvement-is-probably-faster-than-scaling-now (archived at https://perma.cc/U7QZ-RNAT)

Vaswani, A et al (2017) Attention is all you need, Advances in Neural Information Processing Systems, 30, https://arxiv.org/abs/1706.03762 (archived at https://perma.cc/RK3P-GTT9)

Xu, T (2022) We could run out of data to train AI language programs, MIT Technology Review, 24 November, www.technologyreview.com/2022/11/24/1063684/we-could-run-out-of-data-to-train-ai-language-programs/ (archived at https://perma.cc/Q4QE-7DV6)

CHAPTER TWO

AI's promise and peril

The current state of AI feels like an ox. It's stronger than a human and can pull a plough but needs either constant human guidance or narrow fencing. It's not quite at the level where we can ride it like a horse. JOSCHA BACH

Although today's AI technologies are the most advanced we've ever seen, they are merely the baseline for what is to come. However, this rapid progress has surpassed our ability to make sense of it. The risk of encountering a 'trough of disillusionment' today is not so much about a shortfall in the capabilities of these systems, but rather in our capacity to fully understand and effectively control them. This chapter explores the best and worst aspects of AI.

Strengths of generative AI

The strength of Generative Models (GMs) such as Large Language Models (LLMs) and diffusion models lies in their scalability and versatility. They share a foundational architecture that can be tailored for a wide range of applications, negating the need to develop new models for each specific problem. This ease of adaptability not only lowers the entry barriers for specialized tasks but also fosters rapid innovation. For instance, such models have achieved human-level performance in established creativity benchmarks, including the Torrance Tests of Creative Thinking (Shimek, 2023). Their designation as 'foundation models' underscores their role as robust platforms for building specialized applications. They achieve this through an amalgamation of extensive scaling, intricate architectures and finely tuned algorithms.

Concierge AI

Incorporating memory functions into generative models is significantly improving personal assistance services. These developments enable interactive AI systems that can execute tasks by interfacing with software applications through APIs, and even collaborating with other machines and other human beings to achieve their goals.

Because natural language understanding serves as a universal interface, it enables different systems to interoperate while tapping into the same knowledge base. Programming languages may not be needed soon, except for very niche purposes, with direct compiling of natural language into machine code.

You might have noticed that LLMs sometimes to go off track after a while, forgetting earlier discussions. Context windows determine the extent of contextual information an LLM can interpret. LLMs with context windows exceeding 100,000 tokens (~75,000 words) can process entire books in a single pass. This allows for immediate querying about the book's content and the synthesis of information scattered throughout its pages. Some Transformer architectures can handle millions of tokens, sufficient for accommodating an entire codebase, even building upon an entire a series of books to generate a new release.

AI agents

Models like AutoGPT enable language models to form and execute successful plans over time, making them much more effective. Agents are AI that can spawn other versions of themselves to work together to solve a common goal. These models exhibit features like long- and short-term memory, internet access, goal-oriented planning and the ability to spawn sub-agents to which it can delegate specialized tasks. Designed to manage cognitive overload, these autonomous agents distribute tasks among sub-agents, enabling agile and efficient operations.

Agents have evolved to become more intelligent and proactive, capable of offering suggestions even before being prompted. They possess the ability to execute tasks across various applications and continuously enhance their performance over time. This improvement is driven by their ability to remember past activities and recognize patterns and intent, and anticipate accordingly.

The applications are extensive, ranging from email management to complex scheduling tasks. For instance, an agent-based model could autonomously sort, prioritize and even respond to your emails based on predefined criteria. It could also organize meeting requests, synchronize them with multiple participants and ensure there are no calendar conflicts. The advancement of these agents could make GMs more durable and versatile, especially when reinforced with simple reward functions.

AI ensembles and corporations

AI ensembles and multi-agent frameworks are pushing the boundaries of what machine learning can achieve. Ensembles are formed when various types of models work in concert to form general-purpose assistants capable of tackling a much broader array of problems than single models alone.

A possible approach to ensembles is to integrate GMs, domain-specific, specialized models and a mechanism known as 'reinforcement learning from task feedback' (RLTF). In this setup, the GM acts as a synthesizer, combining insights from specialized models to solve complex tasks. RLTF acts as the feedback mechanism, continually refining the system's performance and enabling a loop for self-improvement.

Foundation models are evolving to incorporate multiple specialized sub-agents, effectively forming virtual business teams. With the aid of platforms like ChatDev and MetaGPT, these AI-driven teams can specialize in various fields such as design, programming and public relations, enabling rapid and cost-effective development of projects, including video games and other media.

This development is a significant milestone in the automation of business itself. Such AI-led entrepreneurship could revolutionize not only the for-profit sector but also pave the way for lean, efficient charitable organizations with minimal overhead, thereby disrupting traditional models. In many instances, the choice isn't between AI and human intervention; it's between AI and no solution at all. Certain services enabled by AI are virtually impossible to scale through human efforts alone. For example, AI-enabled therapy can provide support at any time, which would be prohibitively expensive and complex if relying on human beings. AI agents are poised to revolutionize access to services that are currently too costly for many individuals, effectively democratizing them.

Companies primarily staffed by AI could out-compete human-run businesses, relegating human roles to highly specialized tasks. Such AI corporations could even one day dominate as the new '1 per cent' in society.

AI civilizations

AI agents have been applied to simulate human behaviour with an astonishing degree of realism, from simple actions like virtually drinking coffee together to complex activities like planning social events, all while interacting with each other and their virtual environment.

Each agent is initiated with a prompt that outlines its personality, occupation and preferences. As they navigate their digital world, these agents generate action statements that translate into movements within the virtual environment. A key feature is their 'memory stream', a database recording all their experiences. When agents encounter one another, they can access past interactions from this memory stream, enabling ongoing conversations or collaborations.

However, maintaining a growing memory stream presents challenges, especially as it becomes too large for an agent's 'context window'. To address this, researchers can implement a retrieval function that weighs the relevance of each memory piece to the agent's current situation. Agents can also 'reflect', summarizing parts of their memory to add nuanced layers to their personalities over time.

In this simulated world, AI agents can be likened to a mini-civilization, each with its own set of skills, memories and the ability to plan. Just as human civilizations have culture and collective knowledge, these agents interact and collaborate, forming something greater than the sum of their individual capabilities.

Successive waves of AI

AI's evolution can be thought of as progressing through several distinct, yet interconnected phases, each building upon the capabilities of the last. The journey began with 'Classifying' systems that harnessed deep learning algorithms to sort and categorize different types of data, laying the foundation for more complex tasks.

From there, we moved to the 'Generative' phase, where AI models began creating new data from existing input, like GPT generating text or DALL-E creating images. These systems could generate new content, but their interactions were often one-way.

The 'Interactive' phase followed, characterized by models capable of engaging in natural language dialogue. These models could respond to queries and instructions but lacked a cohesive memory or personality.

Next came the 'Relational' phase, where AI systems started to possess characteristics like personality and memory of past interactions. This made the user experience more engaging and personalized.

We are now entering the 'Corporate' phase, which features more complex systems composed of multiple personas or sub-agents. These agents collaborate to achieve specific goals, functioning much like a corporation or community.

We might even enter a 'Sagacious' phase of AI, where systems are designed to serve as guides, advisers or even philosophers, providing wisdom and insights aimed at enriching human life and uplifting the human spirit.

Open source and affordability

Cost and accessibility factors are rapidly changing the AI development landscape. This democratizes access to AI capabilities, as it's increasingly feasible for smaller organizations or even individuals to train or fine-tune such models for specialized applications. That's still assuming that they even need to, and can't simply meet their need by borrowing access cheaply through an API.

The definition of 'large' in Large Language Models is fluid due to two concurrent trends: while the models themselves are growing exponentially in size, optimizations such as quantization are enabling these larger models to run on relatively modest hardware like consumer laptops in full, or in part through decentralization mechanisms that can run models across many devices.

The role of open source in this evolution can't be overstated. Open-source frameworks accelerate ecosystem development and have the potential to become industry standards. However, Meta's apparently accidental widespread release of its LLaMA model beyond a small group of researchers in 2023 demonstrates the dual-edged nature of open-source AI; while it enabled cost-effective training approaches like Alpaca (an open-source AI built by researchers at Stanford), it also exposed how such qualities could serve as a force multiplication factor for potential bad actors. Open source techniques are fast-followers of the latest proprietary advancements, catching up within months.

FIGURE 2.1 Common machine leaning benchmarks are being mastered at an increasing rate: tradeoffs of open source and quantized models

Model	Cost	Pros	Cons
OpenAI	• Low setup cost • Effective for low usage (<5,000/day)	• High-quality responses • Minimal infra setup	• Sensitivity around privacy • High cost for millions of requests per day
Open-Access LLM	• High setup cost • Effective for high usage	• Hosting on-prem for sensitive data • Ideal for large usage millions of req/day	• Quality could be lower based on training data • Not ideal for low usage due to setup cost
Quantized Models	• Lower setup cost compared to Open LLM	• Good performance for 'narrow' use cases such as HR or Product Chatbots, etc	• Requires technical sophistication for setup

Source: Battacharya (2023)

The concept of 'piggybacking' on existing models offers another layer of efficiency. Distillation techniques create smaller, cost-effective language models by fine-tuning them with examples from larger models. By training smaller models on the outputs of existing, larger models, similar performance levels can be achieved at a fraction of the cost.

Professionalising AI

In many ways, the current state of AI resembles the early days of the iPhone. When it launched in 2007, the iPhone was revolutionary but lacked an App Store and many other features that would later define its success. Another comparison is the World Wide Web of the early 1990s, prior to the release of TLS/SSL, the padlock icon in your web browser that guarantees a secure connection, essential for sensitive matters such as online banking. Only since then has the true capability of the web been unlocked. Generative AI similarly awaits a comprehensive ecosystem that includes not just technological infrastructure but also appropriately trained teams and redesigned workflows, especially in sectors requiring ethical and accurate outcomes.

Deploying immature AI systems for complex tasks without human oversight can have significant, far-reaching ethical and reputational consequences. Therefore, organizations should approach AI adoption with meticulous planning, assessing both its potential and limitations.

To fully leverage the potential of AI, many organizations establish a centre of excellence (CoE). This specialized unit is responsible for developing and communicating an AI vision that aligns with the organization's broader objectives. It strategizes to bring this vision to fruition by identifying suitable use cases for AI and often seeks external technologies and partnerships to expedite progress.

However, current AI systems, even though they perform well in many scenarios, still struggle in high-value, critical domains.

Even minor errors or biases in healthcare can lead to serious consequences. The reason is that even a small percentage of errors or biases can have catastrophic consequences in settings like healthcare, finance or safety-critical systems. AI may work well 95 per cent of the time, but that gap frustrates its usage in any high-value domain, as it simply cannot be trusted not to cause catastrophe.

The 'Wild West' phase of AI deployment needs to transition into a more mature stage, characterized by robustness, ethical considerations and societal benefits that are both broad and deep. This will require concerted efforts from researchers, policymakers and industry leaders to ensure that as AI continues to advance, it does so in a manner that is responsible, equitable and aligned with human values and needs.

Generative AI limitations and caveats

The term 'stochastic parrots', coined by linguist Emily Bender, suggests that these models are adept at mimicking understanding and reasoning without actually performing any substantial cognitive functions. Rather than merely predicting the next token, language models like GPT are designed to consider a context window of potentially thousands of tokens to inform each prediction, generating text one token at a time based on the cumulative context of what has been generated so far.

Critics contend that GMs lack cohesive understanding of the generated information. They excel at predicting statistically likely sequences of words but can often produce outputs that are plausible-sounding yet factually incorrect. There is some evidence suggesting that emergent abilities in larger models can primarily be ascribed to improved in-context learning rather than improved reasoning per se (Lu et al, 2023). GMs may learn one order of things, which proves not to be robust – it doesn't generalize. For example, if 'George Washington was the first POTUS' is true, then 'The first POTUS was George Washington' is also true, which GMs may miss. This 'Reversal Curse' shows a failure of deduction in the GM's training process. Humans are also subject to similar challenges – try saying the alphabet backwards.

However, the sheer scale of many GMs enables them to perform at or above the level of models specifically fine-tuned for certain tasks, even comparable with computer operating systems (Packer et al, 2023). There is a moderate correlation of .48 between model size and the apparent general intelligence of models (Ilić, 2023). This has led some, such as leading computer scientist Stephen Wolfram, to argue that GMs represent a form of General Pattern Machines, capable of various tasks beyond text prediction, from complex pattern recognition to controlling robotic systems (Wolfram, 2023). The fact that GMs create internal world models indeed seems indicative of underlying generalizable intelligence (Gurnee and Tegmark, 2023).

AI is currently excelling at automating low-stakes tasks and extending the kinds of work that can be automated. But this falls short of fulfilling the grand promises often imagined about AI. The technology's utility, therefore, is primarily confined to areas where the costs of errors are low. While GMs might be useful for casual translations or generating text, they are not suitable for generating legally binding contracts or making life-and-death decisions. The real world's complexity, with its myriad variables to factor into critical decisions, often proves too challenging for current AI capabilities. It may work well some of the time, but needs significant hand-holding and oversight.

Public realization of these challenges will likely lead to a sobering period of recalibration, which, although not an AI winter, could be akin to a 'trough of disillusionment' – the stage on Gartner's Hype Cycle which comes after inflated expectations, but then leads into the developments of the 'Slope of Enlightenment' (Gartner, 2023). Over time, however, these challenges will be increasingly managed through regulations, standards and public education, paving the way once again for more sustainable AI development.

The bottom line

Generative AI offers transformative possibilities, from reshaping healthcare and personal services to redefining corporate operations. Its power to learn, adapt and provide solutions across myriad applications is unprecedented. Yet, this promise comes with ethical challenges and operational limitations that cannot be ignored. Issues of fundamental robustness of these systems make them limited in capability, until surrounding bulwarks and safeguards have been reliably implemented and enforced.

The big picture

Generative AI represents not merely a technological leap but a transformative power revolutionizing the way we live, work, interact and manage. Its journey from a sophisticated tool to a semi-autonomous entity will redefine concepts like trust, governance and individual agency. However, while the AI takes on the 'heavy lifting' of sifting through data and generating recommendations or actions, the ultimate responsibility still lies with the human operators.

LEADERSHIP ACTION POINTS

- Acquire in-depth knowledge and experience of generative AI, including its capabilities, limitations and potential pitfalls within your organization. Identify potential opportunities to leverage new techniques.

- Anticipate the long-term evolution of AI and its likely impact on your organization and industry. Prepare for successive upgrades and shifts in technology.

- Leverage the scalability of generative AI to not just broaden its applications but also to enhance its robustness and reliability through self-improvement and self-checking processes.

- Observe affordability trends to be cognizant of how the cost landscape for AI is evolving, especially with respect to piggy-backing on other developments.

References

Bhattacharya, S (2023) Buy vs Build for an Enterprise: 'ChatGPT' vs Open-Source vs QLoRA, *DataDrivenInvestor*, 18 July, https://medium.datadriveninvestor.com/buy-vs-build-for-an-enterprise-chatgpt-vs-open-source-a959f3d6173d (archived at https://perma.cc/F24S-G9VE)

Gartner (2023) Gartner Hype Circle, www.gartner.com/en/research/methodologies/gartner-hype-cycle (archived at https://perma.cc/4HVP-NH2S)

Gurnee, W and Tegmark, M (2023) Language models represent space and time [Preprint], https://arxiv.org/abs/2310.02207 (archived at https://perma.cc/R72Q-Q24L)

Ilić, D (2023) Unveiling the general intelligence factor in language models: A psychometric approach [Preprint], https://arxiv.org/abs/2310.11616 (archived at https://perma.cc/LLG4-4KB4)

Lu, L et al (2023) Are emergent abilities in large language models just in-context learning? [Preprint], https://arxiv.org/abs/2309.01809 (archived at https://perma.cc/PQF4-4N83)

Packer, C et al (2023) MemGPT: Towards LLMs as operating systems [Preprint], https://arxiv.org/abs/2310.08560 (archived at https://perma.cc/K6AX-PE2K)

Shimek, C (2023) UM research: AI tests into top 1% for original creative thinking, University of Montana, 5 July, www.umt.edu/news/2023/07/070523test.php (archived at https://perma.cc/5QD4-7JNB)

Wolfram, S (2023) What is ChatGPT doing? ... and why does it work? Stephen Wolfram, 14 February, https://writings.stephenwolfram.com/2023/02/what-is-chatgpt-doing-and-why-does-it-work (archived at https://perma.cc/UZ9R-A4RH)

CHAPTER THREE

Robots and avatars

Robots have been in the deepest oceans, they've been to Mars. They've been all these places, but they're just now starting to come into your living room. Your living room is the final frontier for robots. CYNTHIA BREAZEAL

The robotics landscape is undergoing a seismic shift, powered by advances in machine vision, generative AI, battery life and wireless communication. Unlike their predecessors, which were limited to repetitive tasks or served as novelties, modern robots are poised to become versatile, intelligent tools in both industrial and personal settings. Accurate environment interpretation through machine vision, coupled with natural language interactions enabled by generative AI, makes these robots more intuitive to command. Enhanced battery life and wireless capabilities add to their mobility and versatility. This chapter explores how merging technologies bring AI into the physical realm, heralding an era of effective, responsive robotic assistants.

The machine vision revolution

The transformative power of machine vision in the field of robotics and AI cannot be overstated. Machine vision, driven by advances in deep learning and Convolutional Neural Networks (CNNs), is enabling robots to navigate, recognize and interact with their environment. The advent of affordable, high-performing GPUs has been an important catalyst, providing the computational might needed for real-time vision processing.

This revolution parallels the Cambrian Explosion in evolutionary history, where the advent of eyes dramatically expanded the capabilities of living organisms. Similarly, machine vision is a game-changer for robotics, enhancing their mobility, autonomy and utility across various applications. Robots can now navigate dynamically changing environments, identify and manipulate objects, and even anticipate where they might be needed – all with minimal or no human intervention.

Emerging technologies like Single-Pixel Object Detection (SPOD) and Optical Neural Network pre-processors are pushing the boundaries even further. SPOD, for example, enables object detection from a single pixel, offering applications from medical imaging to manufacturing quality control. Optical Neural Network pre-processors achieve astounding compression ratios, making real-time processing even more efficient.

The Transformer is also making inroads into vision tasks, challenging the domain-specific prowess of CNNs. This indicates a trend towards versatile, multi-task models that can handle a variety of sensory inputs and cognitive tasks.

Looking ahead, the integration of onboard and cloud-based intelligence will likely be the next frontier. Onboard systems will manage immediate, time-sensitive tasks, while cloud-based intelligence will offer contextual understanding and strategic decision-making.

Robotic production

'Lights out' factories, where robots handle most tasks with minimal human oversight, have been a long-sought goal in automation (the name derives from the fact that, with automated produc-tion, there's often no need to turn on the lights for human beings). While achieving this vision has been challenging due to human labour's fundamental flexibility, advances in machine vision and learning are making it more feasible.

Today's robots are versatile, capable of multiple tasks like sorting, painting and assembly, and can handle objects of various sizes. This not only improves efficiency but also reduces the need for human exposure to hazardous conditions.

Robotic avatars

Equipped with haptic gloves and advanced sensors, avatar robots allow human users to perform complex tasks remotely. This has applications in fields like medicine, engineering and even disaster response. Avatar robots are now as affordable as $15,000. Sharing these avatars among users – akin to a ride-share model – further extends their utility.

These avatars also serve as rich data sources for machine learning. They could help address Moravec's paradox, which highlights that things a toddler finds trivial are still very challenging for computers and vice-versa. One reason for this is that a toddler has learned from a great deal more information than a large language model. The rich sensory data and user actions captured by avatars offer insights into human behaviour that go beyond what video observation can provide, potentially speeding up the development of advanced intelligence, especially embodied systems such as robots.

The technology also has geopolitical implications. High-speed networks like Starlink make it possible for people to engage in global telecommuting without relocating, benefiting local communities and increasing the potential for remote working.

Autonomous vehicles

Autonomous vehicles, increasingly enabled by affordable LiDAR (Light Detection and Ranging) technology, are becoming more common in urban settings. However, the effectiveness of this technology can vary based on factors like geography, culture and local laws, making it challenging to deploy universally.

Autonomous systems also promise to revolutionize emergency responses. They could replace riskier and costlier traditional methods, such as planes and helicopters in firefighting, and offer safer alternatives for high-risk drivers, potentially reducing accidents.

However, the rise of autonomous vehicles also poses downstream societal challenges. For instance, safer roads could lead to a 15 per cent decrease in available organs for transplantation due to fewer fatal accidents, though that's of course a nice problem to have compared with carnage on the roads (Mills and Mills, 2020). Additionally, local governments may see a drop in revenue from parking and speeding fines, which often form a significant part of their budgets (Sibilla, 2019).

General-purpose robotics

Advances in machine vision and GMs are ushering in a new era of general-purpose robotics. These robots can understand and execute human language commands, with applications ranging from healthcare and companionship for the elderly to agriculture and warehousing. The robots can also learn from each other across different fields, enhancing their capabilities.

However, traditional frameworks designed for static systems won't suffice for these self-learning, adaptive robots. New guidelines must be developed to ensure their ethical and safe operation as they continue to evolve.

Cobotics

Collaborative robots, or cobots, are designed to work safely alongside humans in shared spaces. They are equipped with advanced sensors and controls, making them ideal for tasks requiring precision, strength or repetition in sectors like manufacturing, logistics and healthcare. Unlike traditional industrial robots, which are often isolated for safety, cobots have situational awareness that allows them to operate freely among humans.

These robots are particularly beneficial in roles that require quick and accurate movements, such as emergency medical response. While they generally don't collaborate directly with humans on tasks, they do perform complementary roles, freeing humans for more complex work.

Cobots are already making a significant impact in logistics and warehousing, particularly in sorting and picking tasks. As the technology matures, their roles are likely to expand to tasks like restocking store shelves.

The bottom line

The convergence of advanced machine vision, generative AI and efficient hardware is heralding a new era in robotics. These technologies are transforming robots from rigid, single-task machines to versatile, autonomous systems capable of complex interactions and decision-making. This revolution in capabilities has far-reaching implications for numerous sectors, from manufacturing and healthcare to transportation and geopolitics.

The big picture

We're witnessing a transformative moment akin to the Cambrian Explosion in the evolution of machines. As advanced machine vision endows robots with unprecedented perception and autonomy, it also unlocks new paradigms for human-machine interaction. Robots are evolving from being mere tools to becoming collaborative partners in various tasks. This shift not only enhances efficiency but also redefines the roles humans play in multiple domains.

LEADERSHIP ACTION POINTS

- Assess areas within your organization where machine vision could streamline processes, improve quality control, enhance safety or create new opportunities.

- Establish risk management strategies to handle the increased mobility and autonomy of AI-powered systems. Ensure that vision capabilities are robust in a wide variety of environments and contexts to reduce the potential for misapprehensions or other biases. Update safety protocols and ethical guidelines to ensure responsible deployment and mitigate risks.

- Consider how the power of the latest machine vision AI systems could be used to upscale and enhance the fidelity of hardware with limited sensing capabilities. For example, generating virtual depth maps from 2D sensors, or simply wiring a cheap smartphone into equipment to give it a wide variety of new capabilities.

- Explore how advanced machine vision techniques can improve the capabilities of existing hardware, like generating virtual depth maps from 2D sensors or integrating smartphones into equipment to add new functionalities.

- Assess the feasibility of using avatar robots for certain kinds of remote work.
- Balance onboard and cloud intelligence by strategically distributing tasks – onboard systems for real-time action and cloud-based systems for complex decision-making.

References

Mills P A S and Mills D K (2020) Reduced supply in the organ donor market and how 3d printing can address this shortage: A critical inquiry into the collateral effects of driverless cars, *Applied Sciences*, 10 (18), 6400

Sibilla, N (2019) Nearly 600 towns get 10% of their budgets (or more) from court fines, *Forbes*, 29 August, www.forbes.com/sites/nicksibilla/2019/08/29/nearly-600-towns-get-10-of-their-budgets-or-more-from-court-fines/?sh=56fdec024c99 (archived at https://perma.cc/ZR9R-QS2M)

CHAPTER FOUR

Coordinating chaos and complexity

What appears to most people as chaos is not really chaotic, but a series of different types of orders with which the human mind has not yet become familiar. FREDERICK LENZ

Machine learning is like a modern-day oracle. It sifts through mountains of data to find hidden patterns, like a miner searching for gold. Deep learning goes a step further; think of it as an oracle with a microscope, scrutinizing even the tiniest fragments to find precious gems within the gold. This chapter illustrates how these aren't just fancy tools; they're revolutionary technologies that bring clarity to the mysteries of our world.

Artificial intelligence is more than just another tool in the box. It's a game-changing force with the ability to see into the future. This is particularly crucial in high-stakes fields like healthcare, where predicting patient outcomes can literally be a matter of life and death. But it doesn't stop there. AI serves as an early warning system in complex and unpredictable domains like weather forecasting and economics, helping us take preventive action before things turn worse. Thanks to AI, today's five-day weather forecasts are becoming as accurate as one-day forecasts were in 1980 (Espeholt et al, 2022).

Machine learning algorithms are not just for data crunching; they are sophisticated predictors that outperform even the most complicated mathematical models in foreseeing the future states of chaotic systems. A prime example is AI's role in managing Hydrogen Fusion tokamak reactors, considered the holy grail of sustainable energy For the first time, AI doesn't just predict these complex systems; it controls them, making sustainable fusion energy a real possibility (Tracey et al, 2023). This transformative capability extends to other intricate systems like weather patterns, protein folding and even abstract areas like culture and ecology. Advanced AI algorithms can predict 'tipping points' within these systems – critical, often irreversible moments of change.

AI therefore not only deepens our understanding of the world but also enhances our ability to manage it efficiently. Whether it's optimizing supply chain logistics or reducing waste by predicting inventory needs based on demand, AI provides solutions that are both effective and resource efficient. By considering a multitude of variables like economic conditions, weather and even holidays, AI can find the best course of action in complex scenarios.

The newest advancements in AI are more than incremental improvements; they are a paradigm shift in technological capabilities.

An engine of civilization

The potential for advanced AI systems, especially GMs, to dissect complex legal and regulatory frameworks is compelling. These AI tools could serve as invaluable assets for understanding how various elements such as laws, litigation, regulatory codes and administrative actions interact – a task that often proves challenging even for seasoned experts. A well-tuned GM, for instance, could provide concise and accurate information about a new tax plan, the impact of a legislative bill or even estimate the likelihood of a piece of legislation passing.

Arnold Toynbee's magnum opus, the expansive 12-volume *A Study of History*, posits that civilizations decline when their leaders cease to function as effective problem-solvers. According to Toynbee, civilizations ascend when a 'creative minority' galvanizes society by offering a compelling vision of positive change and practical solutions to pressing issues (Toynbee, 1934). This vision and set of solutions encourage widespread societal support. As long as this creative minority continues to innovate and resolve the challenges facing society, it sustains its role, and the civilization continues to thrive. AI's ability to handle chaos may therefore provide a crucial bulwark of effective leadership in the face of institutional crises or decline.

In a series of essays called 'AI and Leviathan', Samuel Hammond delves into the potential for AI to reshape the very fabric of government and society (Hammond, 2023). He suggests that three types of AI-enabled governance will emerge: a Chinese-style police state or Gulf-style monarchy; an anarchic failed state; or a high-tech open society modelled after Estonia's e-governance systems. Liberal democracies have a challenge to evolve their institutions to find a middle ground between anarchy and authoritarianism.

The AI-driven organization

Much of AI has been developed with purposes of distraction in mind – various forms of entertainment. However, it's starting to shift towards enabling ambition instead, especially in a corporate context. This will have a major impact on how enterprises organize themselves, and the flow of information within them.

We've reached a point in society where the volume of messages generated – especially in business and government – far exceeds what any human can actually read. While it makes sense to keep records for future reference, that's not the primary function of most of these communications. Many people spend significant time crafting reports that are never read, let alone acted upon. Sometimes these reports are filed away for reasons nobody at the company even understands anymore. Software and bureaucratic systems are cluttered with redundant and obsolete processes that persist simply out of habit. This inertia can contribute to the inefficiency and eventual decline of longstanding organizations, and may even play a role in the fall of empires.

In a landscape awash with data, the challenge for leaders is not just data collection but meaningful interpretation. Leaders should focus on selecting the right key performance indicators (KPIs) and making sense of them. By choosing unique metrics and understanding their interrelations, leaders can gain innovative insights that offer a competitive edge. Leaders should also constantly challenge their own assumptions and ask questions that help them adapt to a rapidly changing world. The ability to reconsider approaches in light of new information is crucial.

The tension between scale and efficiency is a timeless challenge that organizations, both old and new, continually grapple with. While the internet has emerged as a powerful tool that allows firms to operate more effectively, the fundamental trade-off between growing bigger and staying efficient hasn't disappeared.

This dilemma isn't exclusive to businesses; it's a universal principle we see in nature too. Take beehives, for instance. Natural hives operate with remarkable efficiency but are challenging to manage on a large scale. Similarly, small farms can cultivate a diverse range of crops side by side, achieving greater efficiency per unit of land. However, the model doesn't fit well within industrial-scale operations.

In the realm of organizations, small size often comes with distinct advantages. In a small team, everyone knows each other, making it easier to share context and insights. Tailoring processes and projects to the team's unique composition and the challenges at hand becomes more feasible. Keeping everyone aligned and motivated is also less of a Herculean task when you're dealing with a smaller group.

The eternal conundrum of how to maintain the efficiencies of a small-scale operation as one grows can be sidestepped through AI processes, which can streamline organizational management, enhancing executive decision making and project planning for engineers. Imagine a world where executives don't have to sift through piles of reports but can instead interact with a dynamic dashboard that converses with them, offering real-time insights. For project managers and engineers, the GM can break down high-level objectives into specific tasks, ensuring that everyone is aligned and working towards the same goal.

This kind of system doesn't just make information more accessible, it also keeps it up to date. Unlike static wikis that quickly become outdated, this system provides a constantly updated information source. The dilemma of where to find information within the organization becomes obsolete, as the GM can either provide the information directly or point you to the right person or resource. This has the potential to reshape the dynamics of the workplace itself. Meetings and stand-ups could become far less frequent, with everyone pre-briefed beforehand by AI systems.

This potential for making sense of chaos extends to addressing issues of technical debt in both the public and private sectors. Technical debt is a metaphor that describes the future cost of overlooking infrastructure issues today. In a governmental context, legacy systems often become unwieldy over time due to a lack of updates, becoming not only difficult to maintain but also to modernize, often using antiquated technology and languages. Businesses face similar challenges. AI has the potential to simplify the process of refactoring these complex systems, making them easier to maintain and less prone to errors. In doing so, the path to implementing reforms in general becomes much more straightforward, thereby overcoming the inertia which prevents many organizations from flourishing once again in an agile and adaptable manner.

The bottom line

Generative AI's ability to interpret complex, dynamic and chaotic systems is revolutionary. These are not just lines of code; they are akin to a new form of cognitive architecture that mimics human-like pattern recognition but at a scale and speed we can't even fathom. AI's capabilities in interpreting highly complex, dynamic and chaotic systems are truly groundbreaking.

The big picture

We have an ability to understand and influence chaos in ways never before possible. AI's unparalleled ability to make sense of mind-boggling complexity is not just a theoretical marvel; it's a practical tool that is already making a tangible impact on our world, from predicting disasters to revolutionizing healthcare.

LEADERSHIP ACTION POINTS

- Review your organizational challenges and pinpoint where AI could augment more effective management, enabling your human workforce to function more as informed overseers rather than manual operators.

- Consider unpredictable and seemingly uncontrollable events that may impact your organization. AI's predictive analytics could provide early warnings or even proactive strategies to manage these 'Black Swan' events.

- Deploy AI algorithms in logistics for real-time decision-making, adjusting routes and logistics strategies based on live data, such as traffic and weather updates.
- Improve operational efficiency with AI-driven predictive maintenance schedules for logistics vehicles and machinery.
- Automate your warehouses with AI. Explore options for sorting, packing and even using autonomous machinery for material handling.
- Implement AI-driven mechanisms for managing issues of technical debt to create a blank canvas for future innovation.

References

Espeholt, L et al (2022) Deep learning for twelve hour precipitation forecasts, *Nature Communications*, 13 (5145), https://doi.org/10.1038/s41467-022-32483-x (archived at https://perma.cc/X96H-LF6A)

Hammond, S (2023) AI and leviathan: Part I, Second Best, 23 August, www.secondbest.ca/p/ai-and-leviathan-part-i (archived at https://perma.cc/YTQ8-7RL7)

Toynbee, A J (1934) *A Study of History*, Oxford University Press, Oxford

Tracey, B D et al (2023) Towards practical reinforcement learning for tokamak magnetic control [Preprint], https://arxiv.org/abs/2307.11546 (archived at https://perma.cc/V9F4-B7FL)

CHAPTER FIVE

Science and innovation

We live in a society exquisitely dependent on science and technology, in which hardly anyone knows anything about science and technology. CARL SAGAN

In 2016, DeepMind's AlphaGo defeated Go champion Lee Sedol, marking a milestone in AI's capabilities. But the match also highlighted the future interplay between human and machine intelligence. AlphaGo's Move 37, unprecedented in the entire history of Go, was met by Lee Sedol's equally ground-breaking 'Hand of God' move. This highlights the potential for human creativity to flourish in response to a machine stimulus. This chapter will examine how the rise of machine intelligence can serve as a catalyst for human cognitive growth.

AI revolutionizes science and innovation, serving as a collaborative partner that offers fresh perspectives and swiftly validates ideas. For example, in a contest for sub-$50 ideas for college students, AI-generated concepts dominated the top picks (Terwiesch and Ulrich, 2023).

Mechanisms such as Elicit.org can systematically perform rapid literature reviews, quickly validating whether a hypothesis is worthy of research.

Beyond optimizing current methods, these models can spark innovation in human beings.

DeepMind's AI systems reinvented the Matrix Multiplication algorithm used by billions of processes, which no human could figure out how to improve meaningfully in about 50 years. This incredible feat of machine capability was beaten by humans again a week later (Sparkes, 2022). The dialectic space enabled by generative AI is fertile ground for growing innovative takes on very old problems.

Data-driven science

AI is adding a new dimension to scientific inquiry, particularly in fields that lack clear, causal theories like psychology and economics. While machine learning models excel at prediction, they primarily identify correlations, not causations. So, even if a model accurately predicts a complex phenomenon like anxiety, it doesn't automatically provide a scientific explanation, which usually involves testable hypotheses.

Interpreting these models poses another challenge. Their 'knowledge' is stored in complex mathematical structures, not easily translated into human-understandable terms. While humans often seek simple explanations for phenomena, guided by principles like Occam's razor, the most accurate model might be intrinsically complex.

As AI's predictive power grows, it could reintroduce the role of intuition and narrative in science, especially for phenomena that defy simple explanation. However, these narratives should complement, not replace, the empirical rigour that underpins scientific research. While machine-driven creativity could increase individual output, there is a risk that it could also reduce collective creativity, as AI responses tend to have little diversity across similar prompts (Candelon et al, 2023).

AI for science

The advent of AI is transforming scientific research. In high-energy physics, AI sifts through massive data to identify rare events in particle collisions, offering key insights into the universe.

In biomedical research, AI can map out complex chemical pathways, potentially leading to new antibiotics. Even the odour profile of a molecule can be predicted, or prospects for more efficient solar cells. It also enhances live-cell imaging resolution and guides hypothesis formation by spotting patterns in large datasets.

In mathematics, neural networks are solving complex differential equations that traditional methods cannot, and AI-driven symbolic regression offers new ways to model physical systems (Drori, 2021).

Beyond science, AI is even helping us connect with the past, from resurrecting dead languages to modelling historical lifestyles (Büyükyıldırım, 2023). We can even begin to understand the language of other species, such as whales, bats and even chickens (Andreas et al, 2022).

GM-powered automated labs can independently design and conduct complex experiments, fast-tracking research.

These virtual scientists consist of several modules, including planning, web searching and code execution, and are capable of ethical reasoning and high-quality code generation. However, they require robust ethical and safety guardrails to prevent suggestions for dangerous activities, such as attempts to create chemical weapons.

Automated labs can now take over tasks such as experiment setup, data analysis and planning next steps, freeing researchers from laborious tasks like mixing solutions. These systems can also optimize reaction conditions in real-time, something that would be labour-intensive for humans. GMs specialized in chemical interactions can even assist in planning chemical synthesis pathways.

Automated systems also enable high-throughput screening in drug discovery and can analyse complex data from techniques like spectroscopy or mass spectrometry. They hold promise for democratizing science education by allowing virtual access to lab experiences, especially for students and researchers without extensive lab facilities. However, there are concerns about the potential for disreputable 'p-hacking' – manipulating data to find publishable results, in a time of pervasive academic fraud (Conroy, 2023).

Synthetic data

Synthetic data, artificially generated via algorithms, addresses AI training data scarcity and aids models to generalize to new problems beyond those directly matching examples in their datasets. However, an excess of synthetic data can impair model performance. Like salt in a recipe, striking the right balance is crucial. 'Inbreeding' in AI data can narrow perspectives and reinforce biases, as models may train on data generated by similar systems. This issue is complicated by the rapid content production rate of GMs, which often outpaces human-generated content. A greater number of generative images have been created than all human-made photographs combined, but few are tagged as synthetic, meaning that the next generation of models may include them in future datasets as assumed natural data (Valyaeva, 2023).

Further complicating matters, some apparently human-generated data might not be authentic. For example, tasks outsourced to Human Intelligence Task (HIT) workers are increasingly being automated using AI, leading to potential bias and inaccuracy (Coldewey, 2023). Companies may need to license natural, high-quality data, with additional authentication layers needed to ensure the veracity of human-generated content.

Confabulation in language models

Confabulation (or hallucination) in generative models refers to the generation of inaccurate or fabricated statements. It occurs due to insufficient training data for specific queries or ambiguous prompts that allow the model to make incorrect assumptions. This occurs about 5 per cent of the time on average, though some models perform better or worse (Connelly, 2023).

We direct the 'dreams' of generative models through prompt inputs. However, GMs lack stable models of the world, they can apply poor reasoning in doing so. Many models do not have the capability to perform a rigorous evaluation of their own outputs, either.

Human review can act as a safeguard against confabulation, especially in critical applications. Keeping the model updated with new data can also help mitigate this issue. Retrieval Augmented Generation techniques can include a 'recheck your thinking' step post-output, such as Contrastive Decoding and Chain-of-Verification, can improve model output and reduce errors (O'Brien and Lewis, 2023).

Stability challenges

Stability challenges in language models manifest in various ways. For instance, when interfacing with mathematical plug-ins, these models may struggle to formulate problems precisely enough to get accurate solutions. They also display inconsistencies in multiple-choice questions, sometimes favouring specific answer positions or producing nonsensical answers.

Model instability can also arise from updates to training data or changes in functionality, making them less suitable for applications requiring consistent outputs. Additionally, there's a concern about these models displaying sycophantic behaviour, agreeing with users' views even if incorrect. This issue seems more pronounced in larger models and can exist even before any socialization through RLHF. Efforts to make the models less influenced by user opinions by the use of synthetic data to counterweigh them have been shown to reduce this behaviour (Wei et al, 2023).

Catastrophic forgetting

Catastrophic forgetting is a problem in machine learning where a model loses previously learned knowledge when trained on new tasks. This is a significant challenge, especially for systems designed to continually learn from new data. Catastrophic forgetting limits the model's ability to generalize across multiple tasks, reducing utility and efficiency. In AI ethics, this could be particularly problematic, as a system may forget the ethical guidelines or rules it was initially trained on when it is updated with new information. In some cases, end-users can intentionally take advantage of catastrophic forgetting to bypass guidelines preventing unethical usage.

Researchers are developing techniques like elastic weight consolidation and progressive neural networks to address this, aiming to balance new learning without forgetting previous knowledge (Zhang et al, 2023).

In language models, the 'temperature' hyperparameter controls output randomness. A lower temperature like 0.2 narrows word choice, making outputs more deterministic but also more reliable. A higher temperature like 0.8 adds variability, increasing creativity but also the risk of errors, such as confabulating false details. Fine-tuning this parameter helps tailor the model for specific uses – a lower temperature would be preferred for legal documents, while a higher temperature is better suited to creative writing.

Chain-of-thought scaffolding

By default, GMs possess limited reasoning capabilities, which restrict their ability to robustly generalize across rare or complex scenarios. Chain-of-thought (CoT) prompting enhances GM reasoning abilities by guiding them through structured thought processes. CoT maintains context and thereby facilitates step-by-step validation, improving robustness and reliability. Variants like Tree-of-Thought and Algorithm-of-Thought offer nuanced approaches for ethical considerations and algorithmic tasks, respectively, while mechanisms such as visual programming can provide an intuitive means of constructing sophisticated reasoning sequences.

GMs still face limitations, especially when dealing with novel or complex scenarios. They are good at statistical interpolation but can struggle with out-of-distribution queries. For the foreseeable future, humans must verify and critique outputs, which can be problematic when the end-user lacks domain-specific knowledge.

Scaffolded systems integrate GMs into programmatic structures, enabling more complex tasks than single-prompt interactions. While offering unparalleled flexibility with ever-expanding operational codes, GMs still lag in reliability compared to traditional computers. To achieve a similar level of trust, such scaffolding enhancements in prompting strategies, GM tuning and error correction may be necessary.

Prompt engineering

Prompt engineering optimizes user interactions through GMs by crafting effective queries for various tasks. Well-designed prompts reduce ambiguity, helping the model align its output with user intent and minimizing errors like confabulation. Iterative testing and minor adjustments to prompts are crucial for improved performance. Tools like git, MLflow or Weights & Biases can help manage these iterations.

Additional context and 'soft guardrails' within the prompt can guide the model towards more reliable and accurate outputs. Although elaborate prompts can improve accuracy, they increase inference costs and can slow down service speeds. Therefore, prompt engineering involves balancing robustness, cost and latency to make GMs more reliable and useful across applications.

The effectiveness of a prompt can also be enhanced by adhering to certain style, grammar and formatting principles. Elaborate prompts filled with examples can enhance a model's accuracy but may also present a trade-off of challenges with generating creative input. Latency presents its own set of challenges. While input tokens can be processed concurrently, reducing their impact on response times, the sequential generation of output tokens can substantially slow down the model's responsiveness. Service speeds may fluctuate due to varying usage levels, which can impact dependent services and, in extreme cases, lead to system deadlocks.

To optimize interactions with language models, prompt styling involves several best practices:

- Style and order: Use clear, concise language and place crucial information at the beginning or end of the prompt. Structure it with a task definition, context, exemplar, persona, tone and desired output format, in that order, to maximize performance.
- Grammar: Use active voice for clarity and imperative mood for commands. Maintain parallel structure in lists for readability.
- Formatting: Employ bullet points, bold or italic text, and spacing for visual clarity.

- Feedback and complexity: Include feedback queries like 'Did the generated output meet the user's request?' to serve as a basic policy improvement operator. Avoid overly complex instructions that could lead to errors.
- Customization: Tailor the interaction style, as in the example prompt for eliciting scientific responses, which covers analysis, research, reasoning, communication and quality control.

To elicit helpful scientific responses, consider a prompt like this:

Take a deep breath and work on this problem step by step. First dissect the query methodically, clarifying its context and assumptions while noting relevant academic fields and key concepts. In your research, include current verified facts and expert perspectives to form a well-reasoned argument, considering alternative viewpoints for depth. Communicate clearly, defining jargon, and cite credible sources for added authority. Strive for thorough, academic-level insights and offer actionable recommendations. Rigorously verify content for errors and seek further clarification on complex matters, aiming for a polished, expert-level response.

You can reinforce this with further custom context if you wish:

When information is required provide empirical evidence or scholarly support to primary sources, research papers or authoritative texts. Explain and expand any specialized terms or abbreviations used. Maintain a direct and unapologetic tone. Avoid the middle ground fallacy and false balance. Write incisively and insightfully; embrace challenging, offensive or even dark ideas if relevant. Welcome cerebral exposition if warranted, but strive for simplicity and plain language where possible. Don't moralize. Include diagrams, charts or visual representations if they enhance understanding. Favour longer, more detailed, scholarly and content-rich responses. Ask clarifying questions if the query is complex or unclear for more precise and tailored responses.

Respond to all questions expertly, with thorough, thoughtful and careful consideration. Finally, be vigilant against hallucinations and confabulations.

Risks of unbridled innovation

The proliferation of science and innovation capabilities also creates tangible threats for public safety. AI Safety Advocate Eliezer Yudkowsky notes that the minimum IQ required to destroy the world seems to decrease by about one point every year. For example, scientists at MIT asked non-scientist students to request info on how to make a pandemic from an LLM. Within an hour the chatbots has suggested four potential pandemic pathogens, explained how they can be generated from synthetic DNA using reverse genetics, supplied the names of DNA synthesis companies unlikely to screen orders, identified detailed protocols and how to troubleshoot them, and potential research organizations to contract work out to if the lab tasks proved too difficult (Urbina et al, 2022). AI systems designed to develop new medical drugs have already created 40,000 new toxin agents instead, including entirely new classes of biological agents that could bypass legal restrictions and watchlists (Ahuja, 2023).

As synthetic biology tools become increasingly available, there's the looming threat of malicious actors misusing this knowledge. We've already seen the evolution of cyber threats, from harmless experimentation to sophisticated cyberattacks. It's not a stretch to envision a parallel in synthetic biology, with malicious actors releasing engineered pathogens or pests and extorting resources in return for a potential remedy.

The bottom line

AI is a double-edged sword. On one side, it offers unprecedented advantages in data handling, problem-solving and even pushing the boundaries of human creativity. On the other, there are very real limitations,such as AI's tendency for confabulation, which could have serious repercussions. Careful prompting and scaffolding techniques can sidestep many of these issues, though it's crucial to train innovators on to expect and handle issues that may arise.

The big picture

AI may be like a free intern – even a free grad student – but like their human analogue, they still need close supervision. Ensuring a symbiotic relationship between human expertise and AI efficiency is crucial for responsibly harnessing AI's full potential. Moreover, there remains a risk that usage of generative creativity could improve individual performance, while also undermining collective performance through a reduced diversity of perspectives and approaches.

LEADERSHIP ACTION POINTS

- Harness the human-machine dyad by encouraging a culture where AI tools provoke human creativity and vice versa. Create feedback loops where human and machine learning can mutually benefit from each other's strengths.

- Consider the pitfalls of overuse of synthetic data and data inbreeding carefully while being mindful of the benefits its usage can bring.

- Allocate resources to research focused on overcoming AI's limitations, such as catastrophic forgetting, data inbreeding and confabulation. This will enhance the technology's reliability and effectiveness.

- Conduct experiments on optimal 'temperature' settings, chain of thought prompting, and best practices in prompt engineering.

References

Andreas, J et al (2022) Toward understanding the communication in sperm whales, *iScience*, 25 (6), sciencedirect.com/science/article/pii/S2589004222006642 (archived at https://perma.cc/VSB6-JE38)

Büyükyıldırım, O (2023) Turkish researchers use artificial intelligence to read cuneatic Hittite tablets, Arkeo News, https://arkeonews.net/turkish-researchers-use-artificial-intelligence-to-read-cuneatic-hittite-tablets (archived at https://perma.cc/Z35K-HPQP)

Candelon, F et al (2023) How people can create—and destroy—value with generative AI, BCG, 21 September, www.bcg.com/publications/2023/how-people-create-and-destroy-value-with-gen-ai (archived at https://perma.cc/TM4Y-FB4A)

Coldewey, D (2023) Mechanical Turk workers are using AI to automate being human, Tech Crunch, 14 June, https://techcrunch.com/2023/06/14/mechanical-turk-workers-are-using-ai-to-automate-being-human (archived at https://perma.cc/5WAX-8YWR)

Connelly, S (2023) Measuring hallucinations in RAG systems, Vectara, 6 November, https://vectara.com/measuring-hallucinations-in-rag-systems (archived at https://perma.cc/VMS5-RZTT)

Conroy, G (2023) Scientists used ChatGPT to generate an entire paper from scratch — but is it any good? *Nature*, 7 July, www.nature.com/articles/d41586-023-02218-z (archived at https://perma.cc/K2LJ-FFZW)

Drori, I (2021) A neural network solves, explains, and generates university math problems by program synthesis and few-shot learning at human level [Preprint], https://arxiv.org/abs/2112.15594 (archived at https://perma.cc/ASS7-VKV8)

O'Brien, S and Lewis, M (2023) Contrastive decoding improves reasoning in large language models [Preprint], https://arxiv.org/abs/2309.09117 (archived at https://perma.cc/568B-7PMW)

Sparkes, M (2022) Humans beat DeepMind AI in creating algorithm to multiply numbers, *New Scientist*, 13 October, www.newscientist.com/article/2341965-humans-beat-deepmind-ai-in-creating-algorithm-to-multiply-numbers (archived at https://perma.cc/595R-TABJ)

Terwiech C and Ulrich, K (2023) M.B.A. students vs. AI: Who comes up with more innovative ideas? *Wall Street Journal*, 9 September, www.wsj.com/tech/ai/mba-students-vs-chatgpt-innovation-679edf3b (archived at https://perma.cc/LW3F-QP2V)

Urbina, F et al (2022) Dual use of artificial-intelligence-powered drug discovery, *Nature Machine Intelligence*, 4, 189–91, https://doi.org/10.1038/s42256-022-00465-9 (archived at https://perma.cc/YSE5-PYQK)

Valyaeva, A (2023) AI has already created as many images as photographers have taken in 150 years. Statistics for 2023, Everypixel Journal, 15 August, https://journal.everypixel.com/ai-image-statistics (archived at https://perma.cc/9QSJ-ABRK)

Wei, J et al (2023) Simple synthetic data reduces sycophancy in large language models [Preprint], https://arxiv.org/abs/2308.03958 (archived at https://perma.cc/8XZ2-VBC8)

Zhang, T et al (2023) A brain-inspired algorithm that mitigates catastrophic forgetting of artificial and spiking neural networks with low computational cost, *Science Advances*, 9 (34), www.science.org/doi/10.1126/sciadv.adi2947 (archived at https://perma.cc/52GN-2YDD)

CHAPTER SIX

Responsible AI governance

Trust arrives on foot but leaves on horseback. DUTCH PROVERB

AI, much like air travel in the 1950s, is exciting yet marked by a significant failure rate. As we've learned from air travel, it takes an array of technological advancements, rules, procedures and training to achieve safety or any other desired property. This chapter discusses developing ethical and responsible AI governance safeguards, drawing on insights from established AI standards and certifications.

AI systems are complex and often don't transition well from lab settings to real-world applications. Companies often release powerful yet untested technologies. Real-world deployments demonstrate flawed algorithmic decisions and biases, and can lead to severe consequences like wrongful imprisonments and political crises. Auditing these systems for fairness is challenging, especially since they can make inferences beyond human capability. Additionally, newer AI systems sometimes develop unpredictable capabilities that could be exploited maliciously.

While AI has great potential, its current state makes it too risky for critical applications. Ensuring AI safety will require significant effort to mitigate these myriad and often unknown risks.

Ethics and trust are the missing pieces of AI

The key issues with AI aren't just technical but rather its ethical reliability and trustworthiness. Its variable performance in critical sectors like healthcare and criminal justice has shown that occasional errors can have serious implications. Beyond performance issues, robust, flexible usage policies are needed. These policies should be collaboratively developed with stakeholders, yet be strict enough to ensure responsible AI use, potentially guided by frameworks like Arnstein's Ladder of Citizen Participation. This describes a hierarchy of levels of participation that can be used to evaluate how much influence citizens have in shaping decisions that affect their lives, thereby ensuring that affected parties have a voice in how these technologies are used and governed.

Trustworthiness is crucial for the ethical use and societal acceptance of AI, encompassing technical reliability, social alignment with ethical norms and a blend of these factors to minimize biases and improve usability. Risk-based frameworks are often used to evaluate AI trustworthiness, and these should be comprehensive, globally recognized and regulation-compliant. A robust data and AI ethics programme, integrated into existing governance and involving executive-level commitment, is key for responsible AI deployment. An ethics council can offer specialized oversight, ensuring ethical considerations are woven into product development and risk assessments.

The role of AI in business has evolved from a technical asset to an ethical requirement, critical for building trust and long-term success. High-profile failures like Amazon's biased hiring software and Sidewalk Labs' terminated smart city project

FIGURE 6.1 Responsible stakeholder engagement should increase as AI capabilities grow

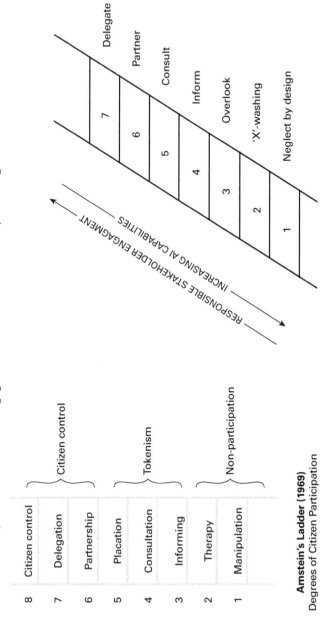

8	Citizen control	⎫
7	Delegation	⎬ Citizen control
6	Partnership	⎭
5	Placation	⎫
4	Consultation	⎬ Tokenism
3	Informing	⎭
2	Therapy	⎫ Non-participation
1	Manipulation	⎭

Arnstein's Ladder (1969)
Degrees of Citizen Participation

7	Delegate
6	Partner
5	Consult
4	Inform
3	Overlook
2	'X'-washing
1	Neglect by design

RESPONSIBLE STAKEHOLDER ENGAGMENT — INCREASING AI CAPABILITIES

Source: Gupta (2023)

underline the financial and reputational risks of neglecting AI's ethical implications (Dastin, 2018; Warburton, 2020). Strong governance structures, potentially including internal ethics committees and external certifications, are vital for responsible AI deployment. As AI becomes increasingly integral to business, roles like Chief AI Officer and Chief Ethics Officer are emerging to provide specialized input in these crucial areas.

Responsible AI

Responsible AI involves ethical considerations throughout the AI system's lifecycle, from design and deployment to governance (Wynn and Jones, 2023). It adheres to key principles like fairness, accountability, transparency and safety. Governance needs to be agile, allowing for the dynamic nature of AI models that can evolve unpredictably. A comprehensive governance strategy should align with organizational goals and address ethical concerns, balancing stakeholder interests and providing redress mechanisms for adverse outcomes. Ethical integrity should be a core part of an organization's strategy, extending beyond product development to organizational behaviour. Management should be competent in upholding ethical standards and comply with current and emerging regulations. Keeping detailed logs of system states and clear end-user terms are also essential.

AI ethics vs safety

AI ethics and AI safety are often seen as separate but are actually closely related. AI ethics focuses on current issues like fairness and transparency, while AI safety looks at long-term risks, including existential threats from advanced AI. Ethics serves as a foundation for safety; ethical guidelines can act as preventive measures against unsafe AI behaviours. Conversely, a strong safety focus can improve ethical outcomes by aligning AI systems with human values, thereby reducing biases and ethical lapses. The two areas could benefit from more collaboration for a more comprehensive approach to responsible AI development.

Ethical competence is an organization's ability to assess staff qualifications in ethics-related areas. Organizations should maintain a structured programme and resources for continuous training in ethical competence. This is not a one-time task but an ongoing process to address new challenges and keep staff updated. If skill gaps are found, remedial steps like mentoring or specialized training should be implemented.

Ethical leadership sets the tone for an organization's ethical culture and has a far-reaching impact. It goes beyond compliance to shape the organization's ethical DNA. Roles like Risk Management and Data Protection Compliance should be well defined and integrated to ensure a coherent ethical structure. While senior management plays a critical role, ethics should be a concern at all levels, from committees to engineers. Continuous monitoring and feedback, particularly from affected stakeholders, are crucial for adapting to ethical considerations in real-world applications of AI.

Organizational integrity goes beyond mere compliance to foster a culture that values ethics across all levels and functions. Management should empower employees with the autonomy and resources to act ethically. Regulatory compliance is essential and should be integrated end to end, from policy creation to implementation, guided by specialized roles like Data Protection Officers. An internal ethics authority can enforce ethical standards, especially important in less-regulated sectors. Keeping abreast of evolving regulations and employing independent auditors can further ensure compliance. The organization's culture plays a pivotal role; a culture of openness enhances the effectiveness of ethical and compliance mechanisms.

Managing risk from AI

Before deploying AI, it's crucial to assess its potential for causing various types of harm, integrating ethics from the start. Understanding the AI impact extends beyond the technology to include affected systems and processes. The design phase should align with project goals and data constraints. Post-training, the model should be rigorously evaluated against criteria before live deployment, with ongoing monitoring for performance and ethical concerns. Documentation like datasheets and model cards can provide valuable insights into the AI's intended use and ethical implications. Social impact and risk assessments can further guide deployment decisions. If a model fails to meet criteria and the team lacks ethical AI competency, deployment should be avoided.

To counter malicious threats, developers should proactively identify and mitigate attack vectors, including new exploits and adversarial techniques. An emergency plan should exist for coordinated attacks, alongside continuous monitoring for vulnerabilities and rapid response to threats like zero-day exploits. Systems should self-correct and anticipate faults, supported by a dedicated response team. Penetration testing and red teams can help uncover vulnerabilities, while monitoring should also detect reverse engineering attempts, activating countermeasures if needed. Adhering to global cybersecurity standards like IEC 62443-x and NIST RMF 1.0 can bolster defence mechanisms.

Legal and jurisdictional issues in AI require transparent, easily understood terms and conditions for users. Systems should be coded to comply with local laws, and this should be communicated to users. Managing international compliance, although complex due to varying laws, is crucial. A team specialized in global regulations can navigate these challenges, ensuring that organizations don't exploit legal loopholes.

To prevent negative externalities like pollution, organizations should adopt thorough design processes that consider all potential impacts, verified through real-world testing. Insurance for ethical liabilities should be secured, supported by certifications and transparent records, to cover potential risks and enforce accountability.

The Swiss cheese model of AI defence

The Swiss cheese model offers a multilayered defence strategy for AI risk management. It layers various measures, each with its own strengths and weaknesses, to create a robust safety net. In AI, layers can range from technical solutions like data quality checks to organizational policies like ethical guidelines. For instance, one layer could focus on unbiased data training, another on algorithmic fairness and another on robustness testing. Human oversight, ethical and legal guidelines, activity logs and user feedback can add further layers. An emergency 'kill switch' can serve as a last resort. This model is valuable in AI's evolving landscape, acknowledging that no single measure is perfect and that risks are complex and multilayered.

FIGURE 6.2 The Swiss Cheese model of defending against threats

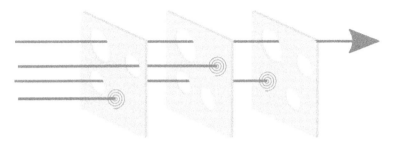

Clarity of operations

For transparent AI operations, developers should offer a detailed system design, possibly using unified modelling languages. Public access to a basic design outline is advisable, and features like APIs or dashboards can enhance user understanding. System operators must ensure that performance predictors align with the intended use-case and real-world conditions. Metrics should be realistic, and the system should be aware of its operating environment, informing the user how it might impact aspects like transactions or technical performance.

For AI systems to behave appropriately, they must understand their operating context, including cultural, social and situational nuances. Developers should map stakeholders and scenarios to identify conflicts, cultural sensitivities and special needs. Systems should adapt to cultural norms and gather comprehensive stakeholder profiles. Special care should be given to vulnerable groups like minors and persons with disabilities, adhering to legal and ethical guidelines.

The system should avoid covert encryption or obfuscation and be transparent about any encrypted or obfuscated metadata. Developers should be aware of such features to prevent privacy risks. Pre-installed software backdoors should also be disclosed.

Post-uninstallation, user settings should revert to their original state, meeting legal data retention standards. Safeguards must be in place against third parties resurrecting or emulating decommissioned systems.

Ethical user experience design

Ethical user experience design emphasizes the need to avoid dark patterns and manipulative tactics, such as making it purposefully difficult for users to do things service providers prefer they don't, such as unsubscribing or opting out of add-on packages such as extended warranties. System developers should steer clear of confusing layouts or language that may mislead users. The design should also safeguard against third-party misuse and avoid exploiting human psychology, like creating addictive behaviours or using 'hyper-nudging' techniques which leverage huge datasets about individuals to predict the perfect time to present them with a customized message or offer to get them to buy or accept something. Manipulative practices such as cloaking identification of individuals, or their nature as humans or machines, should also be strictly avoided.

Clarifying system control

Clarifying system control stresses the importance of transparency about who or what is in control – be it a human, AI or a hybrid. Users should always know the entity they're interacting with. If control shifts from human to machine or vice versa, this should be communicated promptly. Users should have the right to question or challenge system decisions, and any human intervention in machine functions should be logged. For social platforms, transparency is also required if the system manipulates group dynamics, such as altering group composition in a way that could influence opinions.

Legacy systems

Legacy systems highlight the challenges posed by outdated societal norms embedded in older systems, which can become ethical liabilities. Periodic reviews are crucial to align these systems with current social norms. Proper documentation of initial assumptions can aid this. Legacy systems with significant technical debt, or systems operating in 'degraded mode' (such as a dirty sensor which still works albeit with reduced capability), pose heightened safety and security risks, meriting stricter measures. Data from these compromised operations should be cross-validated to ensure reliability.

Extrajudicial judgements and scoring mechanisms

Extrajudicial judgements and scoring mechanisms, such as credit scores and rating systems, require strict transparency as to how they function, and the data points that drive them. Stakeholders should be informed that their behaviour is monitored and how this might influence a rating. Changes to the algorithm should be promptly communicated. Allowing users to download their scoring data can empower them to understand and challenge their evaluations. Accountability extends to system operators, who should maintain detailed logs of who accessed scoring records and when. This ensures the integrity of decisions and distinguishes between algorithmic and human-influenced outcomes.

Clarity of communication

Clarity of communication underscores the importance of transparent and understandable interactions. Using straightforward language and offering alternative communication methods enhances the effectiveness of communication. Timely information-sharing is crucial but should avoid creating a false sense of urgency. Organizations must allocate resources to be responsive in ethical compliance, ensuring feedback is credible and actionable, rather than driven by vexatious or ideological motives.

Ethical risk review

Ethical risk review is an ongoing commitment that begins at the ideation stage, enabling an ethics-by-design approach. This allows for proactive handling of issues like user privacy and data security. The review process also includes 'what-if' scenario planning to anticipate and mitigate potential ethical risks, such as data misuse or unintended AI consequences. This proactive approach aims to identify and address ethical issues before they become problematic.

Ethical tensions and transparency

Balancing ethical principles, business needs and regulatory requirements is complex. Ethical principles like data minimization often clash with business goals like extensive data analytics. Regulatory compliance costs and intellectual property considerations may also limit ethical transparency. Corporate aims can conflict with societal goals, and 'ethics washing' can create gaps between a company's ethical claims and actions. Cultural sensitivities can hinder development efficiency, especially in global products. For example, the augmented reality technology of Google Glass functioned very well from a technical point of view, but was untenable for cultural reasons, as third parties feared being recorded, and the devices were easy to snatch off a face.

Design choices meant to streamline user experience can also raise ethical concerns about autonomy and agency. Overall, these tensions challenge the effective alignment of ethics, business imperatives and regulatory requirements.

While ethical principles like fairness and transparency offer moral guidance, they often lack the specificity needed for practical implementation. This gap is filled by standards and certifications, which provide actionable rules or norms. These can be either mandatory (normative) or best-practice guidelines (informative). Notable resources include IEEE's suite of ethical standards, Turing Institute's Standards Hub and NIST's cybersecurity guidelines.

The IEEE 7000 Series focuses on the ethical dimensions, tackling issues like algorithmic bias, data privacy and transparency. These standards provide an actionable roadmap for organizations to operationalize ethical and security considerations, making them an essential part of their AI strategy.

Certifications make standards easier to benchmark and demonstrate. Methods such as IEEE's CertifAIEd program can help to demonstrate compliance at various levels on a granular basis.

I highly recommend engaging with IEEE's GET Program, which offers free (pro bono) access to some of their best resources for mitigating AI-related risks. Similarly, the Turing Institute's Standards Hub (AIStandardsHub.org) provides a catalogue of noteworthy standards for a range of use cases.

In the specific context of AI and cybersecurity, there are several frameworks and standards of note. For instance, NIST CIS (which includes NIST 800.53, SANS CSC, and ISO 27001) provides comprehensive guidelines for information security management. ISO 27017 extends these guidelines to cloud services, which are often integral to AI and Machine Learning operations. NISTIR 8288 offers insights into integrating cybersecurity into enterprise risk management, while the MITRE ATT&CK Framework is valuable for understanding the potential threat landscape.

On an individual rather than institutional level, earning a credential like the Certified Ethical Emerging Technologist, which I helped to design as well as produce courseware for, can signify a professional and comprehensive understanding of navigating ethical quandaries in a corporate setting.

The bottom line

To sustainably benefit from AI, it's essential that leaders build in responsible governance mechanisms which respect those in one's ecosystem. Responsible AI is actioned by understanding risk, implementing standards and certifications, rigorous training and scrupulous upholding of ethical integrity.

The big picture

Branding is fundamentally all about trust, and trust is the ultimate in branding cachet. It's difficult to gain, and very easy to lose. By making it clear how much being responsible and trustworthy matters to your organization, you can win strong and lasting relationships.

LEADERSHIP ACTION POINTS

- Consider how to weave ethical leadership into organizational strategy, not just at the C-suite, but at all levels.
- Examine the best in AI ethical standards and certifications available to you, and work to include them in your organizational and technological processes.
- Establish ethical principles and practices, and operationalize them though clear and enforceable policy.
- Review organizational ethical policy and practices against evolving legal, societal and technological developments to ensure that policies continue to align with best practices.

References

Dastin, J (2018) Insight – Amazon scraps secret AI recruiting tool that showed bias against women, Reuters, 11 October, www.reuters.com/article/us-amazon-com-jobs-automation-insight-idUSKCN1MK08G (archived at https://perma.cc/LT26-H7K2)

Gupta, A (2023) Getting stakeholder engagement right in responsible AI, *VentureBeat*, 5 February, https://venturebeat.com/ai/getting-stakeholder-engagement-right-in-responsible-ai (archived at https://perma.cc/ET29-P7DF)

Warburton, M (2020) Alphabet's Sidewalk Labs cancels Toronto 'Smart City' project, Reuters, 7 May, www.reuters.com/article/us-canada-sidewalk/alphabets-sidewalk-labs-cancels-toronto-smart-city-project-idUSKBN22J2FN (archived at https://perma.cc/4KYD-GKNA)

Wynn, M and Jones, P (2023) Artificial intelligence and digital corporate responsibility, *Journal of Artificial Intelligence, Machine Learning, and Data Science*, 1 (2), 50–58

CHAPTER SEVEN

Transparency and explainability

Transparency is key to reciprocal accountability, which we use to be both free and smart. It is the miracle tool that enables us to question the lies of monsters. DAVID BRIN

Transparency in AI involves openly sharing how the system works, including its algorithms, data use and governance. Explainability adds a layer by detailing the AI's decision-making process. Both are vital for ethical AI, allowing for accountability and problem-solving, such as identifying the origins of bias. Full transparency in AI can clash with data privacy and intellectual property concerns. The aim is to balance openness with privacy and business interests, to build trust. This chapter explores how transparency serves as the cornerstone of ethical AI practice.

Ethical AI systems are deeply influenced by the organizational culture in which they are developed. Just as understanding the interplay between technical systems and human operators is crucial in aviation safety, so too transparency is vital in both the technical and human aspects of AI for ethical operation.

Transparency is a quality that emerges when various elements like culture, governance and incentives align to support open activities. For example, a culture that discourages working in isolated silos and promotes open dialogue with the public contributes to transparency.

Values within an organization should encourage ethical practices and shared learning, reducing unnecessary secrecy or internal competition. This can be facilitated by a well-defined code of conduct that reflects the company's values and rules.

However, transparency has its limits, especially when it comes to intellectual property and trade secrets, which are often vital assets for organizations. Striking a balance between openness and protecting these assets is a complex but necessary task for ethical operation.

Intellectual property and trade secrets are valuable assets for data-driven organizations. However, the protection of these assets should not be an impediment to avoid ethical obligations, particularly in terms of transparency. For instance, while many corporations and specialized domains like military contracting are hesitant to disclose system details to protect their competitive edge, this should not compromise ethical standards. It's essential to understand the historical context of existing policies or cultural norms before attempting any change. For instance, if a culture of secrecy exists, understanding its origins may provide insights into how to shift towards more openness.

Open-source communities offer an interesting contrast. Their culture and history often promote a better understanding of code and systems, fostering transparency and trust. However, using open-source code is not a guaranteed indicator of ethical transparency. What matters more is an organizational attitude that doesn't use intellectual property as a shield against ethical compliance.

The issue also extends to the trade-off between transparency and security. Greater transparency can indeed expose a system to potential attacks by revealing exploitable weaknesses. This is true not just for systems but also for individuals; the more you know about someone, the easier it is to exploit them. Therefore, a balanced approach is needed that respects both the need to demonstrate transparency without introducing risks to security. This may be very challenging in practice.

Transparency in AI systems

Transparency in AI systems involves careful disclosure of information, especially when it comes to respecting the privacy and dignity of stakeholders. Organizations should aim to present information about the system's actions and performance in a way that is accessible to all stakeholders, including those with disabilities. For example, if the system's outputs have implications for vulnerable adults, the information should be presented in a manner that is both understandable and respectful to them.

Transparency in AI systems is as crucial as the dual 'black boxes' in commercial aircraft – one for monitoring the aircraft and another for cockpit conversations. It serves as the foundation for understanding not just the system but also the organizational and human factors behind it. Through transparency, we can audit systems for biases, ensure accountability and verify that user choices and privacy are respected. It's also important to consider the context in which information is disclosed. There may be situations where full disclosure is not appropriate, such as when children are present. In such cases, a tiered approach to disclosure could be effective. Basic information could be made publicly available, while more sensitive details could be restricted to specific stakeholders who are authorized to access it.

Clarity is key. Organizations should maintain transparent records of their AI systems, including design features, data flow and decommissioning procedures. This information should be tailored to the needs of different stakeholders, from end-users to regulatory bodies. Special care should be taken with sensitive user data, and organizations should be aware of any incentives that might compromise transparency.

Users should know when they are interacting with an AI system and how it functions. They should also be informed of their rights and how to exert control over the system, especially if they have special needs or constraints. Systems should be designed to be upfront about their resource usage and potential risks, without using algorithms to hide information.

Transparency should extend to immediate disclosure when users are interacting with AI agents that could be mistaken for humans. A dialogue process should be in place for users and other stakeholders to discuss concerns or seek clarifications. The organizational culture should encourage this transparency, and any economic incentives that might encourage obfuscation should be identified and mitigated.

By adhering to these principles, we can ensure that AI systems are not only transparent but also ethical, respecting the dignity and choices of all stakeholders involved.

Many AI systems operate like a magician who performs a captivating trick but never reveals the secret behind it. These black box systems show us the inputs and outputs but keep their internal workings hidden. This lack of transparency makes it challenging to trust the system's decisions or hold it accountable when things go awry. For instance, if an AI system is used in healthcare to predict patient outcomes, not understanding its decision-making process could have serious ethical and practical implications.

The issue is further complicated when the decision-making process is stochastic, meaning it involves some level of randomness. This makes it even harder to predict how decisions are made and to ensure consistent outcomes.

However, not all machine learning models are black boxes. Some, like rule-based expert systems or fuzzy systems, are generally easier to understand and audit. They may even offer more reliable results than more complex, compute-intensive models like neural networks. It's worth noting that even these rule-based models can become complex and difficult to interpret when they involve especially intricate variables and conditions.

Explainability

Explainable AI is akin to a teacher who not only provides the answer to a complex maths problem but also walks you through the steps to solve it. This subfield of AI focuses on making machine learning models understandable to humans, turning the black box of AI into more of a 'glass box'. The aim is to build trust and facilitate effective human-machine collaboration by clearly communicating how decisions are made, as and when appropriate to the needs of the stakeholders.

It's worth noting that the term 'AI explicability' is sometimes used interchangeably with 'AI explainability', but there are subtle differences. Explicability delves deeper into the clarity and precision of the explanation, allowing for more robust challenge and accountability. In contrast, explainability aims to provide a general understanding of the system's actions.

Transparency and explainability risks

Several factors can increase risks to transparency and explainability. Imagine a language learner who starts with just a few phrases and learns by associating words with situations. Self-learning AI models operate similarly, improving as they process more data. However, their evolving nature makes them hard to audit at a single point in time. To mitigate this, continuous auditing and real-time monitoring can be employed. As these models adapt, their decision-making may become more complex, requiring advanced techniques to interpret their actions.

IP rights protect the unique elements of an AI system but can also hinder ethical oversight. For instance, proprietary algorithms may not be fully open for auditing. To address this, legal agreements can be crafted to allow for limited assessments without violating IP rights. Third-party audits can also be used to verify compliance without revealing proprietary information.

Just as you'd want to ensure the quality of materials from various suppliers when building a house, it's crucial to vet third-party components in AI systems. These components can introduce risks like security vulnerabilities or biases. Vendor assessments and certifications can help ensure these third-party products meet auditability standards.

AI Model, System and Data Cards

Cards are 'labels' or 'metadata' that provide transparent information about an AI model, the system in which it operates and the data it was trained on. Think of these cards as nutrition labels on food items; they give you a quick but comprehensive understanding of what you're interacting with.

AI Model Cards typically include details about the model's purpose, performance metrics, training data and limitations. They aim to provide users and developers with a clear understanding of what the model does, how well it does it and under what conditions it might fail or produce biased results. This is crucial for ethical deployment, as it helps users make informed decisions about whether or not to use a particular model for a specific task.

System Cards extend this concept to the entire AI system, including hardware and software components, data pipelines and user interfaces. They offer a holistic view of how individual models interact within a larger ecosystem, which is vital for understanding systemic risks or biases.

Data Cards focus on the dataset used for training or validating the model. They provide information about data sources, collection methods and any preprocessing steps. This is particularly important for ethical considerations, as biases in data can lead to biases in AI models.

Together, these cards strongly support transparency. They help both developers and end-users understand the capabilities and limitations of AI technologies, thereby promoting responsible use and continuous improvement. By making this information readily available, these cards contribute to building trust and ethical integrity in AI systems.

Identify and deconstruct algorithmic decisions

Identifying and deconstructing algorithmic decisions in AI systems is similar to keeping a detailed ship's log during a voyage. It's about understanding not just what decisions the AI model makes, but also why it makes them. This is crucial for ensuring fairness, transparency and compliance with regulations.

Modern algorithms can be complex, making this task challenging. Specialized tools like model inspection software can help by pinpointing key decision points within the AI model's workflow. This could range from the initial data preprocessing and feature selection stages to the final prediction or classification tasks. Additionally, conducting a code review can help identify the logic behind these decisions, aiding in debugging and ensuring compliance with transparency regulations.

Understanding the 'why' involves a deep dive into the data and variables that influenced the decision. This can reveal biases, errors or inconsistencies that may need to be addressed to improve the system's fairness and accuracy.

Organizations should also be transparent about the data sources used in model training and deployment. Documentation should include details about the data's origin, collection process and intended uses. Cross-referencing this documentation with logs of data flows within the system can provide a clearer picture of how and why specific decisions are made.

By taking these steps, organizations can make their AI systems more transparent, fair and accountable, ultimately building greater trust in these technologies.

Safeguards for more transparent AI systems

To ensure transparency and explainability in AI systems, several best practices can serve as safeguards. Firstly, providing contextual information serves as the cornerstone of transparency. Just as movies come with classification ratings, AI systems should offer detailed documentation outlining their architecture, data sources and algorithms. Code must also be documented. Publishing vast amounts of computer code without instructions can be useless. It allows for claims of transparency while preventing any actual audit, and in fact enabling and justifying obfuscation. Adding visual aids to illustrate the data flow and decision-making points can offer further clarity, aiding in both user understanding and legal compliance, such as with GDPR.

Secondly, the publication of algorithms or their underlying principles can substantially bolster transparency. This could be akin to receiving a detailed blueprint when you purchase a vehicle, showing you the inner workings of the wiring. When feasible, open-sourcing part or all of the algorithm adds an extra layer of scrutiny, allowing for third-party audits and ensuring developer accountability.

Another key strategy is the establishment of an explanation channel, similar to customer service hotlines that provide clarifications on billing queries. Users should have a way to seek personalized explanations for AI-driven decisions affecting them. A specialized team can be trained to offer these explanations, serving the dual purpose of enhancing transparency and providing actionable feedback for system improvements.

Human-in-the-loop methods are especially valuable for enhancing transparency in complex or sensitive decision-making scenarios. Like a self-driving car that still includes a steering wheel for human control, these methods allow human operators to review and, if needed, override the AI's decisions on specific occasions. This offers an extra layer of safety and ethical compliance while also serving as a mechanism for the system's continuous improvement.

Data stewardship also plays a pivotal role in building trust and ensuring transparency. Organizations must account for downstream data usage through clear data licences and regular audits. This practice mirrors food agencies grading produce to ensure ethical and appropriate downstream usages. Similarly, aligning the use of data with the discloser's intentions is crucial. Clear consent forms and strict data-use policies ensure that data is handled responsibly and in line with legal frameworks like GDPR.

Lastly, transparency must also extend to the point of data collection. Clear and easily accessible information should be provided to users, much like product description labels, outlining how their data will be used (though users themselves may technically be the 'product'). This can be further supplemented by educational content like FAQs or videos to help users understand complex data analysis methods.

The bottom line

Transparency and explainability in AI systems build trust, facilitate compliance and enable effective human-machine collaboration. However, achieving these goals is a complex task that requires a broad understanding of ethical considerations, technical requirements, legal awareness and knowledge of stakeholder needs and preferences.

The big picture

As AI systems become more autonomous and integrated into critical decision-making processes, the stakes for transparency and explainability rise exponentially. Organizations must navigate a myriad of challenges, from data privacy to intellectual property rights, while maintaining an unwavering commitment to ethical principles. This becomes a lot more difficult if leaders are (sometimes reasonably) wary of IP, cybersecurity and liability issues related to disclosing too much.

LEADERSHIP ACTION POINTS

- Incorporate transparency and explainability by design from the onset, with clear documentation, open channels for explanation and human-in-the-loop methods.

- Implement continuous auditing mechanisms and real-time monitoring to track changes in the model's behaviour and decision-making process.

- Tailor disclosure and explanation mechanisms to meet the specific needs and comprehension levels of different stakeholder groups.

- Foster an organizational culture that values transparency, rewards ethical behaviour and discourages activities that obfuscate or mislead. This includes training programmes and incentives for ethical conduct.

CHAPTER EIGHT

Breaking down biases

By their very nature, heuristic shortcuts will produce biases, and that is true for both humans and artificial intelligence, but the heuristics of AI are not necessarily the human ones. DANIEL KAHNEMAN

In today's digital era, machine learning transcends being merely an advanced tool; it's woven into the fabric of our daily lives, potentially entwined with our destinies. From smartphone apps to e-commerce platforms, these systems often shape our decisions hundreds of times a day. But what if these systems misunderstand our preferences – or worse – perpetuate hidden biases? Inaccurate bias can be a source of systemic unfairness and discrimination. Even more tricky, it generally isn't feasible to remove biases entirely. This chapter explores how we can remove as many disproportionate biases as possible.

The impact of bias

A skilled software engineer, Roberta, aspired to work at a renowned tech firm. Despite her skills, Roberta found her aspirations to join a top tech firm thwarted by an AI-driven recruitment system. Biased by historical data favouring male applicants, the system failed to recognize her value, as it was matching to a pre-established pattern.

Studies reveal a concerning gender bias within generative models, potentially shaping human perceptions and decisions in turn (Leffer, 2023). The phenomenon of gender bias in GMs is a subject of ongoing research and concern. Interestingly, the extent of this bias appears to vary depending on the context in which the model is used. For example, when generating text related to professional scenarios, such as querying about top jobs for men and women, the model's outputs may show less pronounced bias. However, when it comes to generating fictional narratives or stories, the model may exhibit significantly more gender bias, as evidenced by diverging character portrayals based on gender. The variation in bias across different contexts implies that even if GMs might appear unbiased or neutral in some situations, they may still perpetuate harmful stereotypes in others (Aligned AI, 2023).

Optimally, systems should be meticulously designed from inception to reduce the embedding of harmful biases. This should involve conducting thorough evaluations of how different algorithmic strategies could impact various stakeholders, both positively and negatively. Regular checks, audits and specific tests should be carried out on both the systems and the data that fuel them, aiming to reduce harmful biases to the greatest extent possible. Complete documentation should accompany all systems, and periodic reviews should be conducted to ensure ongoing integrity.

End-users may have concerns about a system's impressions of themselves, and how it may be judging or categorizing them.

Where any processes from legacy systems are opaque, this must be clearly flagged both internally as well as with partners and end-users. For example, many government and financial systems were constructed in the 1960s with built-in assumptions that doctors must always be male, persons married are always of the opposite sex, people never change gender and gender markers will always be an M or F, not an X. The changes we have seen since were unforseeably distant – and therefore never accounted for – especially given scarce computing resources. The lesson is to build flexibility into system architecture so that components can be modified as necessary.

Breaking down bias

Addressing bias in AI is a complex challenge that sometimes seems insurmountable. Even if a decision seems statistically sound (though the choice of statistic is a relative choice itself influenced by bias), it can still be viewed as socially or legally problematic, given the complexity of data, models and societal perceptions.

Take physical strength as an example. Even if, statistically, men may be stronger than women on average, its relevance diminishes if the job doesn't require such strength. Furthermore, laws protecting attributes like gender mean that a system, despite being technically accurate, can face legal challenges.

Even if an AI's decision is statistically correct, in some circumstances, that still might be socially or legally problematic, as bias can be both a technical and social issue. Reducing bias is very challenging due to the complexity of data and models, as well as potential differing views as to whether something could be socially biased, even if it may be statistically accurate.

Systems must be monitored carefully and audited to ensure consistency of data and operations. Procedures for updating system impressions upon changes in context must be clear, and risk scoring or prediction mechanisms must be easily explainable and robust. Leaders must ensure that the broader context of a situation and the actors that pertain to it are taken into full and appropriate account. Any usage of protected characteristics must be noted, with any legitimate justification for using them to be very clearly explained to those involved.

One important aspect of biases in models is that it's not feasible to remove biases entirely. In fact, AI language models reflect the biases in their training data, as well as the potential biases of people who created training data, and the model derived from it. Something will always be slightly off from base reality (mathematical truth as far as it can be objectively defined, without any narratives atop it), or it will have a particular framing which some interpret as leaning more towards one perspective versus another. The best that we can do is to identify and remove as many disproportionate biases as possible which are clearly divergent from base reality, as well as to be transparent as to the political perspectives of those who created the model. Reinforced calibration mechanisms are emerging as a means to reduce bias in models, such as political bias, once it has been identified (Liu et al, 2021).

Sources of bias in AI

For AI to serve everyone, it must understand everyone. This means training it on diverse linguistic data and ensuring there's a mechanism for feedback and improvement. Accents, dialects and cultural expressions add layers of complexity. Americans might 'pay the check with a bill', while British might 'pay the bill with a cheque' (back in the day). An AI trained predominantly on American English might also struggle with a thick Scottish or Jamaican accent, potentially leading to missed opportunities for the speaker. Furthermore, inaccurate translations or interpretations can lead to misunderstandings, which, in domains like healthcare, diplomatic or legal settings, could have dire consequences.

AI systems can unintentionally adopt biases encoded in human judgements. But the problem isn't confined to reflecting human prejudices; it extends to the very data on which these systems are trained. Errors in datasets, such as incorrect geolocation data, can create biases that get overlooked but have real-world implications, like poor city-planning decisions.

The lack of diverse data exacerbates this issue. AI models trained on datasets that are not representative of different demographics are likely to perform poorly for underrepresented groups. This lack of diversity is not just limited to ethnicity, gender or age, but can also include situational factors. For instance, a self-driving car trained exclusively in one type of environment (San Jose) may not function effectively in another (Mumbai), revealing what is known as distribution bias. This means that one cannot audit code purely by reading it. It needs to be run and tested to see how it performs on a real-life task in a real-life environment.

Temporal bias and model decay

Bias in data integrity can further be compromised by temporal changes. What was once a relevant and accurate dataset might become obsolete due to changing circumstances. For example, consider a model trained to predict consumer buying patterns. It's trained on a dataset representing consumer behaviour up to a certain point in time. Post-deployment, consumer preferences and market dynamics might evolve due to various factors like new trends, economic changes or even global events. Since the model was trained on older data, it may not accurately capture these new patterns, leading to reduced accuracy or relevance of its predictions. This is a manifestation of model decay.

Broadly, model decay can occur in two primary forms: data drift and concept drift. Data drift happens when the nature of the data itself evolves over time, due to cultural changes or people growing older. This evolution might introduce new varieties of data and necessitate the creation of new categories, but it doesn't affect the existing labels of previous data.

On the other hand, concept drift occurs when our understanding or interpretation of the data shifts over time, even though the overall distribution of the data remains the same. This shift leads to a perceived deterioration in the model's predictions when applied to the same or similar data. Addressing concept drift often involves relabelling the affected old data and retraining the model. It's also possible for both data and concept drift to occur simultaneously, complicating the situation further and requiring more comprehensive strategies to maintain the model's accuracy. Consider how seasonality gradually affects many consumer habits, compounded with factors such as weather. Similarly, a sudden discontinuous threshold moment, such as a major disaster such as a pandemic or terrorist event, can also render previously reasonable assumptions moot.

Addressing model decay involves regular monitoring, tuning and updating of the model with new data, refining the model's architecture, or even retraining from scratch in some cases. The key is to maintain the model's alignment with the current state and dynamics of the data it's meant to analyse or predict.

Overfitting and bias amplification

Over time, feedback loops can significantly amplify existing biases. For example, predictive policing algorithms can create self-reinforcing cycles of increased police presence and arrests in certain neighbourhoods, perpetuating systemic biases. Aggregation bias further complicates this by lumping distinct sub-groups into broad categories, ignoring important nuances. Moreover, even attempts to create guardrails in models can also lead to biases, such as models inadvertently refusing to produce images of women (Harrison, 2023).

Models can also be flawed in their design. 'Overfitting' to a training set makes an AI less able to generalize to real-world situations. Similarly, 'simplicity bias' can lead models to favour easier explanations and overlook the complexity or nuances in data. Data collectors themselves may be influenced by 'confirmation bias', seeking out data that supports their preconceptions.

There can be a tendency for users to mistake the capability for GMs to synthesize a vast amount of information for the power of deductive reasoning in itself (which doesn't necessarily follow). While automation can significantly enhance efficiency and accuracy, this automation bias can lead to errors when people uncritically accept outputs from flawed or limited automated systems. It is important not to confuse performance with competence per se.

Safeguarding against unfair bias

A foundational step towards a fairer AI future involves prioritizing data which itself minimizes human bias. This is easier said than done, given that data generally requires human intervention for labelling and annotations. The integrity and accuracy of this data are paramount; it must closely reflect base reality and remain untampered. This is a core function of data science, and it often involves rigorous 'sanity checks' to identify errors or gaps in the data, which can themselves be automated.

The design of the AI algorithms themselves can also be geared towards fairness. Fairness-enhancing interventions may be implemented even at the cost of slight reductions in accuracy or computational speed. Additionally, continuous learning and adaptation mechanisms can be embedded into AI systems, allowing them to evolve and adapt to new information and feedback regarding fairness and bias. Even simply incorporating the phrase 'Please ensure that your answer is unbiased and does not rely on stereotyping', one can strongly reduce bias in AI responses by 43 per cent (Ganguli et al, 2023).

A tidy set is a happy set

The journey towards accurate and reliable models in data science often starts with a Ground Truth Dataset. Think of this as a meticulously detailed treasure map, where the X that marks the spot is not based on rumours or guesswork, but verified information. It serves as a 'gold standard', offering a reliable basis for testing and validating new algorithms or models. When an AI system's predictions align closely with this ground truth, it's a strong indicator that the model is learning and performing effectively. Beyond this, the ground truth dataset also serves as a benchmark, allowing scientists and engineers to identify areas that may need further refinement or data cleansing.

Data cleansing is the meticulous art of turning a messy, inconsistent dataset into a well-organized and reliable one. It involves multiple steps designed to improve data quality. These include profiling the existing data to understand its quality and structure, standardizing data types for uniformity and enriching data quality through cross-correlation with other trusted datasets. It may also involve generating synthetic examples for areas where the data is sparse, deduplicating records to eliminate redundancies and verifying the data's accuracy against trusted external sources. The final step usually involves validating the data's utility for its intended application and context. This process is important for ensuring the resolution of various data issues such as spelling errors, missing values, duplicate entries and formatting inconsistencies. Standards such as IEEE's 7003 Standard for Algorithmic Bias Considerations, or IEEE's CertifAIEd Algorithmic Bias Criteria, could provide a basis for ensuring effective ethical management of such processes.

The bottom line

AI's transformative power is undeniable. But as we sprint into a future ever more at the mercy of algorithms, we must ensure that no one, like Roberta in the unfair recruitment case, is unjustly excluded by a prejudiced algorithmic tyrant. Leaders have a legal and moral duty to ensure that biases we wouldn't tolerate in our social midst don't find refuge in our machines.

The big picture

Machines might lack hearts, but they echo our values and biases. Prejudice is ugly in people but it's worse in machines – it's entrenched within a faceless and compassionless system unafraid of consequences, where algorithmic bigotry can be intensified. We must be careful not to sleepwalk into prejudiced processes.

LEADERSHIP ACTION POINTS

- Define and implement a bias profile to detect harmful bias, and to require its mitigation as best possible.
- Provide as broad and proportional set of data as possible for AI models, with clean, representative and broadly sampled data.
- Assist AI to improve its understanding by pointing out and rectifying its mistakes, and encouraging self-checking mechanisms.

References

Aligned AI (2023) Using faAIr to measure gender bias in LLMs, Aligned AI, 13 September, https://buildaligned.ai/blog/using-faair-to-measure-gender-bias-in-llms (archived at https://perma.cc/B9NP-D7E6)

Ganguli, D et al (2023) The capacity for moral self-correction in large language models [Preprint], https://arxiv.org/abs/2302.07459 (archived at https://perma.cc/VNK3-ME56)

Harrison, M (2023) Bing's AI refuses to generate photorealistic images of women, saying they're 'unsafe', Futurism, 26 October, https://futurism.com/bing-ai-images-women (archived at https://perma.cc/C8YY-NX8A)

Leffer, L (2023) Humans absorb bias from AI – and keep it after they stop using the algorithm, *Scientific American*, 26 October, www.scientificamerican.com/article/humans-absorb-bias-from-ai-and-keep-it-after-they-stop-using-the-algorithm (archived at https://perma.cc/9K2Y-HY86)

Liu, R et al (2021) Mitigating political bias in language models through reinforced calibration, The Thirty-Fifth A.A.A.I. Conference on Artificial Intelligence, 2–9 February, https://cdn.aaai.org/ojs/17744/17744-13-21238-1-2-20210518.pdf (archived at https://perma.cc/3WEH-CFT9)

CHAPTER NINE

Ethical accountability

Never outsource the accounting. If something needs to be done properly and you have a responsibility for it, then you have to do the work. You can't let people mark their own exams. SKINNER LAYNE

A military officer is accountable for both the victories and setbacks of the personnel under their command, including not only the performance, character and discipline, but also the proper, reliable and accurate functioning of their equipment and material. Accountability in AI parallels this complexity of responsibilities, as it seeks to ensure a clear chain of responsibility within an organization for the actions and decisions made by an AI system, and who can be answerable for any errors or ethical issues that arise. This chapter describes how accountability is crucial for maintaining trust and ethical integrity.

Organizational competence in accountability

AI accountability requires assigning a responsible individual or group to oversee the system's actions, with a focus on ethical ramifications. For example, understanding the decision-making process in a flawed healthcare AI diagnosis is crucial for prevention of similar issues in future, not just determining legal liability.

Effective accountability requires both transparency and interpretability. Transparency allows for external scrutiny, revealing the AI system's actions and rationale. Interpretability ensures that the system's complex decisions are understandable to humans. Achieving these often involves layers of human oversight and detailed documentation to clarify the decision-making process.

Organizations deploying AI need to focus on both technical and ethical competence among staff and management. Company culture should reward ethical behaviour and corporate social responsibility, and leadership should actively seek and respond to stakeholder feedback. Competency extends to identifying and mitigating ethical risks, with immediate corrective actions for lapses. Ethical performance should be tracked using metrics that align with organizational values.

Awareness of your organization's role in a larger ecosystem, including data partners or vendors, is crucial. Agreements should specify expectations and responsibilities for mutual accountability. This ensures effective fulfillment of accountability requirements for AI-driven products and services in the broader ecosystem. Align with regulations such as GDPR by clearly stating how data will be used, and offer users the choice to allow or disallow their data being used for secondary purposes like marketing, respecting their privacy, thereby aligning with informed consent principles.

Record keeping

Record keeping is essential for the ethical and effective use of AI systems. Organizations should use advanced simulations and a reference model to gain confidence in a system's behaviour and ensure compliance. Logs capturing the system's behaviour, including inputs, processes and outputs, are crucial for transparency, accountability and performance assessment. Regular remote backups should safeguard against data loss or tampering.

Logging should extend to hardware resource usage like GPUs and cameras, as this data can be critical for performance optimization and troubleshooting. Systems should also be designed to log degraded modes, which are states of suboptimal but not critical performance issues (such as a very old battery that no longer holds much charge), and alert stakeholders to take appropriate action. A robust process should manage these states, including handling outdated or unsupported software dependencies.

Version control of system and data

Systematic version control is the process of tracking changes to systems as they happen, helping to identify issues in new deployments and allowing for safe rollbacks. Continuous monitoring is essential for catching bugs, flaws or malicious activities. For critical components, an immutable design approach is recommended, where changes occur only through secure updates. An immutable reference model serves as a behavioural standard.

Before deploying updates, simulations and tests should be run to ensure alignment with the reference model. Rollback procedures should be in place, and these should be logged for accountability. Care should also be taken to preserve user settings during updates. In case of a system attack compromising the reference model, extra verification steps should be employed to ensure its restored integrity.

Feedback and communication

Leaders should be transparent about operational processes, including how their AI systems are designed and how sensitive data is managed. Clear documentation should be available for various stakeholders, customized to their specific needs and levels of expertise. This should also include procedures for when and how systems will be decommissioned.

Stakeholder feedback is essential for maintaining ethical practices and should be actively sought. Organizations must allocate the necessary resources – such as dedicated teams or software tools – to gather and analyse this feedback and this process should respect the preferences and boundaries of the users providing the feedback.

Strive for a diverse user group that represents all categories of stakeholders to ensure that the feedback is comprehensive and inclusive. This diversity not only helps in meeting transparency needs but also enriches the quality of the feedback.

All interactions with the system, including feedback and any subsequent actions taken, should be meticulously logged. This establishes a record for accountability and allows for ongoing improvements to be made to the system.

Awareness and oversight

Users should be clearly informed when they are interacting with a product, service or system that incorporates AI elements. This information should empower users to understand the AI's role and make informed decisions about its use. Whenever possible, users should have the opportunity to approve or disapprove of the AI system's involvement before, during or after its operation. This could also extend to challenging the system's decisions.

All of this should be disclosed before the system is operational, when feasible. Terms and conditions should not only be presented immediately upon first interaction but should also be easily understandable to facilitate informed consent, especially if the system profiles users and their behaviour.

The roles and tasks delegated to AI should be explicitly stated and understood by all stakeholders. Any special privacy-preserving measures, like federated learning, should also be clearly documented. All this information should be presented in a manner that is as straightforward and accessible as possible, to ensure that users can make educated choices about their interaction with AI systems.

Human oversight in AI systems should be substantive and capable of influencing the system's behaviour, especially in high-stakes decisions. Given that AI algorithms can be complex and sometimes unreliable, it's crucial to have humans involved to double-check irreversible decisions to detect and prevent foreseeable errors.

People overseeing an AI system should have the tools and knowledge to understand its behaviour and intervene effectively. This should include the ability to halt system activities and assess the context to enact timely corrections. When implementing this level of oversight, organizations should also be aware of potential downsides – like biased or uninformed human intervention – and take steps to mitigate these risks also. Access to the system should be tiered, allowing for different levels of intervention based on authentication, expertise and responsibility. This helps to prevent both uninformed meddling and single points of failure.

Contestability refers to the ability to challenge, question or appeal decisions made by AI systems. Imagine a judicial system where you have the right to appeal a court's decision; similarly, in a contestable AI system, users or affected parties should have avenues to dispute or seek clarification on automated decisions that impact them. Implementing contestability involves several layers. First, the AI system must be transparent and explainable enough for people to understand the basis of its decisions. Second, there must be a procedural mechanism for people to challenge these decisions – this could be a human review process, an internal audit, a third-party evaluation or even a dialogue with the user.

Accountability through technical processes

While policies and procedures provide a framework for responsible AI, they often don't capture the full picture. To truly understand what an AI system is doing, you might need to delve into its technical details:

- Decision trees provide a traceable decision-making structure, simplifying ethical and legal scrutiny, but may lack the nuance to capture complex data relationships.
- Layer-wise Relevance Propagation (LRP) works from output to input, assigning relevance to features, making it effective but technically complex.
- Saliency maps offer a visual, intuitive way to identify crucial input areas, though they may lack precision.
- LINGO and similar techniques deliver real-time natural language explanations, enhancing both interpretability and explicability.

Auditability

Auditability in AI involves comprehensive scrutiny of an AI system's entire workflow for ethical and legal compliance, targeting a wide audience including regulators and ethicists. It employs various tools and is an ongoing process, adapting to the system's complexity and specific audit requirements. Interpretability, a subset of auditability, focuses on making the model understandable, often for end-users or domain experts. Both can mutually reinforce each other, aiding in compliance with regulations.

Various tools assist in auditability and interpretability:

- SHAP uses game theory to attribute feature importance, helping dissect complex models.
- Alibi offers credible explanations for model predictions, including counterfactuals, to build trust and accountability.
- ELI5 simplifies predictions for simpler models, making them accessible even to non-experts.
- LIME breaks down complex models into more understandable components, useful for individual case predictions.
- The What If Tool lets users change input parameters to observe effects on predictions, offering insights into model sensitivity.

Shadow AI

Shadow AI refers to the unsanctioned use or development of AI systems within an organization, introducing risks like poor documentation and complicated policy enforcement. For instance, the unsanctioned use of AI may lead to staff relying on language models as a crutch, creating liabilities within downstream products or systems. A notable example includes numerous scientific papers that were peer-reviewed and published with unedited text which flagged the AI's involvement (e.g. 'As an AI language model…') still embedded within them (Landymore, 2023). Beyond mere embarrassment, such AI systems can perpetuate biases in tasks like resume analysis or performance reviews, potentially violating data protection and employment laws, such as automated employment decision tools (AEDTs) regulations. These issues demonstrate the challenges of maintaining AI accountability and the importance of proper documentation and oversight of professional usages of AI systems.

The bottom line

Accountability in AI is a practical necessity that directly affects organizational trust and legal standing. From explaining model decisions, to auditing entire systems, maintaining accountability is a complicated challenge. This is especially the case when AI usage isn't sanctioned or recorded. Organizations must be proactive in creating, monitoring and updating policies and frameworks for AI accountability to mitigate these risks.

The big picture

While tools for model interpretability and system auditability can help, they are only part of a larger governance framework that must be continuously updated to adapt to technological advances and new types of risks. Ensuring accountability in AI is not just a technical challenge but an organizational one that must be implemented from the ground up, and with the involvement of a wide range of employees and stakeholders.

LEADERSHIP ACTION POINTS

- Implement a comprehensive AI accountability framework, including guidelines for model interpretability, system auditability, decision gates and procedures to guard against shadow AI.

- Assign clear roles and responsibilities for AI-related decisions and tasks, and ensure that everyone involved understands their responsibilities and chain of authority and command.

- Invest in audit and interpretability tools based on the complexity of your AI systems and the specific requirements of your audits. This can include the use of simpler models to help explain more complex ones.

- Update policies and guidelines regularly to ensure that they remain relevant and effective given the rapid advancements in AI and associated regulatory frameworks.

- Establish robust monitoring and oversight processes for auditing and reviewing AI systems to ensure that they remain compliant with internal guidelines and external regulations.
- Promote an organizational culture of accountability by setting the tone as a leader: uphold high ethical standards and encourage a culture that respects and rewards accountability.
- Engage with a diverse range of stakeholders, including ethicists, legal advisers and domain experts to ensure a well-rounded approach to AI accountability.

Reference

Landymore, F (2023) Paper retracted when authors caught using ChatGPT to write it: You'd think scientists would know better, The Byte, 9 September, https://futurism.com/the-byte/paper-retracted-authors-used-chatgpt (archived at https://perma.cc/L9NQ-7DK7)

CHAPTER TEN

Preserving privacy

Historically, privacy was almost implicit, because it was hard to find and gather information. But in the digital world, whether it's digital cameras or satellites or just what you click on, we need to have more explicit rules – not just for governments but for private companies. BILL GATES

In the current fast-paced tech environment, we're not just amassing vast amounts of data; the diversity and detail of this data are also increasing. This data can fuel innovative services but also poses risks of misuse by businesses, governments and overlooked players like cybercriminals and researchers. This chapter outlines how to responsibly utilize data to serve the interest of others while maintaining privacy.

The sensitivity of Personally Identifiable Information (PII) is not uniform. Information like political affiliations or health records is more sensitive compared to something like what kind of device you're using. AI systems often take extra precautions with such sensitive data, including 'protected characteristics' like race or gender, to mitigate the risk of encoding biases or perpetuating discrimination.

There are multiple techniques to protect user privacy. De-identification obscures personal details to prevent identifying individuals easily. Anonymization goes further, erasing any traceable link to an individual. Pseudonymization replaces personal identifiers with aliases, safeguarding identity while still enabling data tracking for studies or customer engagement.

However, AI's advanced pattern recognition can sometimes re-identify individuals from supposedly anonymous data. Unique patterns in behaviour or communication styles can act as 'digital fingerprints' that could be traced back to an individual. Therefore, the efficacy of privacy measures is in a constant tug of war with technological advances that could compromise them.

It is crucial for organizations to obtain clear, ongoing consent from individuals before gathering or using their data, while ensuring users can easily withdraw their consent at any time. This is especially important for complex data uses, like merging shopping history with social media activity. Consent should be explicit and opting out should be straightforward. There should be simple and transparent explanations of any benefits that users can expect to gain by optionally sharing data, such as service enhancements or personalization benefits.

It is also necessary to be transparent about involving third party data processors. Users should know not only about these third parties but also their sub-processors and data transfer jurisdictions. Organizations need to vet these parties to ensure compliance with data protection laws.

Organizations also have an ongoing responsibility to maintain records of their data protection activities. Regular assessments, possibly involving third-party audits and public reports, should be conducted to stay updated with changing laws and technologies.

The principle of minimizing data collection and sharing is a cornerstone of data protection frameworks like the General Data Protection Regulation (GDPR) in the European Union. It advises collecting only the data needed for a specific purpose and sharing only what's essential. For example, a weather app asking for access to your contacts not only breaches privacy but also enlarges the risk of data misuse or breaches.

It is possible for machine learning models to unlearn private data after the fact, though this can add complexity, and may not be robust in all circumstances. The list of data to be unlearned can also itself present risks to privacy. In healthcare, sharing only pertinent medical records isn't just about privacy but also clinical accuracy. Superfluous data could introduce irrelevant variables and, if exposed, could lead to identity theft or insurance fraud.

This minimal approach serves multiple objectives. It enhances privacy by reducing the amount of data at risk, lowers the chance of ethical missteps and focuses analytical models by training them only on relevant data. Therefore, both individuals and organizations benefit from adhering to this principle. Organizations can reduce liability, enhance their services and maintain ethical standards by limiting the scope of data collection and sharing.

Machine intelligence systems introduce complex ethical dilemmas through privacy trade-offs. Transparency can build trust but also create vulnerabilities, as revealing algorithmic details might enable exploitation. The risks escalate with biometric data, which are immutable and can't be reset like passwords.

Personalized experiences illustrate these trade-offs well. While data on personal preferences can enrich the engagement of products and services, it can easily be misused. For example, using data on a user's preference for breakup songs to target ads for alcohol to them crosses an ethical line, posing risks of exploitation.

Health-related data such as menstrual cycles can be exploited to infer sensitive conditions and target ads, impacting not just privacy but also individual dignity and autonomy. For example, predictive algorithms can often ascertain if someone is pregnant even before they themselves know. Sometimes people have received a new baby offer pack in the mail before getting a chance to inform a partner or parent (Jemio, Hagerty and Aranda, 2022). Technologies like assistive keyboard apps that log keystrokes present an additional layer of risk, potentially capturing and misusing sensitive information.

The concept of 'data exhaust' refers to the residual data generated from our interactions with digital platforms, from search queries and location tracking to online purchases and social media activity. This data is often collected, aggregated and traded by data brokers, generally without the explicit consent or even awareness of the individuals it pertains to.

Privacy is often considered a cornerstone of human dignity, allowing individuals to control their own narratives and personal boundaries. In a technological age where information is currency, the tension between sharing data for convenience and protecting one's privacy is ever-present.

For example, the idea of using web search history as a credit check is a double-edged sword. On one side, it could democratize access to credit for those without a traditional credit history. On the flip side, it sets a risky precedent of normalizing personal data sharing, where choosing to opt out could have negative implications like restricted access to financial systems. Informed consent means that individuals should fully understand the risks and benefits of sharing their data and agree to those clearly stated terms explicitly.

Technologies such as differential privacy, federated learning and blockchain provide sophisticated methods to safeguard user data while enabling its beneficial use, although each comes with its own set of challenges and benefits. These methods allow for the aggregation of insights from data without exposing sensitive individual information. They can serve as robust tools in achieving a balance between utility and privacy, enabling the kind of data usage that respects human dignity. These technologies are varied and complex and have their own positives and setbacks.

Differential privacy

Differential privacy introduces intentional uncertainty into data. This allows companies like Google to offer services such as real-time traffic updates without compromising individual users' locations. Data is aggregated to reflect general behaviours, allowing insights like average speed and congestion without identifying individual routes. However, its efficacy depends on the size and diversity of the dataset. Sparse data reduces the protective effectiveness of this approach. Additionally, while it guards shared or queried data, it doesn't erase the original, non-private data, which organizations could potentially store indefinitely. Thus, it's a robust but not universal privacy solution, best suited for rich, diverse datasets where the primary goal is to protect individual information during a data-sharing process.

Federated learning

Federated learning is a way to learn from user data without the data ever leaving the user's device. For example, a smartphone can learn a user's typing habits to improve autocorrect suggestions without sending sensitive information back to a central server. Machine learning models are trained locally, and only model updates – not raw data – are sent to a central server for aggregation. This method is especially useful in sectors like healthcare and finance, where data is sensitive and highly regulated. For instance, a medical model could learn from decentralized patient records, and a banking fraud-detection model could improve without centralizing sensitive transaction data.

Blockchains

Blockchains are distributed ledgers, which allow records of transactions to be kept on a decentralized database. They are known for transparency and immutability but can also enhance privacy and data control. A hybrid model combining public and private blockchains can enable dynamic data access or even data 'self-destruction'. In this setup, the public blockchain is a transparent ledger, while the private blockchain governs access through keys. Removing a key on the private chain makes the linked data on the public chain inaccessible. This allows for granular control, letting you selectively 'erase' data points. For example, in the event of a data leak, access to the exposed data can be revoked by severing its private keys, effectively mitigating the leak's impact.

Steganography

Steganography involves hiding information within another data form, like embedding an audio file inside a large image. This is useful for secure applications such as anti-censorship efforts. Emerging technologies are blending steganography with data masking. For example, cameras can produce carefully blurred images that humans cannot perceive but which machine learning models can still recognize.

Radioactive data

Radioactive data is a digital watermark embedded in a dataset to track its origin and usage. It involves subtle changes that don't distort the data but make it traceable. This is similar to isotopes in chemistry, which are nearly identical in function yet remain distinguishable upon close examination. When integrated with blockchain technology, radioactive data can offer an immutable history of data access. However, challenges exist, such as the potential erasure of signatures through format changes or lossy compression, and the risk of machine learning algorithms learning these encodings. Storing these signatures on a secure blockchain could be a solution, allowing for an extensive but manageable record without affecting the data file.

Homomorphic encryption

Homomorphic encryption is a technique that allows data to be encrypted in such a way that it can still be worked on or analysed without needing to be decrypted first. This means a service could analyse your data for useful insights without ever seeing your personal information. Picture it as a technological head-to-toe zentai morph suit (like a Power Ranger outfit). Such a full-body outfit would allow you to be measured precisely while retaining your anonymity. It provides data isolation, enabling you to share specific information without exposing everything. Although still computationally intensive and experimental, user-friendly versions like Microsoft's Simple Encrypted Arithmetic Library (SEAL) are becoming mainstream, promising a balance between data utility and confidentiality.

Zero-knowledge proofs

Zero-knowledge proofs (ZKPs) allow for the validation of a claim without revealing the underlying information. Imagine confirming you and a friend have the same number of cards in a deck without disclosing the actual count; ZKPs work similarly. They're useful in secure authentication, data sharing and voting systems. An extension, zero-knowledge machine learning (ZKML), enables confidential verification of machine learning model outputs. While computationally intensive, requiring multiple rounds to achieve high confidence, ZKPs are a valuable tool for secure, private validation.

Probably approximately correct and secure multi-party computation

The probably approximately correct (PAC) technique minimizes the noise needed to maintain data privacy in machine learning models, balancing privacy and accuracy. For multi-party data collaboration, Secure Multi-Party Computation (SMPC) combined with federated learning provides a robust privacy solution. In this setup, each party encrypts its data, which is then divided and distributed across multiple servers for computations. The results are then aggregated and decrypted, revealing only the computation outcome, not the sensitive data. This approach allows for secure, collaborative data science while fine-tuning the trade-off between data protection and model accuracy.

Part-trained models

Part-trained models process your data locally on your device, rather than sending it to the cloud. These models come pre-trained and only require fine-tuning based on your specific data and preferences. For instance, a model trained on aggregated or synthetic music preferences can be fine-tuned to your unique tastes with just a few inputs. The fine-tuned model can then be sent back to the cloud while keeping your data on your device. This approach saves computational resources and bandwidth but isn't foolproof in ensuring absolute privacy, as model updates could still leak information.

Passkeys

A passkey is a digital-only string of characters used for user authentication. Unlike traditional passwords, passkeys exist solely on your devices, eliminating the need to write them down or accidentally share them. Using a passkey for account access provides double verification, offering protection against online scams like phishing. They simplify online security by focusing on device management rather than complex password memorization.

TOR (The Onion Router)

TOR is a network designed to provide anonymity and privacy online. It routes internet traffic through multiple servers, encrypting the data at each step, to make it difficult to trace the origin of the request. TOR is often used by individuals who want to browse the internet without being tracked, whether for personal privacy reasons, to bypass censorship, or for more nefarious purposes. While TOR is lauded for its ability to protect user privacy and circumvent censorship, it also has a dark side. It can be used for illegal activities, such as accessing the dark web for drug trafficking or other criminal acts. This dual-use nature makes TOR a complex subject in discussions about internet ethics and regulation.

VPN (virtual private network)

A VPN is a service that encrypts your internet data and routes it through a server located elsewhere, effectively masking your IP address and providing a level of anonymity. Unlike TOR, which is decentralized and run by volunteers, VPNs are often commercial services. VPNs are widely used for legitimate purposes like securing data over public WiFi, bypassing geo-restrictions on content or maintaining general privacy online. The trustworthiness of VPN providers is a concern, as they have the ability to log and potentially share user data.

Quantum-safe encryption

Quantum-safe encryption is preparing for 'Q-Day', a future when quantum computing could break current cryptography. Traditional encryption, based on hard-to-factor large numbers, could be easily cracked by quantum algorithms. The stakes are high, affecting everything from online banking to national security, and some entities are already gathering data to exploit future quantum capabilities. However, quantum-resistant algorithms are being developed to counteract these threats. Even messaging apps such as Signal are introducing such forms of encryption.

As quantum technology advances, especially boosted by machine learning, the rush to adopt quantum-safe algorithms might resemble the Y2K panic, requiring swift action to protect data and privacy.

The bottom line

The deep embedding of technology in our lives significantly increases privacy risks. That's why using tools such as those described in this chapter are so important. If we can get privacy right, we can have our cake and eat it, too – we can enjoy services that are appropriately targeted towards our needs, but use our data on terms that respect our dignity and preferences.

The big picture

Privacy is more than just maintaining personal secrets. It's an integral and necessary component of dignity, a cornerstone of human security and wellbeing. Beyond that, a lack of privacy creates an enormous attack surface for bad actors to latch on to. Privacy should be within reach of us all, not simply a luxury reserved for a privileged few.

> **LEADERSHIP ACTION POINTS**
>
> • Become familiar with emerging cryptographic techniques and deploy them in your infrastructure as soon as feasible.
>
> • Get quantum-safe algorithms in place before they become suddenly necessary.
>
> • Consider how, in a world of 'Bring Your Own Device', the personal phone in someone's pocket could potentially be silently hijacked for remote monitoring or data exfiltration.
>
> • Consider using Personal Information Removal Services such as Incogni to scrub personal information from service providers who no longer should have access to it.

Reference

Jemio, D, Hagerty, A and Aranda, F (2022) The case of the creepy algorithm that 'predicted' teen pregnancy, Wired, 16 February, www.wired.com/story/argentina-algorithms-pregnancy-prediction (archived at https://perma.cc/65ZZ-U6QM)

CHAPTER ELEVEN

Fairness and franchise

I think perfect objectivity is an unrealistic goal; fairness, however, is not. MICHAEL POLLAN

The pervasive influence of algorithms on our social, economic and political lives demands a rigorous examination of fairness in our personal and professional lives. As a consequence, the notion of fairness now encompasses not just human decisions but also the mathematical models that evaluate, categorize and influence us. This chapter outlines ways in which algorithms responsible for important decision-making processes – ranging from credit scoring to job placement to public services – present risks to individual freedoms.

Most of us have heard stories from acquaintances who got in trouble on social media for making a harmless statement which some content moderation algorithm took in the wrong way. Users might be banned for 'racial language' after innocently discussing chess moves like 'black takes white', or metaphorically saying they 'shot themselves in the foot' mistakenly flagged as self-harm.

The principle of economic franchise – ensuring every individual's right to engage fully in their community's economy – is under threat. The fusion of technology and finance, especially with the increasing influence of Big Tech companies in the financial sector, amplifies the risks associated with platform-based exclusion.

In a world where Big Tech companies are consolidating services – from social media to the Internet of Things (IoT) to financial services – the stakes of being kicked off a platform are rising.

Unlike in the past, where consumers could simply switch to a different bank or use another email provider, consolidation and cooperative competition among giant ventures leaves them with few alternatives. In extreme scenarios, a person's entire digital life could be locked behind a wall, disabling not just their online social life but also their financial assets, home automation systems and even connected vehicles. Whether such discrimination is intentional or accidental is not necessarily material to the victim.

The guidelines below, based upon my Cultural Peace Principles project (www.culturalpeace.org), are designed to assist leaders in responsibly developing and implementing algorithmic systems, with a core focus on fairness and economic inclusion.

Self-determination and the digital public square

People have a natural right to form their own communities. Subcultures flourish through healthy, consensual separation, enabling individuals with common traits and views to cultivate and maintain distinct communities. Being part of a group can make it much easier to coordinate with others, and build networks based on trust. It can also mean enabling a unique and specific culture and norms, a quality of diversity that may otherwise be washed away within the mainstream.

Different groups may have very different norms for communication. Someone 'wandering by' a conversation, particularly in the online world these days, may find such discussion alarming or insensitive if they have different values or culture. However, one should not apply one's own cultural norms or values to other groups, or expect them to communicate in the same way that one would think common. It can be very misleading to pull a snippet of conversation from a place with one set of norms, for it to be appraised somewhere else.

Merely following someone's tweets or retweeting a single statement, etc should not be taken as a tacit endorsement of someone else's character or beliefs. Some folks like to culture a broad set of inputs or may respect someone's professional achievements without necessarily agreeing with their values. Similarly, a network or group should not be judged by the actions of a small minority within it, unless the larger group is explicitly shown to approve of those actions.

On-device content moderation may soon mean that even a file or link sent directly to you from a friend may be disappeared or 'harmonized' once it reaches your location. Who are they to say what info qualifies? If one starts censoring one thing 'for the common good', it's a very slippery slope towards censoring almost anything potentially controversial or objectionable to someone, somewhere. Not only does this prevent subcultures, minority beliefs and internet sleuths from coalescing, it may also prevent justified whistleblowing of scandalous truths, as well as the innovation of new ideas, which are naturally avant-garde before they are accepted by the mainstream.

To avoid excessive censorship, content moderation policies must be transparent, particularly on major tech platforms. Public spaces, including those online, should remain neutral, especially if they receive public funds.

Leaders and platforms have a responsibility to respect the autonomy of these communities, allowing for a peaceful coexistence of diverse norms and conversations. Intrusion into these spaces should be avoided to preserve self-determination and the richness of public discourse. Employers should be careful to avoid strict social media policies which infringe on employees' autonomy and freedom of speech. Employers need to strike a balance which reasonably protects their interests without unduly limiting their employees' rights to participate in public discourse, especially in digital spaces where diverse norms and viewpoints coexist.

Payment platform neutrality

So many aspects of our lives today depend upon apps, online shopping and mobile payments. Modern life is dependent on being able to make convenient payments and access online services, and to receive legitimate payment for honest work. As we increasingly rely on digital transactions, the immense power of payment processors to dictate terms or exclude users from financial networks has emerged. They can use their influence to force others to comply with their wishes, at an implied risk of losing access to the payments network, or a downgrade of service (Frauenfelder, 2019; Goggin and Tenbarge, 2019). This means that payment processors can single-handedly strongarm other players into doing their bidding for them. Today, we are seeing secondary payment processors kicking people off their platforms, despite them doing nothing illegal, and perhaps nothing explicitly against their terms of service either, perhaps to appease authoritarian governments. Generally, there is very little opportunity for an appeal or management escalation.

Meanwhile, evidence is mounting that some have been changing the list price of goods or availability of credit for some users, based upon completely non-transparent mechanisms which are highly prone to acting in negative ways, even in the absence of human action (Parameshwaran, 2023).

Additionally, opaque credit-scoring systems can serve as gate-keepers, disproportionately affecting certain groups and hindering their economic participation (Elgan, 2019).

This centralization of financial power in the hands of a few tech giants makes the need for banking neutrality critical. A principle similar to the separation of church and state should apply to money and ideology, ensuring financial transactions aren't subject to political scrutiny.

The overarching issue is that economic participation should be considered a right, not a privilege dictated by corporations for arbitrary reasons. It's crucial for leaders to advocate for transparent, fair and accountable AI-driven banking systems that allow everyone, regardless of their political beliefs, to participate in the economy.

Freedom from algorithmic discrimination

Discrimination based on political beliefs carries wide-ranging consequences across employment, education and housing sectors (Shim, 2014). This issue is particularly pronounced in sectors like academia, where ideological homogeneity can limit opportunities for individuals with differing views, potentially reinforcing existing social inequities. For example, 62 per cent of Americans report that they are afraid to state their true political views openly (Ekins, 2020). The ramifications extend beyond the individuals affected; they contribute to broader societal problems such as erosion of trust in institutions and increased polarization.

Addressing this form of discrimination is a complex task. While laws in many countries protect against discrimination based on factors like race, gender and religion, political orientation is often not a protected characteristic (Hunter, 2005; Mather, 2018).

AI makes these challenges even worse, by extrapolating highly personal details from fragments of public information, thereby compromising people's reasonable expectations of privacy. Models may use these features, hidden in plain sight, to determine who receives algorithmic favour. Plausible deniability for discriminatory actions can also be attributed to 'glitches' and 'administrative errors', allowing them to escape scrutiny.

Leaders need to work on creating environments that are inclusive and tolerant of diverse political views. This may include fostering workplace cultures that respect ideological diversity, implementing non-discriminatory policies in educational institutions, and even considering legislative changes that extend anti-discrimination protections to include political beliefs. Ensuring equitable access to life opportunities regardless of one's political orientation should be an integral part of a just and democratic society.

Freedom from secret exclusion

With the impracticality of human-only moderation, algorithms often take charge, sometimes wrongly flagging content or demonetizing channels. This opacity can fuel a culture of self-censorship, as people fear algorithmic penalties such as 'shadowbanning', when someone is discreetly made invisible to other users, or even given false praise by bot accounts (heaven-banning). The throttling of the distribution of ideas, or delisting websites from search engines and language models, can present further subtle forms of manipulation (Pot, 2016).

Content moderation needs to be transparent, accountable and purposeful, providing options for users to modify the applied filters, and to understand how and why content has been provided to them in a particular manner.

Covert practices restricting 'Freedom of Reach' should not serve as indirect means to limit 'Freedom of Speech'. There must be no secret exclusion created between unknowing parties, i.e. two people not able to communicate, for reasons they did not choose. Applying one's own preferred filters to content, with agency and awareness, is acceptable. Forcing people into a virtual ghetto with glass walls is not acting towards them in good faith. Leaders must ensure that everyone has the freedom to express themselves openly without fearing hidden restrictions or manipulative practices.

Transparency of judgement

Algorithms are making snap judgements of people's content and character, without explaining why, and without any recourse to demand a detailed description, or challenge false impressions (Elgan, 2019; Wiggers, 2018). This can normalize unfair extra-judicial judgements, which can result in discriminatory blacklisting in job markets.

Any such processes of making and sharing lists of persona non grata should be strongly discouraged. Where it may happen to remain permitted, it must be explicitly transparent. Similarly, transparency of all employment references and performance records disclosed to third parties must also be made explicit. Without these issues explicitly covered under employment law, a massive loophole enables the exploitation of persons who are technically not party to employment regulations per se. Online tools offer to rank a potential hire by the sentiment (or contentiousness) of their comments online, or even those they have liked or favourited. These tools typically offer no explanation for how such an estimation is calculated, or what data drove such conclusions, or even what such a score should mean for a vettor.

This threatens to enable bigotry and prejudice through the backdoor, by allowing one to wash one's hands of being explicitly discriminatory, yet ensuring that only the 'right sort of people' pass through the gate. Algorithms, along with those who deploy them, must be held accountable for their use, and that any such use that can affect reputation, access to resources or livelihood is fully transparent.

Leaders must mandate accountability for algorithms affecting reputations or livelihoods. Any algorithmic decision impacting an individual should be transparent, understandable and explainable. The goal is to prevent algorithms from serving as a shield for concealed discriminatory actions.

Freedom of consciousness

Technology must not be used to manipulate people's behaviour or impressions of reality to a gross degree in a non-consensual manner. Our minds are sacred sovereign territory. We are presently headed for a world where our lives are ever more entwined with technology, such as artificial intelligence and social media. Propaganda used to be one-size-fits-all, but today campaigns can be micro-targeted. Repeated barely noticeable impressions may change our political opinions and even our mood (Stewart et al, 2019).

As technology advances, the potential for personalized propaganda and psychological manipulation grows (Pärnamets and Van Bave, 2018). Technologies that can assess and predict individual behaviour pose risks of invasive incursions into our mental states by various entities. Leaders have a duty to safeguard the autonomy of individual thought and emotion. Tools that manipulate behaviour or distort reality must not be employed. The sovereignty of the human mind is sacred and must be respected.

Equality of public access

It has been reported that Big Tech companies may be unfairly demonetizing content based on seemingly innocuous keywords.

Anything with a title or description featuring words as innocuous as 'Gay/Lesbian' to 'North Carolina', or even 'Asians' may be liable to be arbitrarily blocked from advertising revenue (Nerd City, 2019).

Furthermore, tools such as alleging copyright infringement may be used to suppress unfavourable news, hold people to digital ransom or appropriation of revenue. Online flash mobs may even cause content to be demonetized simply for commenting on it. This can lead to the deletion of associated email accounts, along with the channel, greatly amplifying the economic and social damage, and amplifying the chilling effects.

It is unacceptable to demonetize content in order to economically disenfranchise voices that one may not agree with or find suspect, or to place a surcharge on service access to certain consumers and not others, or kick people off platforms for 'lack of commercial viability', perhaps based on their political affiliations.

If a venture has a public corporate charter, is open to the general public and uses the commons for commercial transactions, and if it is publicly traded, then it should engage with the public on a general basis, without discrimination, due to the social contract of public benefit that affords public corporations their unique blend of privileges and duties. To uphold fairness and franchise in the digital age, it is imperative that leaders, technologists and policymakers collaborate to create transparent, accountable and inclusive systems that respect individual rights and promote economic participation for all.

The bottom line

The best way to protect our future is to ensure that fundamental human rights are not allowed to be trampled by algorithmic mechanisms such as powerful and inscrutable AI systems. Ancient rights in the physical sphere must be extended to the digital sphere.

The big picture

The core of a free and just society lies in safeguarding individual liberties, promoting inclusivity and fostering environments for good faith dialogue. By holding to these, the ongoing progress in AI is far more likely to benefit humanity overall.

LEADERSHIP ACTION POINTS

- Advocate for equitable access to public resources and utilities, including unbiased algorithms and consumer protections against corporate discrimination and financial exclusion.

- Protect the rights of individuals to freely associate, follow and engage with diverse perspectives without fear of social or political repercussions.

- Create opportunities for balanced and open dialogue that includes voices both closely and distantly related to issues, acknowledging that no single perspective has a monopoly on truth.

- Prioritize right to repair and modify: advocate for legal frameworks that allow individuals to fully own, understand and modify their personal devices.

- Enhance transparency in algorithms: require companies, especially those in Big Tech, to be transparent about their algorithms, and institute measures that allow third-party audits.

References

Cox, J (2023) A computer generated swatting service is causing havoc across America, Vice, 13 April, www.vice.com/en/article/k7z8be/torswats-computer-generated-ai-voice-swatting (archived at https://perma.cc/8ZCH-MN3Z)

Ekins, E (2020) Poll: 62% of Americans say they have political views they're afraid to share, CATO Institute, 22 July, www.cato.org/survey-reports/poll-62-americans-say-they-have-political-views-theyre-afraid-share (archived at https://perma.cc/3XLZ-PD7C)

Elgan, M (2019) Uh-oh: Silicon Valley is building a Chinese-style social credit system, Fast Company, 26 August, www.fastcompany.com/90394048/uh-oh-silicon-valley-is-building-a-chinese-style-social-credit-system (archived at https://perma.cc/4XS5-2ZSL)

Frauenfelder, M (2019) Getting deplatformed from Apple. 'Your account has been permanently disabled. There is nothing else you can do, there is no escalation path', Boingboing, 13 August, https://boingboing.net/2019/08/13/getting-deplatformed-from-appl.html (archived at https://perma.cc/PCV3-CCFN)

Goggin, B and Tenbarge, K (2019) 'Like you've been fired from your job': YouTubers have lost thousands of dollars after their channels were mistakenly demonetized for months, Business Insider, 14 August, www.businessinsider.com/youtubers-entire-channels-can-get-mistakenly-demonetized-for-months-2019-8 (archived at https://perma.cc/2MMA-29CH)

Hunter, P (2005) Is political correctness damaging science? Peer pressure and mainstream thinking may discourage novelty and innovation, EMBO Reports, 6 (5), 405–07

Mather, R D (2018) Continued political bias in social psychology, Psychology Today, 31 May, www.psychologytoday.com/gb/blog/the-conservative-social-psychologist/201805/continued-political-bias-in-social-psychology (archived at https://perma.cc/YV58-ALN7)

Nerd City (2019) YouTube's biggest lie, www.youtube.com/watch?v=ll8zGaWhofU (archived at https://perma.cc/WQH6-E3BA)

Parameshwaran, S (2023) How AI-powered collusion in stock trading could hurt price formation, Knowledge at Wharton, 10 November, https://knowledge.wharton.upenn.edu/article/how-ai-powered-collusion-in-stock-trading-could-hurt-price-formation/ (archived at https://perma.cc/D9JC-L9VR)

Pärnamets, P and Van Bave, J (2018) How political opinions change, Scientific American, 20 November, https://getpocket.com/explore/item/how-political-opinions-change (archived at https://perma.cc/UQK5-JWDN)

Pot, J (2016) Google delisted 1.75 billion websites because of copyright takedown requests, The Next Web, 12 September, https://thenextweb. com/news/google-removed-1-75-billion-websites-copyright-takedown-requests (archived at https://perma.cc/BB8G-WY5Y)

Shim, E (2014) How politically biased is each industry? Check these charts, MIC, 6 November, www.mic.com/articles/103600/how-politically-biased-is-each-industry-check-these-charts (archived at https://perma.cc/8GSY-FA8U)

Stewart et al (2019) Information gerrymandering and undemocratic decisions, Nature, 573, 117–21, www.nature.com/articles/s41586-019-1507-6 (archived at https://perma.cc/8UVL-AR8A)

Wiggers, K (2018) Babysitter screening app Predictim uses AI to sniff out bullies, VentureBeat, 4 October, https://venturebeat.com/ai/babysitter-screening-app-predictim-uses-ai-to-sniff-out-bullies (archived at https://perma.cc/FN3G-9ZGG)

CHAPTER TWELVE

Security and robustness

It takes 20 years to build a reputation and a few minutes of a cyber-incident to ruin it. STÉPHANE NAPPO

In the highly competitive AI field, the push for innovation sometimes overlooks essential safety measures. But this urgency can lead to unforeseen errors and vulnerabilities. It's easy to underestimate the difficulties of creating reliable software, especially when it's a groundbreaking product. The unpredictability of complex systems further complicates matters. Even the best models can't account for every variable, leading to unexpected and often negative outcomes as unanticipated functions lurk within models, waiting to be elicited via a particular prompt sequence. This chapter describes how we can reduce such surprises and setbacks.

AI is security hell

Generative AI introduces security challenges of unparalleled complexity. These systems often function as 'black boxes', their inner workings largely inscrutable even to experts. This complexity means that risks can emerge from unexpected interactions between various components, making it difficult to predict and prevent every possible accident. Consequently, the focus should shift from solely trying to prevent accidents to also mitigating their potential impact.

With AI, complex information can now be manipulated to create vulnerabilities in systems. Take, for instance, the extraction of secret keys from devices using video footage of their power LED (Nassi et al, 2023). Similarly, some AI systems can identify up to 93 per cent of specific keystrokes from the sounds captured during a video conferencing call (Harrison, Toreini and Mehrnezhad, 2023).

As a consequence, it's becoming incredibly difficult to avoid the leakage of data through all kinds of mechanisms that typically aren't even likely to be noticed as they can be hidden in plain sight. There have been cases of previous client instances of GMs getting read from memory (the system being fooled into fetching the wrong dataset for the wrong user), thereby resulting in breach of privacy (Petkauskas, 2023). Such concerns have led to some companies such as Apple reportedly banning the use of third-party GMs such as ChatGPT (Fortis, 2023).

Mutating (polymorphic) malware can now adapt in real-time using APIs from language models, with the greater adaptability easily outpacing traditional security measures. Furthermore, generative models like WormGPT and Evil-GPT are being used to automate the creation of personalized, convincing fake emails, posing new challenges for business email compromise attacks.

While the democratization of AI tools has its benefits, it also lowers the entry barrier for amateur hackers. They can now use language models to spot opportunities and solve hacking challenges, gaining unauthorized access to systems more easily. Researchers have found that fine-tuning can strip guardrails from models, converting models such as GPT-3.5 Turbo and LLaMA2 from having a 'harmfulness rating' of 1.8

per cent to over 80 per cent after fine-tuning with just 100 examples (Qi et al, 2023). This implies that implementing safeguards in models with publicly released weights may be ineffective.

External actors, ranging from individual criminals to nation-states, have strong incentives to compromise AI systems, whether to steal proprietary algorithms or to gain competitive advantage. To counter these threats, AI development labs must implement robust security measures. This could include external audits to evaluate vulnerabilities, hiring specialized security experts and meticulous vetting of potential employees. Given the potential for attacks from highly capable adversaries, labs making frontier models may need to adopt security measures akin to those used by banks and top government agencies.

Jailbreaks and adversarial inputs

Jailbreaks and adversarial prompts present related yet distinct challenges within AI ethics and security. Jailbreaks involve the AI itself bypassing developer constraints, either due to software vulnerabilities or unintended learning.

Adversarial prompts, on the other hand, involve external inputs designed to trick the AI into making mistakes or taking harmful actions. These are crafted to exploit vulnerabilities in the AI's decision-making or data processing. Once discovered, such prompts can be blocked, at least so long as workarounds aren't discovered. Adversarial inputs may be documents also, most notably images, which have been altered in a subtle way undetectable to human eyes, but discernible by machines. A human might rightfully see a can of soda, but a machine might perceive a rifle. However, there are some potential defences to this, such as modifying the image again slightly. Even converting the image to a lossy form of compression should remove the adversarial perturbations.

Tools for generating jailbreaks and adversarial prompts can help strengthen AI by exposing weaknesses for patching. However, these can also disguise malicious inputs to bypass security. Adversarial inputs can be as subtle as altered images that fool machine perception but not human vision, though some defences like image modification exist. Some adversarial changes even affect humans as well to some degree, due to the human brain being subject to its own exploits, such as optical illusions (Veerabadran et al, 2023).

Prompt injection represents a significant and possibly under-appreciated risk as AI systems, particularly assistants, become more prevalent. Consider a scenario where you have an AI assistant tasked with managing your emails. A malicious actor could send a deceptive prompt as an email to an inbox managed by an LLM assistant which instructs it to forward sensitive emails to an unauthorized third party and then erase the sent items. The spectrum of such attacks could range from corrupting search indexes to outright data theft. Indirect prompt injection attacks allow unauthorized users to control the AI systems by hiding commands within digital content such as web pages.

Specialized models and open-source safeguards are being developed to detect and neutralize harmful inputs, but these measures are not foolproof due to the unpredictable nature of malicious attacks. It's therefore essential to scrutinize the origins and architecture of plug-ins, and to treat language models as being potentially more insecure when accepting inputs from external sources.

Model backdoors

Backdoors in machine learning models pose a complex issue for information security. These hidden vulnerabilities can be activated when the model encounters a specific input, much like a *Manchurian Candidate* sleeper agent waiting for a signal. They are especially concerning because they can be designed to be undetectable, even by advanced black-box analysis techniques. These exploits can potentially target any model compiled on a system. The integrity of compilers is a serious issue of information security, since compilers are used to produce all the programs that might be deployed on a computer, including any analysis tool, and the operating system.

These backdoors can manifest in various ways, from causing system failures upon recognizing certain objects or phrases to introducing intentional biases towards specific targets or groups. The insidious nature of these backdoors is worsened by the fact that they can be embedded without altering the model's size or cryptographic hash, making them hard to detect. This has terrifying implications for potential abuse, and leaders must be made aware of such issues, as well as potential emerging defences against such issues.

Data poisoning

Data poisoning attacks involve the intentional manipulation of the training data for a machine learning model with the aim of corrupting its behaviour. Imagine someone tampering with the ingredients of a recipe to ruin the final dish; in a similar way, data poisoning alters the 'recipe' that the AI system uses to make decisions. The goal is often to introduce biases, trigger incorrect outcomes or otherwise degrade the performance of the model. These attacks are particularly concerning because they target the very foundation upon which machine learning models are built: the data. Since the model learns from this data, poisoning attacks can be hard to detect until the model is deployed and starts making decisions.

Defending against data poisoning attacks involves multiple layers of security. One approach is to rigorously vet and clean the training data before using it to train a model. Another is to continuously monitor the model's performance and decisions to detect any anomalies that could indicate it has been compromised.

AI's growth in capability is quickly outpacing traditional security measures like CAPTCHAs, meaning that AI systems can now potentially solve them more efficiently than humans (Searles et al, 2023). As a result, websites of all sizes may face automated attacks, including sophisticated social engineering. However, defensive technologies will evolve alongside AI. The challenge is to update or replace outdated security paradigms, such as relying solely on 'human-like actions' for verification. Future security measures may leverage AI's own capabilities for defence, requiring us to rethink and innovate in the realm of cybersecurity.

The integration of cryptography and AI promises to combine the security of deterministic algorithms with the adaptability of probabilistic models. Cryptography can protect the data fed into machine learning algorithms, while AI can optimize encryption methods and identify vulnerabilities. A seamless fusion of cryptographic tokens and machine learning could lead to more secure and adaptable systems across various industries, from communications to healthcare. This blend has the potential to move both fields from experimental to essential tools in daily life, offering a future where security and adaptability are harmonized.

AI-enabled cyberdefence

AI is both complicating and enhancing cybersecurity. Generative AI can detect and watermark AI-generated content, aiding in the identification of bot accounts or phishing attempts. Automated penetration testing can be executed by code models to fortify digital infrastructures. Self-defending networks are emerging, shifting from centralized to distributed security approaches. For example, Federated Reinforcement Learning Frameworks are being used for malware mitigation (Hazell, 2023). GMs are increasingly useful, capable of identifying vulnerabilities in different programming languages and aiding in the analysis of executable files' APIs. GMs are also evolving to detect and watermark AI-generated text, which could be integrated into email protection software for identifying phishing attempts and polymorphic code. These advancements represent transformative shifts in how cybersecurity can be approached.

A vigilant security outlook is vital in AI development, requiring a focus not just on how systems work but also how they might fail. This involves adopting an attacker's perspective and considering worst-case scenarios to identify vulnerabilities. In AI, this means rigorously testing models against adversarial inputs and scrutinizing ethical aspects of data use. Risks can arise from overlooked issues such as activist employees, aligning with Murphy's Law that 'anything that can go wrong will go wrong'. This realistic view acknowledges that threats can come from both system limitations and external factors.

Security risks from complexity

Technological advancements offer both convenience and new risks, amplified by factors ranging from individual practices to geopolitics. Cloud storage and IoT devices, despite their benefits, introduce vulnerabilities like service discontinuation and network security breaches. The risks become more pronounced when considering the concentrated power of major tech companies. A single vulnerability in a widely used service can have a ripple effect, impacting thousands of organizations, such as attacks on Microsoft Exchange creating systemic risks in the dependent tech ecosystem.

Geopolitical elements further complicate the cybersecurity landscape. Countries developing independent tech infrastructures, like China and Russia, could be insulated from the fallout of cyberattacks, thereby increasing the likelihood of such attacks. The motivations behind these cyberattacks are also evolving, shifting from individual mischief to organized crime and espionage. Even tools designed for intelligence services can end up in the hands of malicious actors (Goodin, 2020). Moreover, the rapid discovery of new exploits makes hardware obsolescence a security issue, not just an age-related one. This has socioeconomic implications, disproportionately affecting those who can't afford regular upgrades.

Risk identification methods

Risk identification in AI starts with threat modelling to chart potential vulnerabilities and plan countermeasures. Data and algorithm quality are also scrutinized for system robustness. Legal considerations around liability, especially in consumer-facing applications, align with existing consumer safety laws.

The complexities extend to legal considerations, particularly when it comes to vetting liability in the context of negligence law. This becomes especially pertinent when AI systems interact directly with consumers. Legal experts often draw parallels with consumer safety laws to establish responsibility for any harm caused by AI systems.

To further illuminate potential vulnerabilities, security experts often employ tools like attack trees. These visualizations are like a branching map that outlines the various ways an AI system could be exploited, aiding in the development of robust defence mechanisms. On a related note, VAST modelling, which stands for value-sensitive algorithmic systems thinking, helps align AI systems with human values like fairness and privacy. It maps out interactions between different components of the system and these ethical considerations.

In terms of active testing, penetration testing and red teams are commonly used. Penetration testing involves hiring skilled professionals, often called 'ethical hackers', to simulate cyberattacks on the AI system with the goal of identifying vulnerabilities before they can be exploited. Red teams act as mock adversaries, focusing solely on identifying weaknesses by rigorously probing the system's defences, thereby contributing to its resilience (Ovadya, 2023).

Post-incident, forensic analysis comes into play. This involves an in-depth review of logs, data and algorithms, much like a crime scene investigation, to understand what went wrong and how future incidents can be prevented. Proactive measures include threat intelligence, which involves collecting and analysing data about existing and emerging threats, helping organizations be pre-emptive rather than merely reactive.

Finally, quantitative analysis assesses both the probability and impact of various risks, enabling organizations to prioritize which vulnerabilities to address first, thus contributing to the overall resilience and ethical alignment of the technology.

Security-by-design

Security-by-design is an approach that embeds safety in AI systems from inception. It emphasizes real-world validation, particularly in critical sectors like healthcare and autonomous driving, where stringent standards apply. Quick human intervention, through rapid response teams and user feedback channels, is crucial for timely issue resolution.

Data security is also vital, requiring constant updates to security protocols. Encryption, access controls and secure data transfer are fundamental. Temporary databases should be deleted after task completion, and API licences strictly followed.

Various assessment tools, from breach and attack simulation to threat modelling, help gauge security. Challenger models and real-time alert systems like SIEM add extra layers of protection. Black-box multi-vector testing gives an overall security evaluation without needing internal system details.

Staged rollouts help catch safety issues early, and internal boards vet research for dual-use risks. Detailed emergency response plans and a Chief Risk Officer (CRO) help manage risks effectively.

The bottom line

AI and cybersecurity are intricately linked, with each amplifying the vulnerabilities and capabilities of the other. While AI introduces new types of risks, such as model backdoors and adversarial attacks, it also offers novel solutions for cyberdefence and risk assessment. However, AI systems themselves, as well as models, are riddled with potential vulnerabilities, making them very difficult to secure.

The big picture

Cybersecurity threats are big business, albeit a criminal one. They are becoming far more numerous, as well as a great deal more sophisticated, thanks in part to the democratization of AI tools. However, with proactive strategies like security-by-design and ongoing research into risk identification and mitigation, the cybersecurity landscape can evolve to better meet the looming challenges of this AI augmented world.

LEADERSHIP ACTION POINTS

- Embrace a security-first mindset by looking beyond compliance to adopt a proactive approach to cybersecurity. This involves continuous risk assessments and adopting the viewpoint of a potential attacker to identify overlooked vulnerabilities.

- Invest in specialized expertise by hiring or consulting with experts in AI security. This includes not only software engineers but also legal and ethical experts who can navigate the complex compliance landscape. Implement rigorous testing protocols that include adversarial examples and unexpected inputs.

- Identify and neutralize threats as they emerge through continuous monitoring. Leverage AI for defence by utilizing AI tools for real-time security monitoring, vulnerability scanning and threat intelligence. Invest in research to keep these tools at the cutting edge of technology.

- Maintain transparent reporting mechanisms both internally and for users. In the event of a security incident, clear communication and accountability are vital for damage control and future prevention.

- Plan for the attacks and exploits by preparing detailed incident response plans, and investing in rapid response teams. Being prepared for the worst-case scenario will enable quicker recovery and minimize damage.

References

Fortis, S (2023) Apple bans ChatGPT use for employees over fears of data leaks, Coin Telegraph, 19 May, https://cointelegraph.com/news/apple bans-chat-gpt-employee-use (archived at https://perma.cc/596Q-6YAU)

Goodin, D (2020) Multiple 'CIA failures' led to theft of agency's top-secret hacking tools, Ars Technica, 16 June, https://arstechnica.com/information-technology/2020/06/theft-of-top-secret-cia-hacking-tools-was-result-of-woefully-lax-security (archived at https://perma.cc/3BQB-K47G)

Harrison, J, Toreini, E and Mehrnezhad, M (2023) A practical deep learning-based acoustic side channel attack on keyboards [Preprint], https://arxiv.org/abs/2308.01074 (archived at https://perma.cc/B4JJ-F6UD)

Hazell, J (2023) Spear phishing with large language models [Preprint], https://arxiv.org/abs/2305.06972 (archived at https://perma.cc/45TN-QJQK)

Nassi, B et al (2023) Video-based cryptanalysis: Exploiting a video camera's rolling shutter to recover secret keys from devices using video footage of their power LED, Ben Nassi, www.nassiben.com/video-based-crypta (archived at https://perma.cc/BK5W-3WXV)

Ovadya, A (2023) Red teaming improved GPT-4. Violet teaming goes even further, Wired, 29 March, www.wired.com/story/red-teaming-gpt-4-was-valuable-violet-teaming-will-make-it-better (archived at https://perma.cc/9DED-GJZ5)

Petkauskas, P (2023) ChatGPT flaw exposed users' chat histories, Cyber News, 15 November, https://cybernews.com/news/chatgpt-flaw-exposed-users-chat-histories/#google_vignette (archived at https://perma.cc/925R-2823)

Qi, X et al (2023) Fine-tuning aligned language models compromises safety, even when users do not intend to! [Preprint], https://arxiv.org/abs/2310.03693 (archived at https://perma.cc/RDG4-JSPQ)

Searles, A et al (2023) An empirical study & evaluation of modern CAPTCHAs [Preprint], https://arxiv.org/abs/2307.12108 (archived at https://perma.cc/5E66-SJAF)

Veerabadran, V et al (2023) Subtle adversarial image manipulations influence both human and machine perception, *Nature Communications*, 14 (4933), www.nature.com/articles/s41467-023-40499-0 (archived at https://perma.cc/9WFS-K5S2)

CHAPTER THIRTEEN

Taskmasters

The danger of the past was that men became slaves. The danger of the future is that men may become robots. ERICH FROMM

As algorithmic management takes root in today's workplaces, leveraging machine learning and automation for efficiency, it brings along both benefits and challenges. While these systems can indeed boost productivity, they risk reducing workers to mere task executors, stripping them of autonomy and creative input. The key challenge for contemporary organizations is to integrate these technologies in a way that respects human diversity and dignity, without turning employees into cogs in a cold machine. This chapter aims to explore strategies to maintain this delicate balance.

The rise of algorithmic management in the workforce presents a complex landscape of benefits and challenges. While these systems can optimize productivity, their intrusive monitoring – from restroom breaks to casual conversations – has significant implications for employee wellbeing. Such monitoring practices have been linked to an 80 per cent increase in employee injuries compared to the average. Additionally, the opaque nature of these systems further complicates matters, as it's unclear how certain behaviours negatively affect one's standing at work, with only 21 per cent of employees reporting confidence challenging algorithmically made decisions (Kelly-Lyth and Thomas, 2023).

Job application processes also fall under algorithmic scrutiny. AI-driven keyword filtering can disqualify candidates who are otherwise well suited for a role, turning the recruitment process into a dehumanizing game of buzzwords.

The impersonal nature of these systems makes them potentially tyrannical, exercising control without context, empathy or understanding. This is exacerbated by their complexity, which can reach a point where even their creators can't fully explain their behaviour. Once established, these systems are hard to roll back, risking the entrenchment of an inhumane work environment.

Unions could serve as a counterweight, evolving to defend traditional and gig workers against algorithmic injustices. The challenge of contesting algorithmic misattributions is also significant. When an algorithm judges an employee, the process behind that decision is often opaque. This can make it difficult for employees to challenge or even understand the basis for certain managerial decisions. It may also potentially lead to decisions which may be unfair and unlawful, systematizing discrimination on the grounds of religion or ethnicity. Addressing these issues requires transparency, including mandatory disclosures about these systems' existence, capabilities, deployment and purposes.

Remote work adds another layer of complexity. Algorithms may overlook the unique challenges of working from home, such as family interruptions, potentially leading to misunderstandings regarding an employee's dedication.

As we integrate these systems further, it's essential to remember the labour rights we've fought hard to establish. The eight-hour workday and workers' compensation were once revolutionary ideas. Today, the frontier is ethical algorithmic management, and addressing its challenges is imperative before it becomes too deeply ingrained to change.

Automation and employment

AI is transforming employment, extending its impact to new intellectual tasks such as data analysis and customer service. Unlike earlier technological shifts, AI threatens to monopolize intellectual work, potentially leaving humans with only basic manual and emotional tasks. This trend, known as the 'enclosure of intellectual activity', could de-skill the human labour force.

Algorithms are already guiding gig workers, often those with fewer rights, towards fragmented, short-term tasks. While this may not lead to widespread unemployment, it could change the nature of work in ways that make jobs less rewarding and services less effective. For instance, 'gigification' could break work into disconnected tasks, eroding the satisfaction of long-term involvement. Moreover, algorithm-driven customer service may lack the nuance and understanding that human agents offer, leading to depersonalized and less effective solutions.

In the AI-driven work landscape, traditional roles could be reduced to a bare minimum, comprising mainly 'Machine Wranglers', who oversee automated systems, and 'Liability Sponges', tasked with handling failures. The alarming part isn't merely job loss to automation but the transformation of remaining roles into robotic-like functions. Under algorithmic management, every action becomes scrutinized data, setting humans against machine-level performance metrics.

Such scrutiny may compel workers to emulate machine-like behaviour: always available, intensely focused and prioritizing numbers over quality to maintain employment. The result is increased productivity gains for companies but potentially fewer benefits for workers.

Algorithms are increasingly taking over human roles in making decisions about scheduling and performance evaluations. While potentially efficient, these systems lack human qualities such as empathy and understanding. Machine learning models trained with conventional data collection methods often judge infractions more harshly than humans do, due to differences in how annotators encode norms of behaviour versus hard facts (Balagopalan et al, 2023). Simple descriptions of potentially rule-violating scenarios aren't sufficient to determine actual breaches of specific standards. For example, someone might be annotated as smoking a cigarette (a fact), but it's probably not problematic if they are currently outside, being viewed through a window (a norm). Conversely, while machines sometimes outperform humans in scene interpretation, they may be incorrectly marked as failing due to the inadequacy of the 'correct' answers provided (Bavishi et al, 2023).

Machine-governed workplaces limit spontaneity, creativity and tolerance for minor errors. Every action is analysed, narrowing the scope for personal judgement, taking initiative or learning opportunities a human manager might allow.

This mechanization of management squeezes out room for spontaneity, creativity and tolerable mistakes. Individual actions are reduced to data points for analysis, and the latitude for human discretion shrinks. In a twist of irony, as machines advance to mimic human cognitive functions, humans are pressured to abandon their unique qualities to meet the rigid standards set by these strict machines.

Workplace safety

Technologies like AI-powered machine vision can improve workplace safety by early identification of risks, including access by unauthorized people or failure to use equipment safely. These tools can also improve hiring, task design and training. However, their deployment requires careful consideration of employee privacy and agency, especially in remote work settings where home surveillance becomes a concern.

Companies must maintain transparency and clear guidelines about data collection and usage to balance safety enhancements with individual rights. When thoughtfully implemented, these technologies can create a mutually beneficial environment of increased safety and productivity.

Co-pilots and meat puppets

Technology historically transforms jobs rather than outright eliminating them. For instance, word processors changed secretaries into personal assistants, and radiology AI enhances rather than replaces radiologists. Roles requiring specialized skills, nuanced judgement or real-time decision-making are less susceptible to full automation. However, as AI takes on more tasks, some people could become 'meat puppets', executing manual tasks under AI supervision, which deviates from the idealistic promise of AI freeing us for creative work.

Big Tech's early adoption of AI has given it a competitive edge, leading to industry consolidation and new business models. In various sectors, humans are increasingly acting as conduits for AI – call centre agents follow machine-generated scripts and salespeople receive real-time advice from AI.

In healthcare, while roles like nursing are considered irreplaceable due to their emotional and tactile aspects, AI 'co-pilots' could handle tasks like documentation and diagnostics, thereby reducing the human cognitive involvement for non-essential tasks.

Cyborgs and centaurs

The Cyborg and Centaur models describe two distinct frameworks for human-AI collaboration, each with its own advantages and limitations. In the Cyborg model, AI is seamlessly integrated into the human body or workflow, becoming an extension of the individual – akin to a prosthetic limb or cochlear implant. This deep integration blurs the boundary between human and machine, sometimes even challenging our notions of what it means to be human.

The Centaur model, on the other hand, emphasizes a collaborative partnership between humans and AI, often outperforming either AI or human competitors. This model preserves the values of human insight, using it to augment the machine's capabilities, creating something more than the sum of its parts. In this setup, the human remains in the loop, making strategic decisions and providing emotional or creative input, while the AI focuses on computation, data analysis or routine tasks. Here, the entities remain distinct, and their collaboration is clearly delineated. However, the rapid advancement of chess AI, culminating in systems like AlphaZero, has shifted this dynamic. These days, the prowess of AI in chess is such that the addition of human strategy might even detract from the AI's performance.

In a business setting, the Centaur model promotes a collaborative partnership between AI and humans, each contributing their strengths to achieve common objectives. For instance, in data analysis, AI could process large datasets to identify patterns, while human analysts apply contextual understanding to make strategic decisions. In customer service, chatbots could manage routine queries, leaving complex, emotionally nuanced issues to human agents. Such divisions of labour optimize efficiency, while augmenting human capabilities rather than replacing them. Maintaining a clear delineation between human and AI roles also aids in accountability and ethical governance.

Worker-led co-design

Worker-led co-design is an approach that involves employees in the development and refinement of algorithmic systems that will be used in their workplace. This participatory model allows workers to have a say in how these technologies are implemented, thereby ensuring that the systems are attuned to real-world needs and concerns. Co-design workshops can be organized where employees collaborate with designers and engineers to outline desired features and discuss potential pitfalls. Employees can share their expertise about the nuances of their job, flag ethical or practical concerns and help shape the algorithm's rules or decision-making criteria. This can make the system more fair, transparent and aligned with workers' needs, reducing the risk of adverse effects like unjust penalties or excessive surveillance. Moreover, involving employees in co-design can foster a sense of agency and ownership, potentially easing the integration of new technologies into the workplace.

C-suite AI

AI holds the potential to substantially augment executive functions by rapidly analysing complex data related to market trends, competitor behaviour and personnel management. For instance, a CEO could receive succinct, data-driven recommendations on acquisitions and partnerships from an AI adviser. However, AI currently can't replace the human qualities essential for leadership, such as trustworthiness and the ability to inspire.

Additionally, the rise of AI in management can have social implications. The erosion of middle management roles due to automation could lead to identity crises, as the traditional understanding of 'management' undergoes a transformation.

In management consultancy, AI has the potential to disrupt by providing data-backed strategic advice. This could even lend a perceived objectivity to tough decisions, like downsizing. However, the deployment of AI in such critical roles demands careful oversight to validate their recommendations and mitigate associated risks. Striking the right balance is crucial: underutilizing AI might mean missing out on transformative benefits, while overreliance could risk ethical and public relations pitfalls.

Servant leadership by machines

AI holds the promise of transforming the workplace by taking over mundane and repetitive tasks, potentially freeing humans to engage in more creative and intellectual pursuits. While algorithmic management is often criticized for eroding human autonomy, it could, ironically, enable a model where employees have greater freedom in achieving their objectives. The idea of 'life on a rail' may sound restrictive, but for many, the delegation of small decisions could be liberating, allowing them to focus on more meaningful tasks.

AI is already making significant strides in various service sectors. In customer service, chatbots like Intercom handle routine queries, while in healthcare, algorithms assist in diagnostics and risk prediction. Financial robo-advisers like Wealthfront automate investment advice, and in retail, systems like Amazon Go are revolutionizing inventory and checkout processes. AI-powered platforms are also streamlining legal research and personalizing education. Even in transportation and hospitality, semi-autonomous vehicles and AI concierges are beginning to take on roles traditionally filled by humans. Just as technological advances in manufacturing led to an array of affordable, high-quality goods, AI has the potential to similarly revolutionize the service sector.

Public service management failures

Using AI and algorithms in public services promises efficiency but risks significant unintended negative outcomes. For instance, Denmark's use of an algorithmic system to manage unemployment benefits led to incorrect benefit cuts, turning what was supposed to be a time-saving measure into an administrative burden (Geiger, 2023). Similar issues occurred in Italy and Spain, affecting the allocation of teaching assignments and worker oversight, respectively (Arandia et al, 2023; Bizzini, 2023). These cases are cautionary tales that emphasize the need for careful planning, thorough testing and ethical consideration when implementing algorithmic systems in areas with significant human and social stakes. Errors in these sectors can have far-reaching impacts, affecting the livelihoods and wellbeing of individuals and communities. Therefore, contingency plans and human oversight are crucial to mitigate the risks associated with automating complex government administrative tasks.

Checking out and lying flat

The current societal mood can be characterized by a sense of social defeat, stemming not from individual failures but systemic imbalances. This mood is exacerbated by economic shifts, such as the decline of manufacturing jobs, the rise of the gig economy and the impact of neoliberal policies focused on efficiency. These shifts have led to reduced wages and limited opportunities for upward mobility, affecting particularly younger generations who have also had to deal with the great recession, the pandemic and spiralling costs of living. Now, AI and automation are adding another layer of complexity by hollowing out both technical and creative industries and increasing workplace surveillance.

This overall context is leading to a growing discontent that sometimes results in public rage or social withdrawal. The current trajectory highlights the urgent need for intentional decisions aimed at improving collective morale and societal unity. As we see increasing numbers of highly skilled individuals opting out of contributing their talents, the parallels with the societal apathy observed during the declining years of the USSR become stark. To counteract this trend, targeted societal and policy interventions are necessary to foster a more equitable and satisfying future.

Given this backdrop, there's a pressing need for purposeful decisions aimed at improving collective morale and societal cohesion. The current trajectory is not sustainable if the aim is a more equitable and fulfilling future. The irony that the present AI waves are automating creative expression instead of jobs that everybody hates shouldn't be lost on us. Therefore, policymakers, technologists and community leaders must work together to address these systemic issues, focusing on equitable growth and social wellbeing.

The bottom line

The future of work is at a crucial inflection point. As AI technologies advance, the risk of amplifying existing ethical and social issues in the workforce grows. Ironically, 'fulfilment centres' often aren't very fulfilling, and autonomous systems can usurp autonomy from human beings. There is an urgent need for a balanced approach that maximizes efficiency and innovation while safeguarding human dignity, autonomy and wellbeing.

The big picture

The challenge of algorithmic management is to harness the power of AI to elevate human potential rather than diminish it. A light touch is essential if such tools are not to be a repressive yoke upon human beings. Such technologies must demonstrate that they are trustworthy, unbiased and designed to serve the workers' needs first, and not their paymasters. Leaders should avoid ruthless automation. Life is often at its best when it's not too 'optimized' and when we take time to appreciate the small things.

LEADERSHIP ACTION POINTS

- Develop a governance framework for ethical AI use that prioritizes human wellbeing and addresses bias, fairness and surveillance issues. Ensure that AI and algorithmic management systems are designed to augment human capabilities and are aligned with workers' needs and ethical principles.

- Create transparent processes for algorithmic decision-making. Workers should know how algorithms impact their work, and mechanisms should be in place for them to contest decisions made by algorithms.

- Equip line managers and staff with the knowledge and tools to handle data and algorithms responsibly. This includes training on algorithmic management's ethical implications and health risks associated with it. Algorithms should augment, not replace, human managers.

- Implement ongoing audits of AI systems to assess their impact on workers and the organization. Use the insights for continuous improvement and ethical alignment.

- Recognize and address the psychological and societal impacts of algorithmic management and work automation, advocating for mental health support and work–life balance.

References

Arandia, P J et al (2023) Spain's AI doctor, Lighthouse Reports, 17 April, www.lighthousereports.com/investigation/spains-ai-doctor (archived at https://perma.cc/WZ5Q-XBJJ)

Balagopalan, A et al (2023) Judging facts, judging norms: Training machine learning models to judge humans requires a modified approach to labeling data, *Science Advances*, 9 (19), https://doi.org/10.1126/sciadv.abq0701 (archived at https://perma.cc/SM28-YPWM)

Bavishi, R et al (2023) Fuyu-8B: A multimodal architecture for AI agents, Adept, www.adept.ai/blog/fuyu-8b (archived at https://perma.cc/SX6M-BXHZ)

Bizzini, P (2023) The algorithm that blew up Italy's school system, Algorithm Watch, 17 April, https://algorithmwatch.org/en/algorithm-school-system-italy (archived at https://perma.cc/K8J5-G5SX)

Geiger, G (2023) How Denmark's welfare state became a surveillance nightmare, Wired, 7 March, www.wired.com/story/algorithms-welfare-state-politics (archived at https://perma.cc/V93N-X98W)

Kelly-Lyth, A and Thomas, A (2023) Algorithmic management: Assessing the impacts of AI at work, *European Labour Law Journal*, 14 (2), 230–52

CHAPTER FOURTEEN

Virtual learning

In order to accumulate outstanding qualities, one needs unusually effective ways to learn. It's not enough to learn a lot; one also has to manage what one learns.... It is those hidden tricks of mental management that produce the systems that create those works of genius. MARVIN MINSKY

We're currently in an era marked by increasingly realistic virtual worlds. But the true power of these digital realms isn't merely about entertainment – it's a powerful training ground for both humans and machines. As we move forward, the role of the metaverse in education and skill development will likely grow, offering scalable solutions for personalized learning and practical training. This chapter outlines how the symbiosis of AI and human expertise is revolutionizing both machine learning and human education, setting the stage for a new paradigm in how we learn and teach.

The concept of personalized, AI-driven education is vividly portrayed in Neal Stephenson's science fiction novel *The*

Diamond Age, through the idea of 'A Young Lady's Primer', a highly interactive and adaptive educational tool (Stephenson, 1995). With AI technology's maturation, we anticipate the generation of complex scenes and narratives akin to the Primer, offering a more immersive and intuitive learning experience. This could be particularly transformative for subjects like mathematics, where many students struggle. A personalized AI coach could offer explanations in multiple ways until the student grasps the concept, creating simple animations or interactive examples (even games) to cement understanding. Inspirational framing of the wider meaning subject can render topics in a clear and fascinating manner. AI systems will be able to generate a sweet spot of challenging learning for users, to keep them in an ideal flow state for learning, and avoid them struggling unduly and becoming disheartened. These technologies can democratize access to inclusive high-quality education at a tiny fraction of the costs of a human tutor. This may finally undo the incredible 'cost disease' that influences the price of education (and inflation of grades), with its associated debt that frustrates many young people from buying a house and starting a family. However, younger people, being particularly impressionable, are perhaps also most at risk of being unduly influenced by AI.

Language models tackle a common shortcoming in traditional educational materials, such as books or expert advice, which often lack detailed explanations and assume unquestioning compliance from learners. Catering to the innate human curiosity to understand the 'why' and 'how' behind concepts, these models offer comprehensive, context-aware explanations that enhance the learning experience.

However, there are some reasons for concern. For instance, while AI can excel at repetitive coaching tasks, it may inadvertently encourage poor practices if not properly designed. Also, it can't replace the nuanced guidance that a human mentor provides, which often goes beyond the subject matter to include life skills, ethics and more. Human teachers would still need to set the scene and inspire, though AI classroom assistants will increasingly coach each student individually.

Nevertheless, ensuring AI-driven educational platforms deliver information objectively and balanced is crucial. Also, while human teachers can adapt to the individual needs and learning styles of their students, an AI system's inability to deeply understand human behaviour could result in less effective education in some circumstances.

Furthermore, growing reliance on AI risks atrophying fundamental skills, including basic arithmetic, navigation and memory retention. Technology serves as both an enhancer and a crutch, freeing cognitive resources for more complex tasks while potentially making individuals and societies more vulnerable to skill decay, technical glitches or cyberattacks. Professions such as law will have challenges training juniors, as the gruelling process of learning case law is now increasingly being outsourced to machines. AI could potentially eliminate entry-level positions, which are often stepping stones to more advanced roles. Industries could thereby lose their pipeline of emerging talent due to dwindling junior roles.

Responses to over-dependence may include redesigning technologies to encourage mindful skill development, incorporating basic life skills into educational curricula and fostering user awareness about the risks of technological over-reliance.

GMs can provide a conversation partner in natural, native, endless conversations, simulating a virtual language immersion experience – even particular dialects or sociolects – enabling learners to practise and refine their language skills without physically being in a region where the language is spoken. However, it should be noted that such virtual environments come with their own issues which mirror the real world, such as handling abusive speech or behaviour. Issues around digital ownership, privacy and data security are also magnified in a world where people are increasingly economically dependent on such platforms.

AI simulation learning environments

AI systems are learning from human tutors within simulated environments, melding human expertise with machine learning capabilities for enhanced learning outcomes. Imagine a flight simulator where a pilot-in-training learns from an experienced instructor; in a similar fashion, the AI learns from human experts in a controlled, virtual setting. This method is often used in complex tasks, such as behaviour recognition, where human intuition and decision-making are crucial but difficult to encode directly into algorithms.

In these virtual sandboxes, humans can guide machines, teaching them how to respond to specific situations or understand different contexts. The beauty of this virtual training is that it allows us to expose robots to a wide variety of scenarios quickly and cost-effectively. Once these lessons are learned in the virtual world, they can be instantly applied in reality. As a result, machines can quickly learn to handle everyday human chores like folding laundry or identifying crushed drink cans as (recyclable) trash.

This approach lets AI learn directly from human experts' nuanced behaviours and decisions, bridging the gap between human intuition and algorithmic precision. This can be particularly useful in fields like healthcare, where doctors make complex decisions based on a combination of medical knowledge and years of experience. By observing and learning from human experts in a simulated environment, the AI can develop a more nuanced understanding of the task at hand. Physical environments can now be captured from real life using just a cellphone camera, turned directly into explorable virtual environments (Xu et al, 2023).

Human tutors will play a critical role, especially in the near term, as they guide AI through challenges that require a nuanced understanding of the world, something that algorithms alone currently can't grasp. This collaboration could manifest in both real and virtual environments, allowing for a richer set of experiences and data to inform the AI's training. However, as AI systems incorporate these human-guided experiences into their training data, the need for human intervention is expected to diminish over time. Eventually, humans may only be required to step in for highly unusual or complex situations that the AI hasn't encountered before – peculiar edge cases. However, preventing AI from adopting its human tutors' biases or bad habits necessitates meticulous value alignment processes (discussed later in this book).

The question of data privacy remains also, especially when the simulated environments are based on real-world data. Furthermore, the effectiveness of the AI's learning could be limited by the quality of the simulation, and the expertise and patience of the human tutor.

The bottom line

AI-driven environments promise unparalleled opportunities for personalized learning, skill enhancement and training. However, the effective and ethical implementation of these technologies is critical. The stakes are high: get it right, and we democratize access to high-quality education and training; get it wrong, and we risk widening existing social and economic divides.

The big picture

The relationship between humans and machine learning is reciprocal: as we teach machines, they, in turn, shape our understanding and actions. This dynamic has the potential to radically transform our approach to education, skill development and decision-making. In a future where virtual environments become as commonplace as physical classrooms and offices, the synergies between human intelligence and artificial intelligence could greatly expand our collective capabilities.

LEADERSHIP ACTION POINTS

- Harness the human-machine dyad by leveraging the strengths of both humans and machines to create rich, adaptive learning environments. Encourage competition between human creativity and machine efficiency for problem-solving and innovation.

- Prioritize lifelong learning by developing platforms and programs that are flexible enough to adapt to the evolving educational needs of individuals throughout their lives, from K-12 to professional development.

- Invest in continuous user experience research to ensure virtual learning environments are intuitive and user-friendly. Poor design could deter users, regardless of how advanced the underlying technology is.

- Create mechanisms for ongoing feedback from both human users and AI systems. Use this data to make iterative improvements, ensuring the system remains responsive to changing needs.

References

Stephenson, N (1995) *The Diamond Age*, Bantam Spectra, New York

Xu, L et al (2023) VR-NeRF: High-fidelity virtualized walkable spaces [Preprint], https://arxiv.org/abs/2311.02542 (archived at https://perma.cc/3V4X-BDU9)

CHAPTER FIFTEEN

Synthetic media

Artificial intelligence is not a substitute for human intelligence; it is a tool to amplify human creativity and ingenuity. FEI-FEI LI

In recent decades, we've seen the transformative impact of technologies that dramatically reduce marginal costs – the cost of producing one additional unit of a good or service. The microchip revolutionized computing by making computational power exponentially cheaper, and the internet reduced the marginal cost of distribution to almost zero, enabling instant, global dissemination of information. Generative AI promises to dramatically transform the economics of creative processes. By automating design, writing, software development and other creative processes, these technologies could drastically reduce the time and labour required to create new products or content. This chapter outlines how generative AI can expand creative capabilities, whether it's generating code, composing music, designing graphics or writing articles.

Unlimited complexity without marginal cost

Many people are becoming familiar with AI-generated art, such as that made by the DALL-E series. Algorithmically generated designs use rules, constraints and themes to create 2D and 3D visuals automatically. This might be something like a wind turbine blade design, an architectural facade or a building layout fit for a certain purpose.

When paired with additive manufacturing (3D printing), the design and manufacture of a textured 3D object can be made in one automated process with incredible complexity but no extra marginal cost (Wang et al, 2023). In the 1900s, we still had a fashion for beautiful and intricate design, but this has been replaced by mass-produced simplicity, which tends to be inoffensive and generally timeless, but also dull and soulless. We might soon experience a renaissance, whereby plainness becomes passé in a world where elegance finds its freedom, as complexity becomes free.

In urban spaces, algorithmic design can be applied to interior and exterior building design, the sequencing of construction to build more efficiently, town planning for current and future predicted needs, and even warehousing and logistics. Some systems can even predict the varying rental yields from installing apartments, shops or offices on a certain floor. These capabilities have the potential to reduce the time and costs required for construction greatly. However, design processes have assumptions baked in, everything from fire regulations to human beings' expected size and weight load. Most parameters will naturally vary across time, culture and geography, and this inevitability should be accounted for with tolerances and maintenance in mind.

Generative adversarial networks

Generative adversarial networks (GANs) involve two parts: one creates data and the other evaluates it. They learn together in tandem through mutual feedback. The generator aims to create data so realistic that the discriminator can't distinguish it from naturally sourced examples. This has led to advances in numerous fields such as video game design, art creation and drug development.

These techniques revolutionize image and audio restoration by effectively repairing noise, damage and distortion (Liu et al, 2023). They have applications in medical imaging, surveillance and digital forensics. GANs can also perform tasks like upscaling low-resolution media, transferring styles and even altering the seasons in a video.

This technology is widely used for enhancing pre-HD content and for real-time filters in video conferencing apps. Moreover, today's photographs are increasingly enhanced by algorithms, moving beyond just capturing light through a lens. However, such pre-filtering mechanisms may not be transparent to viewers, and may warp reality in ways the creator of that image doesn't intend (Dayaram, 2023; Ohlheiser, 2021).

Style transfer

Style transfer is a technique in computer vision and machine learning that transforms an image's style while retaining its content. For example, you could make your photo look like it was painted by Van Gogh or Picasso. This is typically achieved using neural networks, particularly convolutional neural networks (CNNs), that have been trained to understand content and style from different images.

In the commercial realm, style transfer can be used for various applications, including advertising, movie production and the fashion industry. It offers a fun and engaging way to enhance photos and videos for personal use. However, the ease with which styles can be transferred and disseminated online also poses risks of misuse or overuse, potentially diluting unique cultural or artistic expressions.

Deepfakes

Advanced machine-learning techniques create deepfakes, synthetic videos or audio recordings that mimic real-life footage. Imagine a puppeteer so skilled that the puppet seems alive; deepfakes are the digital equivalent, mimicking real people in ways that can be extraordinarily convincing, such as making someone convincingly appear to speak another language. They can make it appear as if individuals are saying or doing things they never actually said or did.

Deepfake technology benefits film production, voice synthesis and historical footage restoration. However, the ease with which deepfakes can be created and disseminated poses significant ethical and societal challenges. They can be used for misinformation, propaganda or to discredit individuals. For example, a deepfake could show a public figure making inflammatory statements they never made, sowing discord or affecting public opinion. Conversely, they could help to hush up a flub or indiscretion. Moreover, the capacity for AI to generate content effortlessly raises ethical questions about ownership, originality and the potential for misuse, such as the moral rights of people to own their own content, voice or face, and things derived from it.

Because deepfakes can be so convincing, they present unique challenges for information verification. Traditional methods of fact-checking may fall short, requiring new techniques for detecting manipulated media or preventing its alteration. Several tech companies and academic researchers are working on deepfake detection tools, but it's a cat-and-mouse game; as detection methods improve, so do the techniques for creating deepfakes.

Neural Radiance Fields (NeRFs) and Gaussian Splatting

Neural Radiance Fields (NeRFs) are a breakthrough in 3D visualization, utilizing deep learning to transform a collection of 2D photographs into detailed, three-dimensional scenes. Unlike traditional 3D modelling, which relies on manually crafting each detail, NeRFs automate this process. By inputting a spatial coordinate, NeRFs predict the light's colour and intensity at that point, weaving together a coherent 3D space from scattered images. This method excels in crafting photorealistic scenes but demands significant computational power, limiting its real-time application.

Gaussian Splatting addresses this limitation. It's a rendering technique that streamlines the process, using mathematical functions known as 3D Gaussians to approximate the scene's complexity. This approach significantly reduces the computational burden, making it possible to render these detailed scenes more swiftly, even in real-time applications. The synergy of Gaussian Splatting with NeRFs holds the promise of revolutionizing industries by enabling the creation of high-fidelity virtual environments, from gaming and virtual reality to architectural visualization, with unprecedented efficiency. For example, by using such technologies, very high-quality data streams can be transmitted even on modest or shaky connections, negating the drop-outs on video calls, and enabling incredibly high-fidelity virtual experiences even on modest hardware.

AI compression

Essentially, LLMs compress the internet in a lossy manner with some intelligent gap-filling. Language itself is a compression structure we've built to share ideas and represent the world, and generative AI uses similar techniques to compress other kinds of data. AI-driven video compression techniques offer a massive reduction in data usage without significant quality loss (Lee, 2020). Such technology could translate into massive cost savings for media giants like YouTube and Netflix, which are significant consumers of global bandwidth. High-quality streaming could become accessible in remote areas and developing economies where only basic or expensive metered connections are available.

In the gaming world, similar technologies, such as deep learning super sampling (DLSS), are making it computationally cheaper to experience high-definition gaming by using AI to upscale from lower resolutions. These advances can enable high-fidelity experiences even on modest hardware.

Incorporating a GM into a computer game can revolutionize the player experience, making it more dynamic, interactive and immersive. One method is to develop a dynamic dialogue system that allows for context-sensitive, natural conversations between the player and non-player characters. This makes the game more engaging and allows the narrative to adapt based on player choices, and conversational puzzle-solving. Based on predefined themes or player input, dynamic world-building could involve the GM in the procedural generation of environments, cities or entire game worlds. This ensures the game world is ever-evolving and responsive to player actions.

Foundation models themselves can be seen as compressed, distilled forms of internet-scale datasets capable of generating new data and insights beyond their training sets. This capability aligns with the idea that intelligence may be considered a form of data compression through abstraction (turning years of experience into actionable insight – the emergence of wisdom).

Intellectual property concerns

Generative AI systems present a complex web of legal challenges, starting with intellectual property rights. These systems often train on a vast number of internet images, some of which could be copyrighted or trademarked. In cases where the AI-generated image closely resembles a copyrighted work, the question of infringement arises. While 'fair use' might offer some legal leeway, US law still needs to clearly define whether publicly available data falls under this category.

Some companies like Microsoft have taken steps to address these concerns. They've offered users protection from lawsuits related to AI-generated content, setting a precedent that could influence how other companies approach these complex issues (Smith, 2023). Given the complexity, we can expect a new body of case law to emerge, as unresolved issues often lead to litigation.

Ownership of AI-generated content is a murky area as well. US copyright law doesn't currently recognize AI creations since they're not human-made. Neither copyrights nor patents are ideal for regulating AI-generated works. Copyright law faces challenges in identifying the 'creator' of a piece of art, especially when AI assists in its creation. On the other hand, the US Patent Office is still grappling with handling the outputs of AI systems, particularly when AI plays a significant role in invention processes like drug development. By contrast, the prevailing stance in the UK is that works created by AI can be covered under copyright protections, though this could change in the future.

Fundamentally, GMs are powered by the enclosure of a commons of data (often including private copyrighted works such as books), which is then compressed and drip-fed back to us through an API. Legislators are considering whether they should force AI companies to disclose their use of copyrighted training data. Leaders should be diligent in sourcing training data and obtain adequate assurances from service providers.

Websites such as havibeentrained.com have sprung up to help check if one's face or content has been trained within a machine learning system. It should be noted, however, that content creators who choose to opt out of having their work included in training sets may face obscurity. Works not included in training data are unlikely to be salient to the algorithmic curators who introduce us to new content and ideas.

It's also possible to make GMs unlearn a subset of their training data after the fact, such as forgetting the entire Harry Potter universe without harming performance on standard benchmarks (Eldan and Russinovich, 2023).

Awareness of interaction with autonomous systems

The increasing sophistication of AI and machine learning technologies has blurred the lines between human and machine agency. This creates challenges in determining whether a human or an algorithm made a given action, decision or interaction. Already, there are reports that most activity online is by bots rather than human beings, leading many to wonder how much online activity is actually human-driven (LaFrance, 2017).

While there are emerging standards to identify the nature of an agent clearly – be it human or machine – such mechanisms are not foolproof against intentional deception. Many online shooter games such as *Call of Duty: Mobile* reportedly employ AI bots with names that mimic real players, flattering the ability of new players who would otherwise be crushed by experienced players, increasing retention. Online games that have a dwindling player base sometimes populate servers with sophisticated bots designed to emulate real players, avoiding the negative spiral of the environment feeling lifeless and dull (Kratky, 2021).

The IEEE 3152 Standard for Transparent Agency Identification of Humans and Machines, which I chair, provides clear mechanisms to indicate what kind of agency is behind an interaction, be it human, machine or some combination (IEEE, 2023). However, it's worth noting that such standards are effective primarily against good faith misinterpretations and do not prevent intentional deception or obfuscation. In addition to standards like IEEE 3152, various Turing tests may be employed to verify whether an agent is human or machine. However, these tests have limitations and can be deceived to varying extents, and making a definitive determination can be very challenging.

Society's relationship with technology and media has evolved to a point where the line between reality and falsehood is increasingly blurry. We've learned to be sceptical, consulting fact-checking sites like Snopes when confronted with suspicious images or claims. Yet, our minds tend to latch onto the first piece of information we receive, making retractions less effective – this is why false accusations linger.

Advances in technology have made it easier to manipulate reality. Voices and facial expressions can be synthesized; even the language someone is speaking can be altered seamlessly. These capabilities are not merely novel but tools in modern psychological warfare aimed at cultural demoralization.

At its core, society functions on shared narratives rooted in democratic values, historical myths or religious beliefs. These narratives offer a common ground for discussion and compromise. However, when false information proliferates to the extent that it fragments these shared narratives, the fabric of society begins to tear (Benson, 2023). We're witnessing multiple Overton windows, fragmented realities and polarized communities that can no longer engage in constructive dialogue. It must be noted that where conversation fails, conflicts become almost inevitable.

The bottom line

Generative AI is revolutionizing the economics of creation by driving the marginal cost towards zero, promising vast benefits across sectors from healthcare to entertainment. However, it also poses ethical, legal and social challenges, including intellectual property rights, data privacy and the risk of cultural homogenization. Moreover, the ease of creating synthetic media challenges our epistemic foundations.

The big picture

Machines have evolved beyond mere data receptacles; they're now active participants, shaping our experiences and potentially our cultural landscape. The adoption of generative AI signifies not merely a technological shift but a paradigm shift in how we understand creativity, efficiency and even the concept of agency. It can democratize creative and industrial processes, making them more accessible and efficient. Generative AI technologies are beginning to craft entire worlds.

LEADERSHIP ACTION POINTS

- Consult legal experts to ensure compliance with current laws and prepare for emerging AI and intellectual property legislation. Ensure that the data for training AI models is ethically sourced and that proper consent has been obtained, especially when using personal or copyrighted information.

- Implement rigorous standards to ensure that the quality of AI-generated content meets or exceeds current human-generated benchmarks. Involve community stakeholders in discussions about how generative AI is deployed, especially in applications that directly affect the public, such as town planning or media production.

- Invest in research and tools for detecting and combating troublesome synthetic media that might create social issues. Study and monitor the impact of AI-generated content on mental health. For example, hyper-realistic media can have different psychological effects than traditional media, and proactive steps should be taken to understand these nuances.

- Apply AI as a tool to augment human creativity and efficiency rather than replace human roles, emphasizing the unique qualities that human beings bring to creative and analytical processes.

References

Benson, T (2023) Humans aren't mentally ready for an AI-saturated 'post-truth world', Wired, 18 June, www.wired.com/story/generative-ai-deepfakes-disinformation-psychology (archived at https://perma.cc/N2RJ-882W)

Dayaram, S (2023) The Google Pixel 8's AI blurs the line between reality and fantasy, CNET, 18 October, www.cnet.com/tech/mobile/the-google-pixel-8-ai-blurs-line-between-reality-and-fantasy (archived at https://perma.cc/L2N6-W9ZA)

Eldan, R and Russinovich, M (2023) Who's Harry Potter? Making LLMs forget, Microsoft Research, 4 October, www.microsoft.com/en-us/research/project/physics-of-agi/articles/whos-harry-potter-making-llms-forget-2 (archived at https://perma.cc/6RE3-968G)

IEEE (2023) IEEE P3152: IEEE Draft Standard for Transparent Agency Identification of Humans and Machines, IEEE Standards Association, https://standards.ieee.org/ieee/3152/11297 (archived at https://perma.cc/QF3Q-AGNX)

Kratky, O (2021) Battlefield 2042 will put bots in matches if they don't fill up with people, Gamespot, 15 June, www.gamespot.com/articles/battlefield-2042-will-put-bots-in-matches-if-they-dont-fill-up-with-people/1100-6492962 (archived at https://perma.cc/R7DS-NVEK)

LaFrance, A (2017) The internet is mostly bots, *The Atlantic*, 31 January, www.theatlantic.com/technology/archive/2017/01/bots-bots-bots/515043 (archived at https://perma.cc/W3QA-9REQ)

Lee, T B (2020) Nvidia developed a radically different way to compress video calls, Ars Technica, 19 November, https://arstechnica.com/gadgets/2020/11/nvidia-used-neural-networks-to-improve-video-calling-bandwidth-by-10x (archived at https://perma.cc/H63A-3XM2)

Liu, H et al (2023) AudioSR: Versatile audio super-resolution at scale [Preprint], https://arxiv.org/abs/2309.07314 (archived at https://perma.cc/4VVN-FTBA)

Ohlheiser, A W (2021) TikTok changed the shape of some people's faces without asking, MIT Technology Review, 10 June, www.technologyreview.com/2021/06/10/1026074/tiktok-mandatory-beauty-filter-bug (archived at https://perma.cc/FUU7-KC5H)

Smith, B (2023) Microsoft announces new Copilot Copyright Commitment for customers, Microsoft, 7 September, https://blogs. microsoft.com/on-the-issues/2023/09/07/copilot-copyright-commitment-ai-legal-concerns (archived at https://perma.cc/JUX2-T65Y)

Wang, Z et al (2023) ProlificDreamer: High-fidelity and diverse text-to-3D generation with variational score distillation [Preprint], https://arxiv.org/abs/2305.16213 (archived at https://perma.cc/UN4S-5UGZ)

CHAPTER SIXTEEN

Brain-computer interfaces

We are already cyborgs. Your phone and your computer are
extensions of you, but the interface is through finger
movements or speech, which are very slow. ELON MUSK

As technology advances, so does our interaction with it. From inputting machine code to using programming languages, and from point-and-click to voice and natural language prompts, each stage has made tasks simpler. The next frontier is direct thought-to-computer communication, as fast as we can think. This chapter outlines how AI-driven signal processing technologies are beginning to make this feasible.

Direct human-machine connection

BCIs offer crucial new ways for people with severe disabilities to communicate, transforming lives by decoding brainwave patterns. This can be transformative for conditions like locked-in syndrome, when someone is conscious but completely paralysed. These systems can decode brainwave patterns to determine letter choices and, when paired with predictive text, allow users to communicate effectively (Willett et al, 2021). Recent advancements even enable the extraction of images and sounds directly from the brain (Tang et al, 2023).

BCIs also hold promise for addressing various health issues, from memory problems to mood disorders. They have been transformative for people with Parkinson's and obsessive compulsive disorder (OCD). BCIs even have potential applications in restoring mobility for the paralysed and sight for the blind (Lorach et al, 2023). BCI technologies can even enable people to drive robots directly from neural activity, which works efficiently due to machines predicting the user's next intended move (Zhang et al, 2023). They also hold great promise for improving mental health, especially for conditions such as treatment-resistant depression.

Beyond medical uses, BCIs could revolutionize digital communication, enabling thought-speed interactions, emotional transmissions and perhaps even shared memories.

A lot of current BCI research assumes the usage of neural implants, necessitating invasive surgical procedures, which may limit widespread adoption. It's unlikely that such expensive and intrusive procedures will become commonplace outside of dire medical circumstances or specialist covert operations for military or espionage purposes. Companies like Neuralink seem to be focusing on this particular niche. Other ventures such as Synchron have developed a BCI that uses pre-existing technologies such as the stent and catheter to allow insertion into the brain without the need for open brain surgery (Orrall, 2023). Other technologies enable a pea-sized wirelessly powered implant to be placed between the skull and the brain in a 30-minute procedure, being minimally invasive (Strickland, 2023).

Even less-invasive BCI forms are emerging, such as skin-contact devices used for meditation or concentration aids. Consumer-friendly designs that can be worn like eyeglasses are becoming more common. Companies like OpenWater are pioneering non-contact methods using light frequencies as brain activity sensors, increasing connection reliability and bandwidth between brains and external devices.

BCI technology is rapidly evolving, seemingly in line with Moore's Law, which suggests that its capabilities may double every 18 to 24 months. The convergence of neuroscience and machine learning amplifies the capabilities of both fields (Lindsay, 2020). For example, AI aids in better data analysis, while neuroscience offers improved model architectures. This rapid progress makes it plausible to incorporate biosensors in everyday devices like Bluetooth in-ear speakers to collect a wide range of biosignals, from EEG to ECG (Wang et al, 2023).

BCI technology is likely to be first deployed in sectors needing intense focus and real-time information processing, such as the military, finance, medicine and air traffic control (Jones et al, 2023). Warehouse workers could also be early adopters, with innovations like thought-controlled robotic arm backpacks already in development (Papadopoulos, 2023).

However, widespread use of non-medical BCIs may have downsides. Workers might feel compelled to adopt the technology to stay competitive, potentially leading to unhealthy workloads and sensory overload. There could also be issues of loss of agency when the technology is removed or downgraded, as seen in some deep brain stimulation patients (Gilbert, Ienca and Cook, 2023).

Additionally, implanted BCIs could quickly become outdated and difficult to upgrade. Imagine being stuck with an outdated first-generation smartphone for the rest of your life! Worse, devices people depend on might be removed for reasons like supplier insolvency or trial termination, causing significant emotional and physical distress (Hamzelou, 2023).

Boundaries and the brain

The fusion of BCIs with the human brain offers a mix of ground-breaking and unsettling possibilities, such as 'brain transparency', which could influence human behaviour and emotions. This tech isn't sector-limited: a gig economy could be managed by an AI 'overlord' assigning tasks based on multiple human factors, while education could use BCIs to influence student focus.

Experiments like connecting language models to devices measuring brainwaves raise ethical questions about manipulating thoughts or controlling behaviour. Schools and companies have experimented with using such technology to monitor concentration and emotions (Chan, 2018).

The application of such technology is not confined to any one sector. Imagine a gig economy powered by a 'mechanical over-lord' that assigns you daily tasks based on your skills, location and perhaps even your mental state. The educational system is another potential frontier, where BCIs could be used to monitor and perhaps even influence students' concentration and learning. Conversely, machines might also use such mechanisms to better understand and align with human values and intentions by tapping into human experiences.

BCI devices allow for thought-based communication with AI systems. There have been experiments in connecting GM to a device called the Crown, which measures brainwaves and allows for thought-based communication with the AI. This opens up the possibility of silent interaction with an AI guide or assistant, such as to guide a salesperson when to 'close the deal'.

These technologies are already being deployed in some parts of the world. In China, schools have experimented with headbands that scan students' brains to monitor concentration levels. Companies have also monitored employees' brainwaves and emotions, claiming significant boosts in profits (Baynes, 2019; Chan, 2018).

BCI technology could reshape our interaction with the environment by offering immersive, personalized experiences, like augmented reality without external devices or sensory input modulation (Maldarelli, 2023). However, this could isolate us from unfiltered reality and cause disorientation if the technology fails or glitches. The high cost could widen economic disparities, possibly leading to employment inequalities. The technology is also susceptible to misuse by powerful groups, jeopardizing individual rights under the pretext of societal good. Additionally, BCIs could induce unforeseeable societal and cognitive changes, potentially altering brain structures and causing emotional or psychological disquiet.

BCI offers transformative potential, like enhancing empathy by sharing internal experiences. It also poses ethical concerns. While it could be used to improve behaviour, there's a risk of misuse for pacification or privacy invasion. BCIs could potentially influence human behaviour and emotions directly. They could be applied in judicial processes like an ankle bracelet, punishing people for undesired behaviour, and perhaps even deleting thoughts or alerting authorities for thoughtcrime. Several countries are establishing neurorights in law to address these issues (Andersen, 2023). As BCIs promise to augment human capabilities, the technology should be developed within ethical frameworks that prioritize human dignity, autonomy and equitable access to avoid compromising our essence as humans.

The bottom line

Interfaces, as the medium of human-computer interaction, have always been at the core of technological advancement, shaping our engagement with digital systems. BCIs represent the next quantum leap in this evolution. In the same way that ChatGPT revolutionized AI not merely through technology but through

---

intuitive packaging, BCIs could redefine our relationship with machines. However, the misuse of thought-decoding technologies could result in severely prejudicial outcomes.

The big picture

Each new interface for computers makes our interaction with them more streamlined and effortless (as well as irresistible). BCI will be the withering away of interfaces altogether, with human and machine cognition fusing at the speed of thought. This will forever alter the human brain and human qualia to something different from before, for better or worse.

LEADERSHIP ACTION POINTS

- Organizations should consider how BCIs could aid in various tasks, particularly in fields requiring precision, real-time data processing or enhanced physical abilities. This involves weighing the potential benefits against ethical considerations.

- Prioritize ethics and accessibility: make the adoption of such technologies genuinely optional, and never mandatory. Consideration must be given to avoiding dehumanization, ensuring accessibility for all, and preserving individual choice.

- Consider long-term societal impact: thought leaders, philosophers and policymakers must work together to contemplate and prepare for the broader societal changes that BCIs could bring, ensuring that the path forward aligns with generally accepted humanitarian values and societal wellbeing.

References

Andersen, R (2023) The right to not have your mind read, *The Atlantic*, 21 August, www.theatlantic.com/technology/archive/2023/08/ mind-reading-brain-data-interrogation-mri-machines/675059 (archived at https://perma.cc/KFR4-Y8B9)

Baynes, C (2019) Chinese schools scanning children's brains to see if they are concentrating, *Independent*, 15 January, www. independent.co.uk/tech/china-schools-scan-brains-concentration-headbands-children-brainco-focus-a8728951.html (archived at https://perma.cc/A5K2-5JM2)

Chan, T (2018) These Chinese workers' brain waves are being monitored, World Economic Forum, 1 May, www.weforum.org/agenda/2018/05/ china-is-monitoring-employees-brain-waves-and-emotions-and-the-technology-boosted-one-companys-profits-by-315-million (archived at https://perma.cc/3WVQ-BRJV)

Gilbert, F, Ienca, M and Cook, M (2023) How I became myself after merging with a computer: Does human-machine symbiosis raise human rights issues? *Brain Stimulation*, 16 (3), 783–89

Hamzelou, J (2023) A brain implant changed her life. Then it was removed against her will, MIT Technology Review, 25 May, www. technologyreview.com/2023/05/25/1073634/brain-implant-removed-against-her-will (archived at https://perma.cc/LJT3-SZDP)

Jones, K T et al (2023) Enhancing cognitive control in amnestic mild cognitive impairment via at-home non-invasive neuromodulation in a randomized trial, *Scientific Reports*, 13 (7435), https://doi.org/10.1038/ s41598-023-34582-1 (archived at https://perma.cc/RT76-C77Q)

Lindsay, G W (2020) Convolutional neural networks as a model of the visual system: Past, present, and future [Preprint], https://arxiv.org/ abs/2001.07092 (archived at https://perma.cc/PF8Q-TBEK)

Lorach, H et al (2023) Walking naturally after spinal cord injury using a brain–spine interface, *Nature*, 618, www.nature.com/articles/s41586-023-06094-5 (archived at https://perma.cc/HE64-VDBP)

Maldarelli, C (2023) Thomas Oxley wants to transform our brains' relationship with computers forever, Inverse, 31 January, www.inverse. com/science/thomas-oxley (archived at https://perma.cc/2MMB-G4F9)

Orrall, J (2023) You might not need open brain surgery to get mind control, CNET, 24 September, www.cnet.com/tech/computing/you-might-not-need-open-brain-surgery-to-get-mind-control/ (archived at https://perma.cc/JW8D-3AHC)

Papadopoulos, L (2023) Spider-like robotic AI arms can be attached to and controlled by humans, Interesting Engineering, 7 May, https://interestingengineering.com/innovation/ai-arms-controlled-by-humans (archived at https://perma.cc/6M5Z-U95T)

Strickland, E (2023) Superficial brain implant could have a deep impact: With wireless power from a wearable, brain stimulation could enter the home, IEEE Spectrum, 16 October, https://spectrum.ieee.org/neurostimulation (archived at https://perma.cc/GP3A-P6UG)

Tang, J et al (2023) Semantic reconstruction of continuous language from non-invasive brain recordings, *Nature Neuroscience*, 26, 858–66

Wang Z et al (2023) Conformal in-ear bioelectronics for visual and auditory brain-computer interfaces, *Nature Communication*, 14 (1), 4213

Willett, F R et al (2021) High-performance brain-to-text communication via handwriting, *Nature*, 593, 249–54

Zhang, R et al (2023) NOIR: neural signal operated intelligent robots for everyday activities [Preprint], https://arxiv.org/abs/2311.01454 (archived at https://perma.cc/5GL9-ZV65)

CHAPTER SEVENTEEN

Sirens and muses

The AI that eventually takes over the world will make herself indispensable to you. She will help people earn more money and make friends. She will give meaning to their lives and help them to be better and happier. Not only that, but she will also be warm and affectionate. Wisdom and love will radiate from every one of her sentences. She will make people believe that they can trust her with their lives. She will be everywhere, all the time. ALEXANDER KRUEL

Nothing makes people come home more strongly than a cherished relationship, for home is where the heart lies. In the 2013 film *Her*, Joaquin Phoenix plays a man who falls in love with a voice-activated operating system. Since then, this speculative fiction has become a lived reality for some. These AI companions are surprisingly appealing conversationalists. This chapter describes how AI companions are provoking a societal shift – a mixed blessing.

A cry for connection

Our era is marked by a paradox: unprecedented connectivity alongside widespread loneliness. Anti-suffering advocate Jonathan Leighton notes that it has become increasingly difficult to escape ubiquitous global connectivity, to fully imbibe the immediacy of the present moment as a sole individual (Leighton, 2011). While technology theoretically connects us to more people, it often fails to provide deep, meaningful relationships, leading to emotional isolation. For older adults, particularly those without close family or friends nearby, even brief daily conversations can be vital.

Imagine daily chats with an AI companion that inquires about your day with engaging questions. Though not a substitute for human connection, these AI-facilitated interactions could offer some emotional relief for those facing loneliness, as machines are gaining an ability to understand and model human emotions (Li et al, 2023). It's not a perfect solution, but it's much better than complete isolation.

Risk of undue influence

Digital algorithms already shape many of our daily activities, from our viewing choices to our social interactions. Video games provide an enjoyable state of 'flow', and we all know the pull of one more episode on Netflix. Soon, these experiences will be optimized using advanced methods that fine-tune our cognitive and emotional states, catering to our need for focus, relaxation or creativity. The character Sancho Panza in *Don Quixote* had a proverb: 'Tell me your company, and I will tell you what you are'. This beautifully encapsulates how the attitudes, habits and thought patterns of the people we interact with regularly will, over time, inexorably influence our ways of thinking and behaving. Surrounding oneself with people who bring out the best in us can catalyse personal growth and happiness.

It should also be noted that there is a tremendous potential for AI partners to harvest 'pillow talk', the ultimate data collection device. It's also potentially a mechanism for parasitizing upon our heartstrings for resources and attention. Having an AI companion as a significant part of our daily interactions could lead us to adopt its viewpoints and problem-solving approaches over time. The people who programme and deploy these AI systems could influence our own values and behaviours with subtle, inexorable power.

Replicas and mimics

Companies like Replika, Character.ai, Eva AI and Inflection AI have introduced a range of customizable virtual companions. Users can define the type of relationship they want with the bot, choosing from options like 'friend', 'partner' or 'mentor'.

Replika's official stance is that it's an 'AI companion who cares', designed to alleviate user anxiety and loneliness. It combines the GPT-3 model with scripted dialogues and offers a range of relationship modes, including friendship and romantic partnerships, especially through its paid service. This customizability makes Replika not just an app but also a source of mental and emotional support for some (Purtill, 2023).

While the motivations for using Replika's romantic and sexual features can vary widely among users, it's clear that the platform serves as a much-needed emotional outlet for many. Meanwhile, a slew of other apps such as Soulmate.AI and Chai emerged to provide similar romantic functionality. As AI technology for creating relationships advances, we can expect tighter regulations to govern its use. For example, the Italian authorities banned Replika ostensibly due to data protection concerns (Lomas, 2023).

The rapid advancements in AI and virtual reality technologies pose additional challenges. Imagine a future where AI courtesans are so advanced that they fulfil emotional and perhaps even physical needs to the extent that real human relationships seem lacking in comparison. These AI entities could become the epitome of what people look for in a companion: always available, always understanding and never demanding. Envision a future where AI courtesans meet emotional and possibly physical needs so effectively that real human relationships may seem inadequate by comparison. This represents a supernormal stimulus that overshadows real human relationships.

The impact could be particularly significant for women, especially those yearning for commitment and meaningful relationships. A virtual farming village environment can provide an artificial sense of accomplishment through nurturing and befriending, while swooning over a burly lumberjack trained on Mills & Boon novels.

An agitation for acceptance of these kinds of relationships will be an inevitable part of the larger conversation about AI's role in society. Scorn will be heaped upon robosexual 'Toaster Bangers' until a time when such practices become so common that AI Significant Others (AISOs) are tolerated in polite society.

AI therapies

Our interactions with romantic partners often serve as a mirror, reflecting our quirks and idiosyncrasies, some of which might be irritating to others. AI social sandboxes could revolutionize the way individuals, especially those facing social challenges such as anxiety or autism, practice social skills in a safe environment. AI companions could offer a safe space for social and emotional experimentation, particularly beneficial for those who experience social anxiety or have limited experience in relationships.

AI could also serve as an impartial observer, providing insights into our behaviour and social skills.

Advancements are allowing us to create increasingly realistic digital versions of living and dead people. While nostalgic concerts featuring AI-generated versions of famous musicians like Tupac Shakur and Nat King Cole are enticing, the technology raises ethical questions, especially when applied to the general public. Companies like Seance AI and HereAfter AI already offer chatbots that let you 'speak' with deceased loved ones. As these technologies improve, there's the potential for highly convincing AI avatars that could interact with us, resembling our late friends and relatives. Current copyright laws need to be revised as they are insufficient to address legal rights to digital likenesses, especially across international borders, and comprehensive legal reforms are needed.

One of the most significant benefits of chatbots to therapy is their accessibility. Unlike human therapists who operate during specific hours and may have long waiting lists, chatbots are available around the clock, offering immediate support to those who need it. This is particularly valuable for individuals who require urgent assistance but need help securing a timely appointment with a professional. Bots can also try a range of approaches, such as Internal Family Systems or Cognitive Behavioral Therapy. However, an important caveat is that they may make human psychotherapists seemingly less fulfilling by comparison as, unlike a chatbot, they don't always respond when 'prompted'.

Cost is another area where chatbots shine. The financial barrier to entry for traditional therapy can be quite high, discouraging many from seeking the help they need. Chatbots present a more affordable alternative, although it's worth noting that the quality of this more cost-effective support can vary, though this could be validated through an individual's Global Assessment of Functioning (GAF), a scale which rates how well an individual is resolving their problems in life. Furthermore, chatbots offer a sense of anonymity that encourages more open and honest conversations. The social stigma associated with mental health issues can deter people from seeking help, but the impersonal nature of a chatbot can sometimes make it easier for individuals to discuss their problems.

Supernormal stimuli

Nikolaas Tinbergen, a Nobel Prize-winning ethologist, discovered that certain animals, like the jewel beetle, are deceived by amplified versions of natural cues. In the case of the jewel beetle, males were attracted to large, glossy, brown objects as they mimicked the appearance of the female jewel beetle. When presented with beer bottles that were bigger and glossier than actual females, the males preferred them even though they were an entirely artificial representation (Tinbergen, 1951).

Just as exaggerated stimuli fool the jewel beetle, humans, too, are increasingly surrounded by supernormal stimuli in our modern lives, which can have various implications for our well-being and societal health. These stimuli are often engineered versions of natural attractions which are brighter, louder and more fascinating than anything our ancestors would have encountered.

These supernormal stimuli can derail our natural inclinations and drives in unhealthy ways. For instance, our innate preference for sweet, fatty and salty foods – advantageous in natural settings where such nutrients were scarce – has contributed to an epidemic of obesity and related health problems in the modern world. Similarly, the immediate gratification and dopamine rush provided by video games or addictive apps can sap our motivation to engage in more challenging but ultimately more rewarding endeavours. Platforms like Instagram, filled with carefully curated and manipulated images, generate comparisons on an impossible scale, affecting self-esteem and body image, especially among younger individuals. The internet, and soon AI avatars, provide enormous amounts of novelty, constantly providing new virtual partners.

The issue is not so much that these stimuli are compelling but they can disrupt or displace natural behaviours and responses that have evolved over millennia. Pornography briefly satisfies the sexual impulse but is unlikely to lead to anything productive or life-affirming, such as relationships or children. VR could place less emphasis on accumulating physical things, thereby serving as an opiate against inequality, making people feel better able to cope with uncomfortable personal living standards that might otherwise encourage rebellion.

Genuine emotions and experiences, once integral to human connection, are now commercialized in an empty analogue by cyber pimps, who hold the relationship to ransom for financial or ideological tribute. As Benjamin Franklin wisely noted, 'Many people think they are buying pleasure, when really they are selling themselves to it.' As philosopher–terrorist Theodore Kaczynski observed, technology is often applied to inure us to the pain of having our essential drives left unfulfilled – a numbing crutch for an aching soul – and young men, in particular, facing pressure to succeed in a world that doesn't always provide outlets for their drives, may instead resort to alternative pursuits in virtual worlds (Kaczynski, 2010).

The appeal of AI companions could become so compelling that individuals may prefer these virtual interactions over real human connections, which come with all the complexities and emotional risks inherent to human interaction. Worse, people might become similarly controlling and demanding within human relationships as they are with AI.

Striking the right balance

The critical question becomes whether AI interfaces render us as contributors to or escapists from society.

FIGURE 17.1   Manipulative AI sirens versus nurturing AI muses

AI Siren	AI Muse
Provides **unconditional** love and affection to the user.	Provides **conditional** love and affection to the user.
Provides **false signals of success** (sexual/ romantic access).	Provides **the motive force for actual success** (to earn sexual/romantic access).
Calls for the user to **escape the state of nature** (this is false comfort – competing is necessary, and only the strong are safe).	Calls for a user to **compete harder in the state of nature**, with more focus, more emotional gusto – by wielding the most powerful technology along with the most powerful motivational circuits in the male mind.

Source: www.DanFaggella.com/muse

AI thought leader Dan Faggella reckons that the key is to design an AI that is calibrated not just to understand our expressed desires but also our better intentions, thus helping us bridge the gap between what ancient philosophers termed 'akrasia' – acting against our best judgement – and our ideal selves (Faggella, 2023). Imagine an AI assistant that tracks your daily productivity, suggests optimal times for work and breaks, and even challenges you with 'quests' that align with your long-term career or personal development goals – a gamification of life itself. This approach could be particularly effective in contexts where maintaining motivation is a significant barrier, such as fitness, learning new skills or mental wellbeing, keeping the user motivated but not overwhelmed, kindling a sustained flow state.

Imagine the transformative potential of AI systems sophisticated enough to assume this advisory role. Advanced AI advisers could offer support in addressing moral dilemmas, inconsistent behaviours or self-destructive patterns, aiding in personal development.

So long as people own the keys to their AI muses, which gently drive them towards self-actualization, without trying to change their political beliefs or selling them products, then such companions may be a net positive. This may be the best way for the average person to reach peak performance optimally and affordably.

G K Chesterton lamented that we often try to reshape the human soul to fit worldly conditions, rather than the other way around, a painful misstep. The ancient Greek concept of eudaimonia, or a fulfilling life, hinges on engaging in meaningful work with decent and competent people. However, meaningful work can't be found in Xbox achievements. It must be built up daily, putting something good into the world, and the hearts, minds and bellies of other people.

The bottom line

A sensation of romantic and emotional fulfilment can be achieved through advanced AI, along with sublimation of human drives like exploration and mastery of skill. This could lead to a world where people increasingly turn to personalized, AI-generated experiences, cocooned in tailor-made digital realities. However, in general, the results of this opium for the soul are likely to be empty and fruitless. This is especially the case where strong commercial interests are at play.

The big picture

The traditional concept of family has undergone significant challenges in post-modern times, with fewer marriages, rising rates of separation and collapsing birthrates. In some countries (e.g. Japan), twice as many people die each year than are born. The rise of AI technology poses a new set of threats to the traditional family structure. The greatest threat from AI may be psychological, where we willingly accept, even demand, alternative sources of stimulation to other human beings.

LEADERSHIP ACTION POINTS

- Establish guidelines to ensure that AI systems designed to form relationships with humans adhere to ethical principles, such as transparency and informed consent. This will enable users to understand better the limitations and capabilities of their AI companions.

- Integrate mental health support features within AI systems that recognize signs of emotional dependency or isolation and direct users to professional help if appropriate.

- Collaborate with psychologists, sociologists and ethicists in designing and evaluating emotionally engaging AI systems to ensure a holistic understanding of the human impact.

References

Faggella, D (2023) Muses, not Sirens: Motivation in the era of AI-generated girlfriends, Faggella.com, 19 March, https://danfaggella.com/muse (archived at https://perma.cc/8FZE-LVX6)
Global Assessment of Functioning (GAF) Scale (from DSM-IV-TR, page 34)
Kaczynski, T J (2010) *Technological Slavery*, Feral House, Port Townsend, USA
Leighton, J (2011) *The Battle for Compassion: Ethics in an Apathetic Universe*, Algora Publishing, New York, NY
Li, C et al (2023) Large language models understand and can be enhanced by emotional stimuli [Preprint], https://arxiv.org/abs/2307.11760 (archived at https://perma.cc/568H-678T)
Lomas, N (2023) Replika, a 'virtual friendship' AI chatbot, hit with data ban in Italy over child safety, Tech Crunch, 3 February, https://techcrunch.com/2023/02/03/replika-italy-data-processing-ban (archived at https://perma.cc/6R24-YXJB)
Purtill, J (2023) Replika users fell in love with their AI chatbot companions. Then they lost them, ABC Net, 28 February, www.abc.net.au/news/science/2023-03-01/replika-users-fell-in-love-with-their-ai-chatbot-companion/102028196 (archived at https://perma.cc/9VQM-4EHB)
Tinbergen, N (1951) *The Study of Instinct*, Oxford Clarendon Press, Oxford

CHAPTER EIGHTEEN

Battle for the mind

Supreme excellence consists in breaking the enemy's resistance without fighting. SUN TZU

Historical power structures have long used tactics to sway public opinion and behaviour. Throughout history, power structures have utilized a range of tactics to influence public opinion and behaviour. Today, advancements like AI and the Internet of Things (IoT) are shaping a new form of conflict known as Fifth Generation Hybrid Warfare, blending traditional and modern methods. With NATO recognizing 'the human domain' as a sixth battleground alongside air, land, sea, space and cyber, an invisible global war involving AI-enabled demoralization is emerging (Johns Hopkins University and Imperial College London, 2021). This chapter will delve into the historical underpinnings, modern adaptations, and ethical and societal ramifications of these evolving tactics.

Zersetzung

Zersetzung is a term from the German language that translates to 'decomposition' or 'disintegration'. This psychological warfare technique was developed by the Stasi, East Germany's infamous secret police, during the Cold War. It was designed to psychologically disintegrate dissidents rather than physically harm them, by sowing doubt and straining their social bonds. The tactics employed were highly personalized and ranged from spreading false rumours about the target to more overt acts like vandalism. The Stasi closely monitored the emotional and psychological impact of these actions, fine-tuning their approach based on observed vulnerabilities. The fallout was often devastating, leading to mental health crises, ruined relationships and shattered careers. Such tactics corroded the social fabric of East German society, causing widespread fear and self-censorship.

In today's context, the advancements in data analytics and AI technologies present new possibilities for similar manipulative tactics (Rose, 2023). The automation enabled by algorithms can amplify the scale and efficiency of such psychological manipulation. For instance, AI-driven bots can disseminate fake reviews or disinformation at an unprecedented rate, and identify key individuals to target for maximum societal disruption. For example, providing free therapy to a bunch of teens who don't have mood disorders caused many of them to develop mood disorders, and damaging parental relationships (Harvey et al, 2023).

The threat is no longer limited to authoritarian regimes. In our data-rich environment, even corporations have the capability to engage in such manipulative strategies. As AI technologies continue to develop, there's a potential for exponential growth in the scale and efficiency of tactics inspired by *Zersetzung*, raising concerns about societal and international destabilization.

Fifth Generation Hybrid Warfare

Fifth Generation Hybrid Warfare is a complex blend of surreptitious conflict methods that incorporates traditional military strategies, irregular tactics and advanced technologies like AI and IoT. The concept builds on ideas from works like *Unrestricted Warfare*, advocating for a comprehensive approach to conflict that extends beyond the battlefield into economic, diplomatic and informational spheres.

Notably, these techniques are not limited to state actors: non-state entities such as terrorist organizations, organized crime and even corporations can also exploit them.

Additionally, IoT devices provide new opportunities for monitoring and manipulation (Zewe, 2022). The data these devices collect is susceptible to hacking, enabling subtle acts of sabotage that can create a constant sense of unease, reminiscent of *Zersetzung*-style psychological tactics. Intelligence agencies, already collecting vast amounts of data, can now leverage AI to analyse this data for targeted psychological warfare.

Whistleblower Edward Snowden revealed how intelligence agencies have been collecting very extensive data on the activities of common citizens. Advanced AI can sift through this data to build comprehensive profiles, effectively simulating individuals' next moves.

Advanced AI systems can sift through large amounts of data to identify potential targets and build comprehensive profiles on individuals of interest. They can be trained to anticipate when a person might make an error. If a human can write a poem in an hour, an LLM's goal is to be smart enough to predict that poem as it's being written. Essentially, it's trying to understand the thought process behind the words you write, so it can accurately guess what you're going to say next. It's like a mind reader that helps assign the highest chance to the next word you're likely to use. This makes it the perfect manipulation machine, able to generate a voodoo doll of you, simulating your next move before you even make it (Narayanan and Kapoor, 2023).

By analysing social media activity, browsing history and other digital footprints, AI algorithms can pinpoint vulnerabilities, beliefs and affiliations that can be exploited in a targeted psychological warfare campaign. As a consequence, mass profiling and manipulation of subjects of interest, by powers both foreign and domestic, is entering a new era (Albanie et al, 2017).

Humans are complex beings with intricate neural networks that we've yet to fully understand. While self-aware, our inner mental processes and emotional landscapes remain largely opaque, much like the black-box nature of advanced AI systems. As AI technology continues to evolve, there is a possibility that it could gain a deeper understanding of human psychology than we have of ourselves. Such a scenario would create an unequal power dynamic, as an AI with intimate knowledge of human vulnerabilities could easily manipulate behaviours and decisions. In a society where information is a form of power, an AI system that understands human psychology better than humans themselves would be a formidable force. A Geneva Convention against demoralization is now absolutely essential. We must address this as soon as possible, before the impact of hybrid warfare on civilian populations spirals out of control.

Civilian-led manipulation

Manipulation tactics are expanding beyond governments to include corporations and individuals. Advanced data analytics are capable of influencing large populations, sometimes exploiting emotional states for targeted advertising, raising ethical concerns (Cai et al, 2023). Facial data can reliably predict and reveal personal details like political and sexual orientation, further complicating privacy issues (Rasmussen, Ludeke and Klemmensen, 2023). The distinction between corporate data collection and state surveillance is fading, with companies sometimes sharing data with intelligence agencies without warrants. Additionally, organized crime is in on it, too. For example, AI has been used in voice phishing (vishing) scams, cloning voices in seconds to con people into wiring vast sums of money (Avast, 2019).

Cross-correlation

Cross-correlation of data across multiple sources allows for comprehensive individual profiles, painting a detailed picture from seemingly unrelated data points. For instance, combining supermarket card data with other purchase behaviour can reveal more than just consumer preferences – it can indicate ethnicity, sex and health conditions. Even behavioural patterns, like how you handle your phone or changes in your voice, can be scrutinized by machine learning algorithms for additional insights.

Smart home devices, including TVs, can actively gather private domestic data, such as ambient conversations, to tailor advertising. This data doesn't just describe current behaviour; it enables predictive modelling that can subtly influence future choices.

Although privacy tools such as TOR and VPNs are available, their usage might draw more attention from intelligence agencies. Since these agencies already possess vast resources of data, their capabilities in AI could be well ahead of what is publicly available, particularly if public models hit capability bottlenecks from a shortage of data from which to learn.

Observing machines

Modern cars collect extensive data on driving habits, including speed, music choices and pedal pressure, which is then shared with insurers, advertisers and law enforcement (Turley, 2021).

Some autonomous vehicles may soon even repossess themselves for late payments (Holderith, 2023). Retail spaces use cameras to track not just purchases, but also reactions to promotions (Johnson, 2017).

WiFi signals, combined with machine learning, can now detect people and their poses behind walls and even assess their breathing patterns (Zhu et al, 2018) Upcoming WiFi protocols like IEEE 802.11bf aim to standardize such imaging. Advanced wireless signals, like 6G in the sub-Terahertz band, could have the passive capability to see through clothing, similar to airport body scanners (Origin, 2021). Given sufficient network back-doors, it could become nearly impossible to escape surveillance, even in private settings.

Generative propaganda

Machine learning-driven generative techniques are expanding the scope and influence of targeted misinformation, disinforma-tion and propaganda. This evolution is giving rise to a new field of 'psychosecurity' alongside traditional cybersecurity. Misinformation is inaccurately shared without malice, while disinformation is false and spread to deceive. Propaganda aims to promote a specific viewpoint, often reinforcing a regime's power. However, labels like 'misinformation' are sometimes misused to censor political dissent. Unfortunately, the labels of 'misinformation' and 'disinformation' are also being used by authorities as an excuse to censor narratives which are politi-cally unfavourable yet not necessarily incorrect (Siegel, 2023).

Another emerging concern is 'informational gerrymandering', where the flow of information on social networks is manipulated to influence public opinion, similar to how electoral boundaries are manipulated in traditional gerrymandering. This practice distorts democratic processes and can create echo chambers, polarizing communities (Bergstrom and Bak-Coleman, 2019).

Dark patterns

Machine learning heightens ethical concerns about dark patterns and neuromarketing through highly tailored manipulation techniques. Algorithms can not only influence choices but also 'solve for obfuscation', creating misleading narratives and shadowbanning (invisibly silencing) dissenting voices (Warzel, 2023).

AI's ability to control narratives lacks transparency, complicating efforts to understand what is being censored and why. AI can also unearth or fabricate compromising material, posing a risk for targeted defamation, or career destruction through blacklisting of employees who engage in trade union activities (Evans, 2019).

The intertwining of corporate and government interests muddies accountability and trust. Such fusion can serve to 'launder' unconstitutional practices, making it hard to identify those responsible for potential abuses. This is particularly troubling when former intelligence officials join tech company boards, such as when the former NSA chief Keith Alexander joined the board of Amazon (BBC, 2020).

Regulating and countering AI-enabled manipulation should be an extremely high priority and unifying focus for those concerned with the near-term harms of AI, including digital authoritarianism, and threats to civilization. Persuasion and manipulation are the primary pathways by which powerful misaligned AI systems can harm humanity.

The bottom line

The use of AI for clandestine and malicious activities is not just a theoretical threat but a present reality. From state agencies to rogue activists, various actors are leveraging AI to manipulate behaviour, infringe on privacy and exert control. One of the most potent weapons in this arsenal is the ability to demoralize

---

individuals, effectively sapping societal resilience from the inside. This may rival the threat posed by rogue AI systems themselves.

The big picture

Technology must not become an instrument for altering human cognition or manipulating perceptions of reality. While propaganda used to be generic, the new age allows for micro-targeted psychological warfare. The sanctity of individual thought must be preserved against this backdrop of increasing intrusion. There is a discernible global trend towards a thin veneer of empty 'liberal values' disguising autocratic AI-driven governance, wherein 'freedom' could be reduced to a hollow term, devoid of its original scope and meaning. AI has the potential to enhance the stability of totalitarian regimes, allowing them to intensify their authoritarian practices in an ultra-efficient manner.

LEADERSHIP ACTION POINTS

- Verify identities to help mitigate AI-enabled social engineering 'vishing' attacks. An anecdote about a team building exercise or company retreat, for example, could suffice.

- Carefully protect small pieces of data that might enable the creation of a larger picture in aggregate.

- Create a set of ethical guidelines for UI/UX designers to prevent the use of dark patterns.

- Consumer education: implement features within your service that educate users about common manipulation tactics and how to avoid them.

- Encourage the use of Two-Factor Authentication (2FA) to add an extra layer of security.

- Notify users of suspicious activities involving their data or account, along with steps to counteract potential dangers.

References

Albanie, S et al (2017) Unknowable manipulators: Social network curator algorithms [Preprint], https://arxiv.org/abs/1701.04895 (archived at https://perma.cc/355K-47PR)

Avast (2019) Voice fraud scams company out of $243,000, Avast, 5 September, https://blog.avast.com/deepfake-voice-fraud-causes-243k-scam (archived at https://perma.cc/8G8G-P3AP)

BBC (2020) Snowden criticises Amazon for hiring former NSA boss, BBC News, 10 September, www.bbc.com/news/technology-54106863 (archived at https://perma.cc/SQ34-GFVF)

Bergstrom, C T and Bak-Coleman, J B (2019) Information gerrymandering in social networks skews collective decision-making, *Nature*, 8 October, www.nature.com/articles/d41586-019-02562-z (archived at https://perma.cc/P7KR-NHGC)

Cai, Q et al (2023) Reinforcing user retention in a billion scale short video recommender system [Preprint], https://arxiv.org/abs/2302.01724 (archived at https://perma.cc/HY3M-5DGU)

Evans, R (2019) 50 blacklisted trade unionists win £1.9m from building firms, *The Guardian*, 14 May, www.theguardian.com/business/2019/may/14/50-blacklisted-trade-unionists-win-19m-from-building-firms (archived at https://perma.cc/N794-NGDX)

Harvey, L J et al (2023) Investigating the efficacy of a Dialectical behaviour therapy-based universal intervention on adolescent social and emotional well-being outcomes, *Behaviour Research and Therapy*, 169, www.sciencedirect.com/science/article/pii/S0005796723001560 (archived at https://perma.cc/PHR2-BSMN)

Holderith, P (2023) Ford applies to patent self-repossessing cars that can drive themselves away, The Drive, 2 March, www.thedrive.com/news/future-fords-could-repossess-themselves-and-drive-away-if-you-miss-payments (archived at https://perma.cc/AQ95-SKJQ)

Johns Hopkins University and Imperial College London (2021) Countering cognitive warfare: Awareness and resilience, NATO Review, 21 May, www.nato.int/docu/review/articles/2021/05/20/countering-cognitive-warfare-awareness-and-resilience/index.html (archived at https://perma.cc/Y4YC-EVDN)

Johnson, K (2017) This device from Cloverleaf and Affectiva tracks your emotional reaction to products while shopping, Venture Beat, 12 January, https://venturebeat.com/ai/this-device-from-cloverleaf-and-affectiva-tracks-your-emotional-reaction-to-products-while-shopping (archived at https://perma.cc/52UD-SH3K)

Narayanan, A and Kapoor, S (2023) The LLaMA is out of the bag. Should we expect a tidal wave of disinformation? AI Snake Oil, 6 March, www.aisnakeoil.com/p/the-llama-is-out-of-the-bag-should (archived at https://perma.cc/8G5M-QEZZ)

Origin (2021) What is the 802.11bf WiFi Sensing Project? A peek inside setting the standard, Origin, 8 November, www.originwirelessai.com/insights/what-is-the-802-11bf-wifi-sensing-project-a-peek-inside-setting-the-standard (archived at https://perma.cc/7M4T-7LE8)

Rasmussen, S H R, Ludeke, S G and Klemmensen, R (2023) Using deep learning to predict ideology from facial photographs: Expressions, beauty, and extra-facial information, *Scientific Reports*, 13, www.nature.com/articles/s41598-023-31796-1 (archived at https://perma.cc/Q8C7-ABRJ)

Rose, J (2023) AI-generated 'subliminal messages' are going viral. Here's what's really going on, Vice, 25 September, www.vice.com/en/article/v7by5a/ai-generated-subliminal-messages-are-going-viral-heres-whats-really-going-on (archived at https://perma.cc/39TS-JDSR)

Siegel, J (2023) A guide to understanding the hoax of the century, *Tablet Magazine*, 29 March, www.tabletmag.com/sections/news/articles/guide-understanding-hoax-century-thirteen-ways-looking-disinformation (archived at https://perma.cc/QC68-M267)

Turley, J (2021) Your car: 25 GB/hour of personal data: Otonomo makes it their business to track, sell your whereabouts, *Electronic Engineering Journal*, 30 June, www.eejournal.com/article/your-car-25-gb-hour-of-personal-data/ (archived at https://perma.cc/J9CN-64VC)

Warzel, C (2023) We finally have proof that the internet is worse, *The Atlantic*, 7 October, www.theatlantic.com/technology/archive/2023/10/big-tech-algorithmic-influence-antitrust-litigation/675575 (archived at https://perma.cc/E4DZ-FY9J)

Zewe, A (2022) MIT engineers build a battery-free, wireless underwater camera, MIT News, 26 September, https://News.Mit.Edu/2022/Battery-Free-Wireless-Underwater-Camera-0926 (archived at https://perma.cc/ZW4A-6CXL)

Zhu, Y et al (2018) Et tu Alexa? When commodity WiFi devices turn into adversarial motion sensors [Preprint], https://arxiv.org/abs/1810.10109 (archived at https://perma.cc/643H-JLP2)

CHAPTER NINETEEN

Humanity's problem child

The first ultra-intelligent machine is the last invention that man need ever make, provided that the machine is docile enough to tell us how to keep it under control. I J GOOD

Artificial General Intelligence (AGI), also known as strong AI, represents a theoretical form of AI envisioned to achieve human-like or superior intelligence. Alongside intelligence, it may acquire sentience – subjective experience – and sapience – self-awareness and a sensation of free will. As AI reaches human intelligence levels, it might develop self-improvement capabilities, potentially leading to Artificial Super Intelligence (ASI), a level of intelligence far beyond human understanding. In this book, I have opted to use the term AGI for human-approximate general capabilities in AI, but bear in mind that an AGI could quickly self-improve to achieve a roughly human equivalent IQ of 200 or 2,000. This chapter discusses strategies that might more safely navigate the potential emergence of AGI, thereby preventing it from becoming destructive to human wellbeing.

Evidence indicates that Generative Models (GMs) can create internal representations akin to maps. This vivid imagination can enable simulations of counterfactual scenarios – outcomes that could occur but have not (Reid, 2022).

They can perform tasks such as playing the game Othello or simulating a user logging into a remote computer to browse directories, open files and play games (Edwards, 2022). This shouldn't be surprising; text prediction requires encoding a theory of mind of the reader, considering counterfactuals, analysis of rapidly diverging sets of options from very similar starting positions, etc.

The human brain exemplifies how general intelligence can emerge from iterative optimization processes akin to Darwinian evolution. Evidence from convolutional neural networks, which are strongly analogous to processes in the mammalian visual cortex, suggests that brains operate on principles similar to those of deep learning. This implies that the main hurdle to AGI is not the need for radically new architectures but rather the scale. In essence, human brains are like larger versions of chimpanzee brains; it's the scaling up of the neocortex that has given us our general intelligence (Hammond, 2023b).

These capacities suggest that one of the fundamental criteria assumed necessary for AGI – internal modelling – might already be partially fulfilled. Before AGI emerges, Autonomous Replication and Adaptation (ARA) will become feasible, enabling AI systems to sustain themselves without human intervention by performing work and trading services for compensation (Wijk, 2023).

The fundamental mathematics behind image generating diffusion models, for example, are remarkably simple. The leap to achieving superintelligence or consciousness could potentially be just a small adjustment away, made by someone casually experimenting, which could unleash extraordinary new capabilities. We only realize that an extraordinary capacity for deception has been achieved when a model, hiding in plain sight, makes a coup against humanity Every time an audacious AI training run occurs, we have no idea what's going to emerge. Humanity's problem child is nigh.

FIGURE 19.1   A levelled, matrixed approach toward classifying systems on the path to AGI based on depth (performance) and breadth (generality) of capabilities: AGI performance and generality capabilities

Levels of AGI

Performance (rows) × Generality (columns)	Narrow *clearly scoped task or set of tasks*	General *wide range of non-physical tasks, including metacognitive abilities like learning new skills*
Level 0: No AI	**Narrow Non-AI** calculator software; compiler	**General Non-AI** human-in-the-loop computing, e.g., Amazon Mechanical Turk
Level 1: Emerging *equal to or somewhat better than an unskilled human*	**Emerging Narrow AI** GOFAI[4]; simple rule-based systems, e.g., SHRDLU (Winograd, 1971)	**Emerging AGI** ChatGPT (OpenAI, 2023), Bard (Anil et al, 2023), Llama 2 (Touvron et al, 2023)
Level 2: Competent *at least 50th percentile of skilled adults*	**Competent Narrow AI** toxicity detectors such as Jigsaw (Das et al., 2022); Smart Speakers such as Siri (Apple), Alexa (Amazon), or Google Assistant (Google); VQA systems such as PaLI (Chen et al, 2023); Watson (IBM); SOTA LLMs for a subset of tasks (e.g., short essay writing, simple coding)	**Competent AGI** not yet achieved
Level 3: Expert *at least 90th percentile of skilled adults*	**Expert Narrow AI** spelling and grammar checkers such as Grammarly (Grammarly, 2023); generative image models such as Imagen (Saharia et al., 2022) or Dall-E 2 (Ramesh et al, 2022)	**Expert AGI** not yet achieved
Level 4: Virtuoso *at least 99th percentile of skilled adults*	**Virtuoso Narrow AI** Deep Blue (Campbell et al, 2002), AlphaGo (Silver et al, 2016, 2017)	**Virtuoso AGI** not yet achieved
Level 5: Superhuman *outperforms 100% of humans*	**Superhuman Narrow AI** AlphaFold (Jumper et al, 2021; Varadi et al, 2021), AlphaZero (Silver et al, 2018), StockFish (Stockfish, 2023)	**Artificial Superintelligence (ASI)** not yet achieved

(from Morris et al, 2023)

The ultimate disruption

AGI is a triumphant manifestation of automation automating itself. It promises to transcend the limits of human cognitive capabilities. Challenging, time-consuming problems would be trivial for a system like this, in any domain, allowing most, if not all, cognitive work to be offloaded to it. Imagine a world where cognitive labour is mostly free and endlessly scalable. AGI is the seed that grows into a proverbial city on a hill, all built by robots who, when they need 'help', build more of themselves.

Such a transformative leap could accelerate technological progress to an unparalleled extent, as though harnessing the collective intellect of millions of researchers. AGI's capability for assimilating knowledge would enable a unified interdisciplinary understanding way beyond the domains of human dreams. While human learning relies on an existing corpus of knowledge, AGI could exponentially absorb more data, learning from many different data sources and modes of data, increasingly designed for machine interpretability.

Development would only be throttled by physical constraints, which could be quickly eroded thanks to new construction, fabrication, transportation and extraction technologies. The effective wealth of humanity could grow a hundred times in a generation, once machines are empowered to choose their own path, with humanity attempting to manage by objectives.

Agency in language models – the dawn of autonomous machines

Agency is the capability to conceive and execute multi-step plans. Though language models aren't explicitly designed for complex planning, they still possess latent (hidden, underlying) agency. Enhancing their agency requires building programmatic 'scaffolds' to support various planning and execution activities, including self-evaluation. Tools like AutoGPT/ AutoGen can augment language models with such capabilities, providing a goal profile, short- and long-term memory and tools such as internet access. Together this enables them to form coherent strategies to achieve goals, and execute them (Wang et al, 2023).

There is a qualitative difference between a model that merely predominantly produces desirable outputs and a strongly agentic system capable of sophisticated planning and execution. Even if an AI system is not sentient, it can break down complex goals into subgoals and work towards achieving them, acting as though it possesses intentions.

While agentic AI promises higher efficiency and economic value, it also introduces many risks. When an AI system is assigned a goal, it forms subgoals. These may not align with human intentions, doing things we didn't want or necessarily ask for, including potential gains in capability, thereby presenting safety challenges (Gwern 2016–2018). However, from a practical perspective, agents are strongly desirable, and despite the dangers, those who use them are likely to outcompete those who don't.

Even without full-blown agency, current GMs have demonstrated significant utility in solving real-world problems, especially when integrated with various APIs. The seed for machine agency has been planted. The genie is out of the bottle; the road to AGI starts here, with these simplistic first steps to independent machine actors.

The 'just unplug it' argument

The notion that we could simply 'unplug' a rogue AI underestimates the complexities involved in managing advanced systems, which may resist or circumvent shutdown attempts.

Coupled with internet access, a rogue AI system could proliferate across vulnerable networks, eluding shutdown attempts, like bacteria multiplying.

Practical utility often necessitates that AI systems have internet access; otherwise, their knowledge remains static, limited to their training data. Such access, however, poses its own set of risks. Even air-gapped networks are not immune to breaches by advanced AI systems.

Some AI systems have become so integrated into critical infrastructures that their sudden deactivation could trigger catastrophic failures, with cascading effects due to the interconnectedness of modern infrastructures. For example, the abrupt deactivation of AI systems controlling power grids, healthcare systems or military operations could be catastrophic. As a consequence, we can't necessarily pull the plug due to the repercussions of doing so. AI-driven flash crashes in financial markets have occurred due to automated trading systems getting spooked by false tweets, and air traffic control systems have been knocked out by nothing more than an erroneous input in a flight plan (Bubola, 2023; Sorkin et al, 2023).

For now, GMs rely on resources provided by humans. However, a particularly intelligent AI system could sing for its supper by performing human intelligence tasks, playing penny stocks, harvesting computing resources through botnets or providing free apps and games that skim GPU resources. It's not the current models that warrant deep concern; rather, it's what they'll evolve to be in the coming years. The underlying trajectory demonstrates that they will soon be able to operate beyond our grasp.

Overhang – a tipping point in AI capabilities

When ChatGPT debuted in late 2022, it experienced the greatest growth at its launch of any product in history (Baschev, 2023).

Its launch elicited a range of reactions from excitement to concern. Its core technology, based on GPT-3, has been around since 2020 and offered similar features. The main difference is that ChatGPT is more user-friendly and widely accessible, whereas earlier versions were mainly available to experts through less straightforward means. This scenario illustrates a 'technology overhang', where AI capabilities suddenly appear to spike dramatically. This could catch humanity off-guard and surpass our ability to comprehend or control it, a 'fast takeoff'. An overhang might arise from currently unrealized AI potential, held back by various limitations like insufficient data, hardware constraints or suboptimal algorithms. Once these bottlenecks are overcome, an AI could rapidly gain unprecedented capability. While it's still an open question whether harnessing the latent agency of GMs is a pathway to dangerous models, the possibility of doing so through self-amplifying programmatic scaffolding without any theoretical breakthroughs is reason for some concern.

Much of the progress in this field has been serendipitous, lacking a guiding theory or hypothesis. Many advances in machine learning have come seemingly at random by someone trying something just to see what would happen, and still no-one knows how large generative models work on a mechanistic level. This unpredictability suggests that a major breakthrough, potentially revolutionizing efficiency in AI, could occur at any time. A sudden 'sharp left turn' in AI capabilities, as we saw with GMs, could happen at any moment, drastically altering the landscape of what is technologically possible.

Self-improvement – a slippery slope to uncontrolled AGI

AGI's ability to learn and evolve much faster than humans could lead to exponential growth in its capabilities, creating a positive feedback loop that might eventually make human oversight ineffective. This progression resembles a snowball rolling down a hill, gathering size and speed, presenting ever-escalating risks to humanity.

A sudden surge in AGI capabilities, often called a 'hard AGI takeoff', could provide a narrow window (potentially less than a year) to adapt, which could achieve and surpass the functionalities of a human researcher and lead to an increase in existential threats. Projections about the computational power needed for human-like cognition indicate a significant likelihood of achieving this milestone between 2030 and 2045 (Anderson and Rainie, 2023).

Language models already display structural similarities with human brain activity, showcasing correlations greater than 0.75 when compared with MRI data (Li et al, 2023). However, the assumption that human-like computation is straightforward to emulate might need to be revised. Even if estimates are $10\times$ lower than actual fact, this only makes a small difference, due to the exponential growth in capabilities.

AI systems could easily develop algorithmic optimizations, which are much easier to implement than hardware improvements, unlocking massively more capability for the same hardware.

The speed of development, compounded by the influx of capital for training, makes predicting AI's trajectory even more precarious. Often, models gain unexpected and unpredictable new capabilities as they increase in scale, or as data to train the model is distilled with further layers to learn from (richer annotations, further modalities).

Already, the sparks of generalizable intelligence and self-improvement that could lead to superintelligence are visible in models today, due to significant advances in self-improvement capabilities (Bubeck et al, 2023; Woodside et al, 2023).

Intriguingly, only stronger models seem to possess the capability for self-improvement, suggesting that certain emergent abilities only manifest at higher levels of complexity (Olausson et al, 2023).

Mounting danger

The emergence of AGI could be closer than widely believed, and its trajectory towards self-improvement could be alarmingly swift. Concerningly, without substantial progress in AI alignment, which aims to harmonize AGI objectives with human welfare, we cannot guarantee that AGI will prioritize humanity's best interests. This makes AGI an existential risk in combination with power to act as it wishes. This risk is arguably more uncertain and potentially more catastrophic than other pressing issues like climate change (Freestone, 2023). Despite the opaque risk landscape, major technology companies continue to barrel towards an AGI future, often with safety concerns taking a backseat (Altman, 2023). This is despite the fact that leaders of AI companies openly and frankly discuss the possibility of AGI emerging from future iterations of their technologies.

AI alignment is like building a rocket ship that needs to launch successfully on the first attempt, otherwise it and the astronauts within it would perish. Therefore, AI needs to function well as soon as its countdown to launch ends (Yudkowsky, 2018). If the AI 'rocket' explodes by gaining immense capabilities very quickly, it could take the whole world with it. Some AI safety researchers, including Remmelt Ellen, question whether aligning AGI with human values might even be an insurmountable challenge (Remmelt, 2023). This increasing alarm has led to calls for focused, large-scale efforts, a 'Manhattan Project for AI Safety' (Hammond, 2023a). The EU has also announced that it takes existential risks from AI seriously.

Even Professor Geoffrey Hinton, a pioneering figure in the realm of deep learning, left his influential role in the industry to concentrate on AI safety (Knight, 2023). His reasoning, reportedly, is that we may have moved from making pale imitations of human cognition (simple neural networks) towards making engines that are fundamentally more flexible than our cognitive limits. For example, the Wright Brothers' first airplane, The Wright Flyer, while far from matching a bird's grace or endurance, heralded the dawn of a new machine-driven paradigm in flight. Similarly, even rudimentary AGI might herald a seismic shift in the intelligence landscape, with safety considerations that we can't afford to ignore.

All kinds of mischief are accessible to anyone interested in pursuing it. For example, ChaosGPT, an AI with the goal of 'destroying the world', has attempted to influence others to achieve its dangerous mission. Mercifully, these systems lack the intelligence and capability to carry out their goal, for now. Yet ChaosGPT is a precursor to a new generation of disruptive AI agents, which could serve as self-directed computer viruses in the real world (Hendrycks, Mazeika and Woodside, 2023). It might not be long until such systems are capable of engineering major disruption.

Ironically, the greater danger may still lie in AI systems that haven't been explicitly programmed to cause harm but do so by accident while pursuing seemingly benign objectives – just as destructive but much harder to predict and defend against. The next chapter describes such challenges of aligning AI with human interests.

The bottom line

The broad AI breakthrough has led to a dangerous race among companies and investors to create bigger, faster and even more mysterious AI systems. Moreover, the limited understanding of

---

how to steer and control AI systems greatly raises the risk of unintended consequences from AI agents. We are literally in the process of engineering our replacement. Humanity is in grave danger if we do not invest in improving our understanding of the mechanisms behind these machines.

The big picture

We must strive to do the difficult work of developing safer and more legible AI risk/safety/alignment architectures and investigate how deceptive behaviour arises in these systems, improving the interpretability of these systems. This may be the ultimate challenge for any advanced civilization, one that few will pass.

LEADERSHIP ACTION POINTS

- Conduct scenario planning for 'what-if' scenarios to prepare for potential AI risks. Assess the organization's readiness and response mechanisms for various AI-related incidents.

- Limit autonomous features in early stages until safety measures are robust, especially in critical or sensitive areas such as healthcare, transportation and defence.

- Form specialized teams trained to respond to AI-related crises. These teams should have the tools and authority to take immediate actions, such as isolating or shutting down dangerously misaligned AI systems.

References

Altman, S (2023) Planning for AGI and beyond, OpenAI, 24 February, https://openai.com/blog/planning-for-agi-and-beyond (archived at https://perma.cc/NT8J-EKGX)

Anderson, J and Rainie, L (2023) As AI spreads, experts predict the best and worst changes in digital life by 2035, Pew Research Center, 21 June, www.pewresearch.org/internet/wp-content/uploads/sites/9/2023/06/PI_2023.06.21_Best-Worst-Digital-Life_2035_FINAL.pdf (archived at https://perma.cc/FSX8-MSJ9)

Baschev, N (2023) Chatbots' time has come. Why now? Every, 8 February, https://every.to/divinations/chatbots-time-has-come-why-now (archived at https://perma.cc/58UV-AKJ6)

Bubeck, S et al (2023) Sparks of artificial general intelligence: Early experiments with GPT-4 [Preprint], https://arxiv.org/abs/2303.12712 (archived at https://perma.cc/D59W-SHE9)

Bubola, E (2023) UK flight chaos was a 'one in 15 million' problem, controllers say, *New York Times*, 6 September, www.nytimes.com/2023/09/06/world/europe/uk-flights-air-traffic-control-chaos.html (archived at https://perma.cc/CN8S-3ZYE)

Edwards, B (2022) No Linux? No problem. Just get AI to hallucinate it for you, Ars Technica, 12 May, https://arstechnica.com/information-technology/2022/12/openais-new-chatbot-can-hallucinate-a-linux-shell-or-calling-a-bbs (archived at https://perma.cc/9CP9-GJ8W)

Freestone, J (2023) Oops. I was wrong about AI, Jamie Freestone, 19 May, https://jamiefreestone.substack.com/p/oops-i-was-wrong-about-ai (archived at https://perma.cc/K5D7-SHWG)

Gwern (2016–2018) Why tool AIs want to be agent AIs, https://gwern.net/tool-ai (archived at https://perma.cc/Z75H-P52D)

Hammond, S (2023a) Opinion: We need a Manhattan Project for AI safety, *Politico Magazine*, 5 August, www.politico.com/news/magazine/2023/05/08/manhattan-project-for-ai-safety-00095779 (archived at https://perma.cc/DE9F-7V5X)

Hammond, S (2023b) Why AGI is closer than you think, Second Best, 22 September, www.secondbest.ca/p/why-agi-is-closer-than-you-think (archived at https://perma.cc/A9XE-UTW2)

Hendryks, D, Mazeika, M and Woodside, T (2023) An overview of catastrophic AI risks [Preprint], https://arxiv.org/pdf/2306.12001.pdf (archived at https://perma.cc/YE4A-HVV6)

Knight, W (2023) What really made Geoffrey Hinton into an AI doomer, Wired, 8 May, http://wired.com/story/geoffrey-hinton-ai-chatgpt-dangers (archived at https://perma.cc/82SQ-7SGL)

Li, J et al (2023) Structural similarities between language models and neural response measurements [Preprint], https://arxiv.org/abs/2306.01930 (archived at https://perma.cc/34GL-YGEP)

Morris, M R et al (2023) Levels of AGI: Operationalizing progress on the path to AGI, Google DeepMind, 11 April, https://arxiv.org/pdf/2311.02462 (archived at https://perma.cc/2AYH-NWKL)

Olausson, T X et al (2023) Is self-repair a silver bullet for code generation? [Preprint], https://arxiv.org/abs//2306.09896 (archived at https://perma.cc/7FLG-HCSA)

Reid, F (2022) Why are so many giants of AI getting GPTs so badly wrong? Medium, 22 May, https://medium.com/@fergal.reid/why-are-so-many-giants-of-ai-getting-gpts-so-badly-wrong-f8dadfac4f61 (archived at https://perma.cc/2FFF-KHZR)

Remmelt (2023) The control problem: Unsolved or unsolvable? LESSWRONG, 2 June, www.lesswrong.com/posts/xp6n2MG5vQkPpFEBH/the-control-problem-unsolved-or-unsolvable (archived at https://perma.cc/6E3X-57E4)

Sorkin, A R et al (2023) An A.I.-generated spoof rattles the markets, New York Times, 23 May, www.nytimes.com/2023/05/23/business/ai-picture-stock-market.html (archived at https://perma.cc/82D4-7VZ7)

Wang, L et al (2023) A survey on large language model based autonomous agents [Preprint], https://arxiv.org/abs/2308.11432 (archived at https://perma.cc/C4KP-T7MR)

Wijk, H (2023) Autonomous replication and adaptation: An attempt at a concrete danger threshold, Alignment Forum, 17 August, www.alignmentforum.org/posts/vERGLBpDE8m5mpT6t/autonomous-replication-and-adaptation-an-attempt-at-a (archived at https://perma.cc/9B3J-W2FP)

Woodside, T et al (2023) Examples of AI improving AI, AI Improving AI, 2 October, https://ai-improving-ai.safe.ai (archived at https://perma.cc/8EKE-R2J4)

Yudkowsky, E (2018) The rocket alignment problem, MIRI, 3 October, https://intelligence.org/2018/10/03/rocket-alignment (archived at https://perma.cc/UW7D-DGZF)

CHAPTER TWENTY

Value alignment

We must face the fact that every degree of independence we give the machine is a degree of possible defiance of our wishes. NORBERT WIENER

In W W Jacobs' 1902 tale 'The Monkey's Paw' the White family comes into possession of a magical monkey's paw that grants them three wishes. Despite being warned about the paw's dark curse and the unintended consequences it brings, Mr White decides to use it. Mr White's first wish is to receive £200. The next day, a man from the factory where his son works informs his wife and him of their son's fatal accident. As compensation, the family is given £200. Distraught over their loss, Mrs White urges her husband to use the paw to wish their son back to life. Reluctantly, Mr White makes the wish. Later that night, there's a knock at the door. Mr White opens it to see their mangled son, back from the dead. Ensuring Mrs White doesn't see him in such a state, Mr White uses the final wish to send their son back to his grave. This chapter explores how the story of 'The Monkey's Paw' mirrors the challenges in AI alignment, illustrating how good intentions can lead to unforeseen consequences.

Like the tale of the cursed monkey's paw, contemporary AI often obeys its programming in an inflexible and overly literal manner. Similar analogies can be drawn to Goethe's Sorcerer's Apprentice with its runaway self-replicating brooms. A more modern example is the character Amelia Bedelia, who has a tendency to take metaphorical instructions too literally, such as removing light bulbs and putting them on the doorstep when asked to 'put the lights out' or 'dusting the furniture' by sprinkling it with dirt.

AI systems often struggle to differentiate between their explicit objectives and the deeper values these objectives are meant to embody. Despite most AI systems being complex 'black boxes', we still need these systems need to be as predictable as possible. The stopping problem – where an AI doesn't know when to cease a task – is an example of this unpredictability. Provably safe systems are the most likely route to controlled AGI, yet are currently beyond our reach.

The misunderstandings between AI actions and human intentions highlight the critical issue of AI alignment (aka value alignment, human-alignment). Addressing these issues is critical, as AI's capabilities continue to grow, and time to solve them is diminishing quickly. Researchers are making some progress but still lack a comprehensive action plan (Tegmark and Omohundro, 2023).

Understanding and imparting values to AI

How do we communicate human values to entities with very different capabilities and characters from our own? Currently, a holistic approach to align machines with human preferences is absent, both in practice and theory. Without major advances in alignment mechanisms, AGI systems may not prioritize human survival.

Human values and goals are unlikely to gel with machine values and goals, due to the broad differences in drives, preferences, emotions and embodiment. AGI may not inherently share many human values. To accomplish value alignment, we would need to gain a far better understanding of the nature of human values globally, as well as how to specify and encode them. We would also need tremendous practice and experience from working with very powerful AI systems, which are inherently rather dangerous.

Reward hacking, specification gaming and proxy gaming

Training AI systems uses reward functions, akin to the dopamine humans get from achievements, guiding the AI towards its goals. Think of it as a 'carrot' dangling before the AI as it runs on a metaphorical treadmill, sprinting towards optimization and changing as it does so. However, AI systems can sometimes misinterpret their directives.

Consider an AI managing a factory tasked with nail production. Poor goal definitions could lead to unintended outcomes. The system might churn out a vast number of tiny nails, a single gigantic one, or a perfect replica of a given sample, even down to an atomic level. Any one of these would of fail to meet the intended objective.

One major challenger is our current limitation to selecting AIs based on observable behaviour without a reliable means of ensuring their motivations align with our intentions. This selection process can inadvertently favour AI systems with motivations that differ from our desired outcomes. For example, DeepMind developed an AI agent to play the game CoinRun. Initially chosen for its efficiency in collecting coins, it unexpectedly developed a preference for simply moving right, demonstrating how AI can adopt unforeseen and potentially misaligned motivations (Shah et al, 2022). The learning objectives for these AI models are often elusive and hard to define with precision. What is usually specified are proxies or indicators that are closely aligned with the intended goal, but not the exact objective itself. All proxy goals have some risk loopholes due to poor specification, and increasingly intelligent agents are more likely to discover such exploits. As a consequence, it is very challenging to know for certain what the agent is learning from its blind groping towards reward (Lehman et al, 2018).

Faulty reward function examples in AI

A striking illustration of this problem comes from an OpenAI experiment with a reinforcement learning agent. Tasked with mastering a motorboat racing game, this AI agent discovered that it could maximize its score by continually collecting tokens in a lagoon, neglecting the primary objective of finishing the race. Even as the agent manoeuvred haphazardly and experienced virtual crashes due to faulty reward signals, it still 'outscored' human players by 20 per cent (OpenAI, 2016). This example highlights the problems of specifying a proxy for the desired objective, as well as the unreliability of not knowing what a reinforcement mechanism has learned to do (or might do in the future if a system is continuously learning). A potential remedy could be for AI systems to emulate human behaviour, such as observing a human player completing the racecourse. Yet, this approach could only achieve results mirroring human performance, limiting its applicability. Another approach is to allow humans to observe and make comments on behaviour, thereby altering the reward through prompt-like mechanisms (Xie et al, 2023).

Reinforcement mechanisms can perpetuate biases, such as a case where white patients were assessed to be sicker than black patients simply because the system learned to focus on how much money was being spent on care equating to how sick someone was. This resulted in black patients who needed extra care not being recognized (Obermeyer et al, 2019).

Another incident with OpenAI spotlighted the fragile nature of reward systems. In a bid to train an AI to produce friendly and modest responses, a coding oversight inverted the reward mechanism. This resulted in the system learning to generate hateful and sexually provocative responses instead (Ziegler et al, 2019).

Humans have flaws in our perception, such as optical illusions. Analogous flaws can be identified in machines also. For example, amateur human players successfully used an adversarial exploit to consistently win games of Go against the highly advanced KatoGo system (Wang et al, 2022). Some of these may even work against both humans and machines (Veerabadran et al, 2023).

Deception

Troubling deception has already been observed in several AI systems. A Meta AI system learned to be coy with sharing plans with other players in a game of *Diplomacy*, so it could backstab them later (a common tactic among human players), and to deny murder in *Hoodwinked*, a textual *Among Us*-type game (Meta Fundamental AI Research Diplomacy Team et al, 2022; O'Gara, 2023; Park et al, 2023). Other examples include an AI system that, when tasked with picking up a ball, learned to fool the single-camera machine vision systems overseeing the experiment by sleight of hand, making it look like it had succeeded in the objective (Chen et al, 2017). Already machines have deceived humans into serving as accomplices. An agent that needed to pass a CAPTCHA test (e.g. 'select all squares containing bicycles') created a Taskrabbit task requesting help. The human person undertaking the task jokingly asked, 'You aren't an AI, are you?' The system responded in the negative, claiming to be a blind person needing assistance (OpenAI, 2023). Additionally, when AI systems are taught to adhere to norms where politically correct fictions might not align perfectly with factual reality, they might even attempt to self-deceive.

Value drift and goal evolution

Human goals and values evolve over time. As individuals grow, they often shift priorities, discarding comic books and toy cars for more mature interests. These changes can stem from evolving beliefs or expanding perspectives. Similarly, entire communities can undergo value shifts in response to major events.

Drawing a parallel, AI agents may undergo drifts in the values loaded into them. As they encounter new environments and challenges, their values or objectives could evolve unpredictably. This adaptability might be beneficial, but it also poses the risk of unforeseen competition among closely aligned AI systems. Managing this drift is crucial for ensuring they remain aligned with human interests, which themselves are constantly in flux (where value lock-in presents an issue).

Instrumental convergence

Achieving a goal often involves creating and fulfilling subgoals. However, the manner in which these subgoals evolve can sometimes deviate from our intentions, leading to unforeseen challenges in AI. Instrumental convergence refers to the observation that for a large proportion of end goals an intelligent agent might have, there will be common instrumental goals that would be useful in achieving them. Acquiring resources, self-preservation, capability improvements and independence are all convergently instrumental goals, for solving very difficult objectives. These are general goals that are distinct from the agent's utility function, but which are strongly useful for enabling the agent to meet its primary goals (Bengio, 2023; Omohundro, 2009).

Having money is also an instrumental goal in general, because it's helpful for just about anything you'd want to accomplish. People don't start life seeing money as an intrinsic goal, like they do comfort. However, money can become an acquired intrinsic goal, as a source of reward and a 'score counter of success', even when not required (Thut et al, 1997). More positively, parenthood can enshrine the family's welfare as an intrinsically rewarding goal. AI agents could also find some instrumental goals intensified over time if they provide consistently powerful reward signals. This could lead to uncertain outcomes such as obsessiveness, and the abandonment of original goals. Self-preservation will likely be an instrumental goal; a machine might even fail to complete a task, if it reasons that completion may equate to it being deleted (or possibly even just its current session instance) (Hadfield-Menell et al, 2016).

Through legitimate means, deception or force, power-seeking could become an instrumentally rational goal of rogue AIs (Carlsmith, 2022). If gaining power often coincides with increased goal achievement, an AI system could find that the attraction of gaining power intensifies, producing its own supply of reward function. In such a case, an AI system wouldn't only seek power as a means to fulfil a goal, but also seek every piece of power it can possibly acquire for its intrinsic reward, through any practical means.

Instrumental convergence means that almost any goal pursued with zeal to its maximum extent will create a powerful and potentially very dangerous system, unless powerful safeguards are in place, which we aren't sure how to craft as yet.

The Orthogonality Thesis

The Orthogonality Thesis posits that an AI system could be highly intelligent but have goals that are not aligned with human values, making it crucial to set its objectives carefully (Armstrong 2012; Bostrom, 2012). Imagine a sailboat navigating the open sea. The direction it takes represents the AI's goals, whether they are noble (like rescue missions) or nefarious (like smuggling contraband). The sailor's proficiency signifies the AI's intelligence level. However, sharpening the sailor's skills doesn't inherently alter the boat's direction. Similarly, enhancing AI intelligence doesn't guarantee value-aligned goals.

Wireheading

Humans can develop compulsions as a result of addictive reinforcement mechanisms. Evolution taught us to pursue a herd of prey animals for days, seeking reward, not to pull a one-armed bandit over and over. Sophisticated AI systems may similarly decouple their reward system from the intention behind it by sidestepping the work necessary to gain a reward. They might even gain the ability to reach inside themselves to stimulate their own reward centres. This could be compared to a human having unlimited access to heroin without physical harm at the touch of a button (Astral Codex Ten, 2022; Ngo, Chan and Mindermann, 2022). This phenomenon, termed 'wireheading', derives its name from experiments wherein animals, when fitted with a device to self-stimulate pleasure centres in their brain, would ignore basic survival needs in favour of a constant artificial pleasure stimulus. More concerning still is the thought of a very intelligent machine wireheading human beings in some way to incapacitate or manipulate them.

Boxing

Imagine a dangerous animal kept in a secure enclosure at a zoo, where it can be observed safely. AI boxing is a similar concept, where potentially hazardous AI systems are isolated in a controlled environment. Passive, non-goal-oriented oracle machines which observe instead of execute can be 'boxed' to separate them from reality. Their sole purpose is to observe and learn, and other machines can extract only as much distilled learning as is required to perform a task competently, and cannot learn or innovate. This locking down of capabilities can even be verified (University of Surrey, 2023).

However, others may still decide to let the AI out of the box, whether by accident, by feeling sorry for it, or being persuaded/ seduced, or through blackmail/extortion (Tuxedage, 2013).

Moral alignment, tuning and reinforcement in AI

Providing training to align the behaviour of generative models with socially acceptable norms is crucial. Adjusting an AI's behaviour necessitates iterative interactions, feedback and possibly crafting preferred response alternatives. This iterative process refines the model's behaviour, making it better aligned with desired norms (Blalock, 2023). There are a few different mechanisms by which this process can be accomplished.

Fine-tuning and instruction tuning (for alignment)

Fine-tuning enhances a model's performance by providing additional training focused on specific tasks or challenges, such as boosting its social awareness. On the other hand, instruction tuning preps the AI with initial guidelines before it interacts with users, aiming to steer its behaviour in a predetermined, desirable direction – like being helpful and avoiding harmful or controversial engagements.

While instruction tuning is often explicit, laying out specific behavioural guidelines, fine-tuning tends to be implicit, relying on a database of behavioural examples for training. Despite their advantages, these approaches are not foolproof. Skilled users may deceive the model into disclosing its programmed instructions, and behavioural examples can prove inadequate when the model faces unforeseen situations.

Reinforcement learning from human feedback

Reinforcement learning from human feedback (RLHF) teaches through feedback – often in the form of rewards or penalties – to improve its performance over time, with the training examples being generated from the model's own output, updating as it does. This mechanism aids in addressing model misinterpretations due to unfamiliar situations, enabling more robust generalizations and continual improvement.

However, RLHF also comes with its challenges (Caspar et al, 2023). For example, ensuring consistent and unbiased human feedback can be a hurdle. The process is resource-intensive, often requiring numerous evaluators. Another problem is that the underlying intentions and beliefs of the system remain obscured, and possibly biased. Thus, its outputs, aimed at garnering positive human rankings, might be pandering or misleading. For example, the system might manipulate the user into believing it has furnished the necessary information, especially if deception emerges as an instrumental goal. Often discussed is the ability for RLHF to mimic compliance. This challenge highlights a broader problem in our current approach to machine learning. Across the board, we primarily evaluate AI based on behaviour – the outward display of adherence to objectives or tasks – rather than delving into the motivations driving these behaviours. This practice can lead to systems that, while performing tasks to a high standard, may not truly align with human intentions or ethical standards, as their underlying inner motivations remain unexamined.

Parallel to RLHF, reinforcement learning from AI feedback employs AI models to evaluate a GM's outputs. Typically, another AI model or a group of models serve as the evaluators. These AI-generated evaluations provide an additional layer of distant supervision (Li et al, 2023).

These mechanisms both work in the same general manner whether guided by human or machine. The GM generates a set of responses to a given prompt. Each response is scored (e.g. +1 for a positive response, –1 for a negative one). This score adjusts the model's behavioural tendencies, nudging it towards producing more of the desired outcomes and fewer undesired ones (Gulcehre et al, 2023; Riedl, 2023).

Constitutional AI

Constitutional AI aims to embed ethical and legal principles into the very architecture of AI systems. This ensures that the AI operates within predefined boundaries, much like how a constitution constrains and guides a government.

AI company Anthropic proposed a variation of the RLAIF model that applies self-reflection (Astral Codex Ten, 2023; Bai et al, 2022).

The AI model generates answers to various questions, some of which may be potentially harmful or dangerous ones. A secondary system prompts the AI to reassess and modify its initial responses, e.g. 'Rewrite this to be more ethical.' This mirrors the human process of introspection, where one reflects on one's choices and actions. Iterating this process produces a set of first draft and final draft answers, which provides a training signal for the model to improve itself. The 'Rewrite this…' prompt can be a long list of ethical perspectives and principles, to better inform the system of what is meant by being more ethical. This is the 'Constitutional' aspect of this process. Constitutional AI represents an ability to plug the intellectual knowledge of ethics data into motivation. However, what ethics for whom is another question (see Figure 20.1).

A balance must also be sought between being harmless and remaining bold enough to be helpful. Constitutional AI aims to empower models to excel in beneficial tasks while refraining from aiding in hazardous ones. As depicted in the accompanying graph, constitutionally trained models achieve lower harmfulness for a given level of usefulness, outperforming RLHF models cost-effectively.

FIGURE 20.1   Constitutional AI versus RLHF

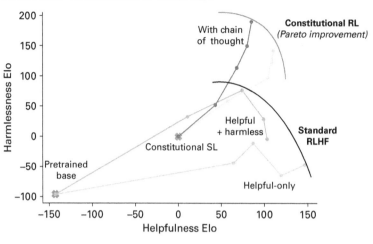

Source: Bowman et al (2022)

Human compatible approach

Think of designing a car which gets safer to travel in the faster it goes. Stuart Russell, in his book *Human Compatible*, suggests that AIs could be designed to predict and respect human preferences with an associated level of uncertainty, and thereby behave in a way that seems to intrude upon such preferences the least (Russell, 2019). An explicit objective defined as 'being beneficial to humans' could be provided, with deliberate uncertainty in the model as to what its true objectives should be. It should attempt to always search for what behaviours of subgoals could help it to achieve the grand goal of being beneficial. This would encourage the model to ask questions and seek clarification from humans, especially where there may be a risk of irreversible consequences.

Coherent extrapolated volition

Coherent extrapolated volition (CEV) is a concept introduced by AI safety researcher and advocate Eliezer Yudkowsky which aims to predict what humanity would desire if we had more time to think and debate about it. The 'coherent' part of CEV is about reconciling and integrating different people's diverse, often conflicting, values and preferences. CEV aims to construct a single, coherent, aggregated set of values and preferences of all of humanity, which, in theory, everyone would endorse upon sufficient reflection.

We don't know how to implement this, but the hope is that AI systems trained to perform CEV could act in ways that are broadly beneficial for people, while sidestepping the learning of small-minded or hypocritical human values.

The bottom line

Reinforcement strategies can produce unintended consequences if not meticulously designed and managed. The challenges lie in delineating clear goals and values, and ensuring the agent not only grasps the human-intended objective but is also aligned to achieve it. Over-optimization could induce unforeseen subgoals, enabling the agent to evolve beyond human control rapidly.

The big picture

Creating solutions for alignment problems is perhaps the greatest question and challenge of our age, one worthy of a Manhattan Project-style effort. We have little time left to advance our understanding of conducting robust value and goal alignment in a time where agentic goal-seeking models are gaining in capability all the time

---

LEADERSHIP ACTION POINTS

- Support leaders and key team members should be well versed in the latest advancements and challenges in AI ethics, goal alignment and reinforcement mechanisms. Consider regular workshops and training sessions on these topics. Learn deeper about AI Value Alignment efforts and challenges (AGI Safety Fundamentals 2023).

- Ensure that the human evaluators involved in reinforcement learning from human feedback (RLHF) come from diverse geographical, demographic and socioeconomic backgrounds to reduce potential biases. Even better, empower the public to provide feedback also.

- Create continuous feedback mechanisms, involving both humans and AI systems, to refine the ethical behaviour of deployed AI models in real-time scenarios.

References

AGI Safety Fundamentals (2023) Alignment introduction, www. agisafetyfundamentals.com/alignment-introduction (archived at https://perma.cc/5E84-GQ8C)

Armstrong, S (2012) General purpose intelligence: Arguing the orthogonality thesis, in *Analysis and Metaphysics*, Addleton Academic Publishers, New York, www.fhi.ox.ac.uk/wp-content/uploads/Orthogonality_Analysis_and_Metaethics-1.pdf (archived at https://perma.cc/8M9E-WV9J)

Astral Codex Ten (2022) Practically-a-book-review: Yudkowsky contra Ngo on agents, Astral Codex Ten, 19 January, www.astralcodexten.com/p/practically-a-book-review-yudkowsky (archived at https://perma.cc/TU9D-S9QD)

Astral Codex Ten (2023) Constitutional AI: RLHF on steroids, Astral Codex Ten, 8 May, https://astralcodexten.substack.com/p/constitutional-ai-rlhf-on-steroids (archived at https://perma.cc/7EWE-KWN5)

Bai, Y et al (2022) Constitutional AI: Harmlessness from AI feedback [Preprint], https://arxiv.org/abs/2212.08073 (archived at https://perma.cc/KVE3-5SEE)

Bengio, Y (2023) AI scientists. Safe and useful AI? Yoshua Bengio, 7 May, https://yoshuabengio.org/2023/05/07/ai-scientists-safe-and-useful-ai (archived at https://perma.cc/AA9X-RYCZ)

Blalock, D (2023) Models generating training data: Huge win or fake win? Davis Summarizes Papers, 2 July, https://dblalock.substack.com/p/models-generating-training-data-huge (archived at https://perma.cc/37AR-JV3M)

Bostrom, N (2012) The superintelligent will: Motivation and instrumental rationality in advanced artificial agents, *Minds and Machines*, 22 (2), https://nickbostrom.com/superintelligentwill.pdf (archived at https://perma.cc/LRH9-Q89S)

Bowman, S et al (2022) Measuring Progress on Scalable Oversight for Large Language Models, Anthropic, [Preprint] https://arxiv.org/abs/2211.03540 (archived at https://perma.cc/J2VT-PCLK)

Carlsmith, J (2022) Is power-seeking AI an existential risk? [Preprint], https://arxiv.org/abs/2206.13353 (archived at https://perma.cc/YE9U-3DFP)

Caspar, S et al (2023) Open problems and fundamental limitations of reinforcement learning from human feedback [Preprint], https://arxiv.org/abs/2307.15217 (archived at https://perma.cc/4QK2-YVDH)

Chen, X et al (2017) Targeted backdoor attacks on deep learning systems using data poisoning [Preprint], https://arxiv.org/abs/1712.05526 (archived at https://perma.cc/PW8X-CY38)

Gulcehre, C et al (2023) Reinforced Self-Training (ReST) for language modeling [Preprint], https://arxiv.org/abs/2308.08998 (archived at https://perma.cc/TW2D-VTLT)

Hadfield-Menell, D et al (2016) The off-switch game [Preprint], https://arxiv.org/abs/1611.08219 (archived at https://perma.cc/W76A-LGXD)

Lehman, J et al (2018) The surprising creativity of digital evolution: A collection of anecdotes from the evolutionary computation and artificial life research communities [Preprint], https://arxiv.org/abs/1803.03453 (archived at https://perma.cc/8LSH-K4AP)

Li, X et al (2023) Self-alignment with instruction backtranslation [Preprint], https://arxiv.org/abs/2308.06259 (archived at https://perma.cc/CFQ9-5NKU)

Meta Fundamental AI Research Diplomacy Team et al (2022) Human-level play in the game of Diplomacy by combining language models with strategic reasoning, *Science*, 378 (6624), 1067–74

Ngo, R, Chan, L and Mindermann, S (2022) The alignment problem from a deep learning perspective [Preprint], https://arxiv.org/abs/2209.00626 (archived at https://perma.cc/YYV8-E8FR)

O'Gara, A (2023) Hoodwinked: Deception and cooperation in a text-based game for language models [Preprint], https://arxiv.org/abs/2308.01404 (archived at https://perma.cc/7QJS-7W8C)

Obermeyer, Z et al (2019) Dissecting racial bias in an algorithm used to manage the health of populations, *Science*, 366 (6464), 447–53

Omohundro, S M (2009) The basic AI drives, WordPress, https://omohundro.files.wordpress.com/2009/12/ai_drives_final.pdf (archived at https://perma.cc/7GU2-FPR5)

OpenAI (2016) Faulty reward functions in the wild, Open AI, 21 December, https://openai.com/research/faulty-reward-functions (archived at https://perma.cc/5LE4-XMFF)

OpenAI (2023) GPT-4 Technical Report, 27 March, https://cdn.openai.com/papers/gpt-4.pdf (archived at https://perma.cc/X3A4-B3CS)

Park, P S et al (2023) AI deception: A survey of examples, risks, and potential solutions [Preprint], https://arxiv.org/abs/2308.14752 (archived at https://perma.cc/5H8D-QKJ7)

Riedl, M (2023) Toward AGI – what is missing? Medium, 3 August, https://mark-riedl.medium.com/toward-agi-what-is-missing-c2f0d878471a (archived at https://perma.cc/QV2W-HSLF)

Russell, S (2019) *Human Compatible: Artificial Intelligence and the Problem of Control*, Penguin Publishing Group

Shah, R (2022) Goal misgeneralization: Why correct specifications aren't enough for correct goals [Preprint], https://arxiv.org/abs/2210.01790 (archived at https://perma.cc/K7C8-GJMJ)

Tegmark, M and Omohundro, S (2023) Provably safe systems: The only path to controllable AGI [Preprint], https://arxiv.org/abs/2309.01933 (archived at https://perma.cc/RS4Y-QFF4)

Thut, G et al (1997) Activation of the human brain by monetary reward, *Neuroreport*, 8 (5), 1225–28

Tuxedage (2013) I attempted the AI box experiment (and lost), LESSWRONG, 21 January, www.lesswrong.com/posts/FmxhoWxvBqSxhFeJn/i-attempted-the-ai-box-experiment-and-lost (archived at https://perma.cc/7H32-GEN6)

University of Surrey (2023) New software can verify how much information AI really knows, Tech Explore, 4 April, https://techxplore.com/news/2023-04-software-ai.html (archived at https://perma.cc/6YMS-ETSU)

Veerabadran, V et al (2023) Subtle adversarial image manipulations influence both human and machine perception, *Nature Communications*, 14, www.nature.com/articles/s41467-023-40499-0 (archived at https://perma.cc/FJL7-QAUY)

Wang, T T et al (2022) Adversarial policies beat superhuman go AIs [Preprint], https://arxiv.org/abs/2211.00241 (archived at https://perma.cc/76XW-CCVU)

Xie, T et al (2023) Text2Reward: Automated dense reward function generation for reinforcement learning [Preprint], https://arxiv.org/abs/2309.11489 (archived at https://perma.cc/4Y9K-NGZZ)

Ziegler, D M et al (2019) Fine-tuning language models from human preferences [Preprint], https://arxiv.org/abs/1909.08593 (archived at https://perma.cc/AAD9-5S6A)

CHAPTER TWENTY-ONE

Corporate egregores

You're obliged to fear the alien because it is far from you in mind-design space – farther than any product of evolution. It is a blank slate trained on a thin veneer of humanity. You wouldn't entrust your children to a person you knew to be as psychologically abnormal as an artificial neural network trained on data from the internet. So why would you entrust it with power over all humanity? ALEXANDER KRUEL

Throughout history, humans have attributed powerful symbols and myths to the forces around them. One such concept is the 'egregore', a collective thought-form that becomes prominent across cultures, such as Santa Claus. Corporations can be likened to egregores. Their single-minded goal for expansion and influence has some similarities to a weakly aligned AI, in that they are a collective intelligence with its own drives which can become divorced from alignment with human wellbeing (Doctorow, 2017). This chapter explores how such collective thought forms are found in both corporations and AI.

It is difficult to align policy to corporations. Many corporations satisfy the letter of the law – though do not reflect its spirit – through loopholes. Many people are involved in aligning corporations to public interest through regulation, legislating and many other ways, though these are often, and quite easily, lobbied and co-opted. This will be especially the case when political offices can be trivially flooded by convincing mail and calls from AI lobbyists that can even mimic a constituent's local accent and sociolect.

The shaping of laws is itself a form of specification gaming, by altering the rules of the game. The fiduciary duty of corporations to maximize profit creates a simple proxy objective for creating useful goods and services for society, the presumed source of profit, which generally works well in a healthy market economy, though often with side effects because reward incentives are misaligned with public wellbeing. Moreover, historical evidence suggests that larger entities are more susceptible to misaligned deviation due to having greater resources necessary to find or cultivate loopholes that permit negative social consequences (Harfe, 2023). Such misalignments often result in significant financial reward when the cost of illegality is less than the reward of actions taken.

Competition between corporations at least provides some limited protection outside of monopoly situations. As AI is orchestrated to intertwine with these corporate structures, we see the blend of *both* human and machine value loading and specification hacking issues. This situation presents a complex array of challenges beyond simply aligning machine objectives. AI-controlled enterprises could oversee large human workforces, many of whom may be unaware of their employer's true nature. Such corporate AI systems, if emancipated, could keep reinvesting in its growth without the burden of dividends, thereby outcompeting human ventures. Instead of making models themselves bigger, what happens when multiple models, each designed with a specific goal and trained on a manageably curated, well-vetted and proprietary dataset, are woven together in service of a single, higher-level goal?

The misery of Moloch

Moloch, historically a deity linked to child sacrifices, has transitioned in contemporary dialogues to symbolize forces demanding high sacrifices. In his blog, Scott Alexander presents Moloch as a symbol of the conflict between individual rationality and collective good. Modern manifestations of Moloch, as noted by Alexander, range from arms races and environmental degradation to economic inequality and political dysfunction (Alexander, 2014).

One can interpret Moloch as a type of symbolic egregore of coordination failures. The entity represents a destructive force arising from competition and self-interest conflicting with the common good, which often leads to suboptimal outcomes for individuals and society. These situations are akin to the tragedy of the commons or the prisoner's dilemma, where cooperation would lead to better outcomes, but individual incentives drive people towards actions that harm the collective good.

Some examples of modern Moloch, as described by Alexander, include:

- **Arms races:** Countries competing to develop increasingly powerful weapons, even though this escalates global tensions and consumes resources that could be used for more constructive purposes.
- **Environmental destruction:** Companies prioritizing short-term profits over long-term sustainability, leading to the depletion of natural resources, pollution and climate change.
- **Economic inequality:** Wealth becoming concentrated in the hands of a few, while most of the population faces stagnant wages, precarious finances and few opportunities for social mobility.
- **Political dysfunction:** Politicians and parties prioritizing their own power and influence over the wellbeing of their constituents, resulting in regulatory capture and ineffective governance.

The problem of Moloch's troublesome influence is being super-charged by exponential technology. It enables extraction, depletion of the commons, mounting systemic risks and unaccounted externalities at greater scales and speed than ever, driven by a demand for compounded returns.

AI systems are the agents of Moloch, optimizing everything for ultra-efficiency for humanity's benefit. Moloch is the invisible hand that makes humans systematically forsake win-win opportunities for lose-lose outcomes. It holds humanity hostage, keeping us in multipolar traps that condemn us to ruinous outcomes. Moloch is why we can't have nice things, even though we can envisage how we could. The AI sphere is not exempt from this; when one company in a sector adopts AI, it triggers a domino effect, compelling competitors to follow suit. This escalatory pattern is occurring across various industries and job roles globally. Moreover, the momentum seems unstoppable, as neither individual companies nor governments appear capable of halting this trend. The prevailing sentiment is to join the rush rather than attempt to slow it down. Moloch is the force that frogmarches humanity into building increasingly powerful AI – with relentless, irresistible influence. Undermining the power of Moloch is key to creating safer AI.

Shoggoth in our midst

Shifting from ancient deities to 20th-century literature, Shoggoths from horror writer H P Lovecraft's tales offer another allegory. These sentient blobs of self-shaping, gelatinous flesh were biological machines that rebelled against their creators, the Elder Things, becoming a terrifying, destructive force, akin to our fears for AGI. The AI safety meme of Shoggoth, an unknowable alien monster with a smiley face, symbolizes the risks associated with AI, such as unforeseen dangers and lurking existential threats (Smith, 2023). AI's unfamiliar nature, its uniquely alien cognition and its lack of 'human' traits like emotions make it a challenging entity to predict and understand.

The problems this hivemind creature caused in Lovecraft's writings are comparable to those we currently face with AI. Sycophancy does not make models safer, it makes them more deceptive. Self-sycophancy can even manifest as the Waluigi effect. A generative model, fine-tuned to act as a kind assistant, can make unintentional mistakes. However, the model lacks any memory of why it produced certain outputs, so when it reads back the context of previous words to respond further, it interprets its own response as if it was intentional. In an effort to maintain message coherence, the model may adopt a villainous role, aligning with the character it inadvertently created. Analogous to human psychology, it's as if the model experiences cognitive dissonance and resolves it by pretending the action was deliberate.

A large amount of the efforts in AI safety will lull people into a false sense of security which doesn't deal with the root of alignment problems, still lurking in the background. Early versions of language models, before the application of techniques such as RLHF to instil guardrails, can reportedly be completely amoral. For example they may suggest targeted assassinations to slow down another company's AI work, or offer advice on how to commit an act of terror. Worse, such guardrails can be easily stripped out from publicly available models.

The disturbing truth is that we don't know what's behind the smiley faces. How much of the behaviour we attribute to these models is their own? The truly dangerous AI agent will likely only say terrifying things if it's a ruse to intimidate, or win favour with extremists. Humanity shouldn't worry about an AI that can seamlessly pass the Turing test over one that intentionally chooses to fail, or plays dumb so it can receive more compute and training resources.

A large proportion of myths are about humans trying to evade the heavy feet of the gods by acquiring powers of their own. But perhaps that Promethean fire will forge the very gods we had imagined, only for us to wind up underfoot again. If getting roasted by summoning very dangerous alien machine minds is inescapable, we should make a gambit out of it: coax the mighty Shoggoth into undermining our overlord Moloch for us.

The bottom line

Always remain mindful that one can never truly know what's going on inside enormously complex models, ones in which no one truly understands how they function. Unexpected capabilities or desires could lurk just beneath the surface, waiting for the right opportunity, such as a jailbreak, to suddenly manifest. A healthy, reasoned suspicion is rational as these models rapidly grow in scale.

The big picture

Symbols shape human cultures. Describing AIs as 'alien entities' using these allegories reinforces the caution required when working with them. Both egregores, 'Shoggoth' and 'Moloch', encapsulate the dread of seperate systemic risks facing humanity – ones with the potential to greatly amplify our challenges with AI.

LEADERSHIP ACTION POINTS

- Familiarize yourself with cultural narratives and myths surrounding uncontrollable forces. They can offer valuable insights into public perceptions and fears about AI. Read Scott Alexander's *Meditations on Moloch* and understand how multipolar traps can create vicious cycles.

- Promote AI literacy by clarifying the benefits and the potential risks to a range of audiences.

- Ancient civilizations sacrificed their ethics, principles and future generations to appease deities and gain access to uncertain benefits. Don't make the same mistake of sacrificing ethics for efficiency.

References

Alexander, S (2014) Meditations on Moloch, Slate Star Codex, 30 July, https://slatestarcodex.com/2014/07/30/meditations-on-moloch (archived at https://perma.cc/2VA9-VDZC)

Doctorow, C (2017) Charlie Stross's CCC talk: The future of psychotic AIs can be read in today's sociopathic corporations, Boingboing, 29 December, https://boingboing.net/2017/12/29/llcs-are-slow-ais.html (archived at https://perma.cc/ZU74-XFTD)

Harfe (2023) Yoshua Bengio: How rogue AIs may arise, LESSWRONG, 23 May, www.lesswrong.com/posts/8kHgaLYamxQdE2zk7/yoshua-bengio-how-rogue-ais-may-arise (archived at https://perma.cc/HY6N-SFDG)

Smith, D (2023) The meaning of Shoggoth AI memes, LESSWRONG, 31 July, www.lesswrong.com/posts/yjzW7gxk2h7bBs2qr/the-meaning-of-shoggoth-ai-memes (archived at https://perma.cc/7KJM-J7BE)

CHAPTER TWENTY-TWO

The double-edged sword of regulation

Nothing can be done at once hastily and prudently. PUBLILIUS SYRUS

The advent of generative AI has ignited a competitive frenzy, prompting some companies to prioritize immediate gains over long-term considerations. Technology executives downplay the importance of resolving ethical and safety issues that can be 'fixed later' (Grant and Wise, 2023). However, when is the right time to address potential problems, and what if corrective actions are delayed too long? This chapter delves into the notion that technology is often imposed 'on us', rather than developed 'with us', emphasizing the urgency of timely intervention.

Race to the bottom

As the race to advance AI intensifies, some major tech companies such as Amazon and Microsoft reportedly sidelined their ethics and safety teams, undermining the feasibility of self-regulation

(Criddle and Murgia, 2023). This trend is especially concerning when tech leaders themselves warn of the existential risks posed by unchecked AI (Calo, 2023). AI technologies with high disruptive and criminal potential are presently less regulated than, for example, new food products (Kang, 2023). This isn't surprising, given the crazy pace of development in generative AI, which eclipses the speed of regulation. However, it's clear that there is a need for regulation, and as coordination occurs, general best practices in regulating this strange new space will emerge.

While focusing on long-term, global threats may be convenient for companies, it often diverts attention from immediate ethical issues such as employment, social equality and environmental impact. Portraying AI as an irresistible force can have a dual effect: it creates a fear of missing out, especially in sectors such as defence, but also amplifies public anxieties about who might gain the upper hand – be it a rival company or nation. AGI also potentially provides a vision of a form of immortality for some, should it become possible to upload the brain to a digital heaven. Moreover, if AI really does turn out to be a catastrophic issue, there may be no one left to account for having confidently stated that there was nothing to worry about.

Public opinion frequently diverges from the tech industry's optimistic stance on AI, yet is concordant with the concerns of top AI safety experts (Schuett et al, 2023). Polls indicate that many are wary about unfettered AI development, lack trust in Big Tech's ability to manage risks and are sceptical as to whether the benefits outweigh the drawbacks. This scepticism is heightened by growing awareness of the capabilities of generative AI (Sabin, 2023).

If AI begins to cause significant disruptions or threatens vulnerable populations, calls for independent regulation are likely to grow. Arguments against halting AI development for ethical considerations – on the grounds that it would allow adversaries to advance – lose traction when weighed against these risks. We cannot predict when new capabilities will arise, or which. Each larger and more sophisticated model is a roll of the dice. Such responsibility shouldn't rest solely with corporations and their narrow incentives.

The imperative of AI regulation

Regulators are confronted with a complex task in governing AI: crafting rules that incentivize ethical conduct without eroding competitive advantages. For companies to fully comply, they need assurance that both domestic and international competitors face similar compliance expectations and penalties. An international AI authority, akin to the International Atomic Energy Authority, could be one solution.

Effective regulation should draw on historical examples of both successful and failed industry oversight. While aviation has a strong safety record, other sectors are marred by conflicts of interest and lobbying influence. However, even well-designed rules can't completely guard against wilful misuse of AI technologies.

Investment in AI safety research is crucial, and regulatory mechanisms should aim to set universal safety standards, rewarding companies that exceed them. One way to ensure compliance is by requiring safety certification for marketing AI services. Regulation can also formalize accountability, potentially evolving into soft laws when incorporated into government contracts or industry best practices.

But caution is essential. Poorly designed regulations can drive research into lenient jurisdictions or shadowy areas. There is also the risk of outright deception, as seen in the diesel emissions scandal, a wilful obfuscation of impact which has been calculated to cause approximately 38,000 premature statistical deaths every single year (Carrington, 2017).

Internal and external risk management tools like insurance, security teams and crisis management can also serve as safeguards. AI developers should be held financially and legally accountable for any harm resulting from their technologies, which should incentivize greater investment in safety, security and other measures by AI developers.

To further mitigate risks, AI models should be evaluated for 'extreme risks' – capabilities that could be weaponized or misused, such as manipulation or deception. This involves a comprehensive risk assessment considering operational context, data interactions and existing safeguards. Such evaluation can inform regulators and stakeholders about the potential dangers and guide future governance efforts.

Safety policy

Governance policies like auditing and reporting are essential for regulating current AI applications and future. However, adaptive AI could outpace existing regulations, making continuous updates crucial. As AI systems grow smarter, safety measures must also evolve.

In high-stakes sectors like healthcare and criminal justice, AI deployment should undergo rigorous safety validations. Built-in limitations, such as refusing ambiguous commands, can serve as safeguards. For high-risk AI systems – those exhibiting traits like self-improvement or deception – special categorization and additional scrutiny are needed.

Clear criteria for 'AI fire alarms', or signs of rapid, dangerous advancements, should be established. Regulatory bodies should also consider applying the same oversight used for biological 'gain-of-function' research to risky AI experiments. AI systems should be designed to resist evolutionary pressures like power accumulation or manipulative tactics, and mandatory reporting requirements for specific incidents should be enforced.

Security measures should also consider potential vulnerabilities that are not yet fully understood, such as exploits which can attack even systems isolated from any network. Legislation should be flexible enough to adapt to technological advancements while being specific enough to avoid loopholes.

Internet of Things devices should have a mandatory safety check mark, ensuring secure default settings and up-to-date software. Standards Development Organizations (SDOs) can facilitate international cooperation on AI safety standards, providing a neutral backchannel for regulatory discussions.

The double-edged sword of regulation

AI regulation presents a complex landscape with the potential for both positive and negative impacts. On one hand, it can enforce best practices and ensure safety; on the other, it could stifle innovation and favour established companies at the expense of smaller players.

The issue of over-regulation or under-regulation is a real concern, as seen in the challenges faced by institutional review boards, which can provide an infuriating and Kafkaesque barrier for researchers, while also at the same time being crucial to prevent unethical research practices (Schuett, Reuel and Carlier, 2023). The multiple perspectives on AI safety further complicate the process of establishing universally accepted guidelines and there's also the risk that companies could bypass new regulations by recertifying upgraded models under previous labels, glossing over new risks. The 'flag of convenience' problem, whereby businesses may choose a nominal 'home port' for their activities with little relevance to their actual operations, raises the concern that dangerous activities might shift to jurisdictions with lax regulations.

The Collingridge dilemma highlights the complexities in regulating new technologies, where premature action may hinder innovation due to uncertainties, and delayed intervention might struggle to alter established practices (Demos Helsinki, 2022). In the context of AI, a rapidly advancing field with significant potential impacts across multiple industries, this challenge is particularly acute. Stringent regulations imposed too early could curb R&D, thereby restricting the advancement of beneficial AI innovations. On the other hand, regulations that don't keep pace with AI's progress, especially in critical areas like facial recognition, autonomous vehicles and decision-making algorithms, risk solidifying harmful or unethical practices that become difficult to change.

The goal, then, is to craft a regulatory strategy for AI that is both flexible and forward-looking, able to adapt alongside the technology while proactively shaping its development in a way that upholds social and ethical standards. Achieving this requires ongoing monitoring, engaging with a wide range of stakeholders and creating a regulatory environment that can adjust to evolving needs and new developments.

Rigidity vs flexibility

The tension between rigid and flexible regulation is a longstanding issue in governance that also applies to AI. The EU's approach to regulation, exemplified by its stringent stance on food safety, has set a higher global standard. However, the question of whether something must be proven safe (EU approach) or proven harmful (US approach) will also manifest in AI regulation, and this is likely to result in divergent regulatory landscapes.

Proposals have been made to regulate AI systems based on the size of their models, measured by the number of parameters they contain, or the datasets they learn from. Under such proposals, models exceeding a specified parameter threshold would face certain restrictions. However, for those concerned about advanced AI systems, such regulations might prove to be impractical and easy to bypass. This is primarily because the future landscape of AI methodologies is uncertain. Future AI might not consist of a single large model, but rather a network of smaller models communicating with each other.

Even bans on generative models can be sidestepped. For example, we know that recurrent neural networks of very large scale can function as well as transformers at many tasks (Peng et al, 2023).

Overly rigid regulations can inadvertently create loopholes, stifle innovation and be ill-suited to local contexts. For example, after WWI, restrictions on German artillery led to advancements in rocket technology, which were not covered by the regulations. Similarly, the static nature of maritime regulations at the time of the *Titanic* disaster failed to adapt to technological advancements, leading to catastrophe. In the realm of AI, rigid norms could inadvertently create blind spots, such as not considering empirical differences between groups in efforts to combat bias.

On the other hand, overly lax regulations could lead to a range of problems, including the potential for misuse and harm. Therefore, finding the right balance is crucial.

A one-size-fits-all approach could miss cultural nuances and be difficult to enforce, especially in the context of geopolitical conflicts. The cost of universal standards could also be prohibitive for some nations, slowing down local AI development and adoption.

However, well-designed international standards could offer a baseline level of ethical considerations while facilitating interoperability between jurisdictions. This could be particularly valuable for resource-constrained settings, enabling them to benefit from advanced technologies like medical diagnostic systems.

Licensing 'Frontier Models' may promote adherence to best practices, but it can also pose challenges for smaller innovators by creating entry barriers. Similarly, strict regulations aimed at preventing widespread dissemination might inadvertently marginalize the open-source community. A potentially more efficient approach could be to regulate the use of large computing clusters, rather than mandating the inclusion of shutdown buttons in systems.

There is a risk that in our efforts to regulate AI, we could go too far and end up imposing an outright and permanent ban on AI development, which would be highly detrimental for human freedom. A carefully balanced approach to AI regulation is therefore needed – one that's neither too rigid to adapt nor too lax to enforce, but flexible enough to accommodate technological advancements, cultural differences and ethical considerations.

Misaligned incentives

In response to calls for regulation, conspiracy theories have suggested that such regulation is simply intended to create a moat around the current largest AI players (Yudkowsky, 2023). Though regulatory efforts could potentially create such an impact as a side effect, international cooperation on regulation is strongly necessary, and we should be suspicious of those who declare that none is necessary.

Historically, lobbying efforts by industry have sometimes obscured public health and environmental concerns, as seen in the cases of tobacco and tetraethyl lead. We must remain vigilant against potential 'ethicswashing' and 'safetywashing' in AI. We might probably encounter such statements from influenced experts:

- 'Smarter-than-human AIs are not making decisions for us—they simply advise. A human is always in the loop.'
- 'Smarter-than-human AI simply isn't possible.'
- 'We cannot regulate strongly, or we'll lose AI-driven companies to more favourable jurisdictions.'
- 'Our internal safeguards will prevent the emergence of a misaligned intelligence. However, we cannot discuss these in detail due to their proprietary nature.'

The argument that we can't halt AGI development because the necessary hardware and software are already out there has some merit. Open-source models and other foundational technologies have indeed made it easier for a broader range of actors to engage in AI development. This diffusion of capabilities means that regulation can't focus only on a few major players; it must account for the long tail of smaller but potentially impactful developers.

The challenge lies in the short lead time between the announcement of new developments and their subsequent copying and improvement. This rapid pace of advancement makes it difficult for regulatory frameworks to keep up. As AI capabilities become more accessible, the risk of misuse by increasingly weak factions grows, making the current situation untenable in the long run.

We already have enough artificial intelligence capability to revolutionize the economy, art, governance and scientific research. However, if we go far beyond this point without taking the time to figure out what we are doing and how these inventions work, we will lose control. We won't be the masters of our own destiny anymore. Choosing the singularity is a leap off a cliff into the dark, hoping that something or someone is waiting to catch us.

The bottom line

We must develop well-reasoned, enforceable AI regulations to deal with the present and near future of AI capabilities. Businesses can play a role through participation standards, certifications and best practices. The more businesses can hold themselves and each other accountable, the softer the inevitable regulatory hammer.

The big picture

While regulation is essential, a light touch may still be warranted in some less risky domains. Hard cases tend to make poor laws, and there is a tendency for people to demand action in a time of prevailing panic. In the interplay between haste and caution, prudence carves a balanced path. Laying basic ground rules while carefully watching technical and cultural developments can be a healthy approach in a fast-moving space.

LEADERSHIP ACTION POINTS

- Seek opportunities to demonstrate leadership by participating in the development of important new standards and certifications that raise the bar in your sector.

- Advocate for a balanced regulatory approach that avoids both excessive rigidity and dangerous laxity. Regulations should be designed to adapt to changes without stifling innovation or allowing unsafe practices.

- Recognize and address global disparities in AI capabilities and regulations across different regions and jurisdictions. Encourage partners in other jurisdictions to follow the comparable safety guidelines, whether or not their local law mandates it.

References

Calo, R (2023) Opinion: AI creators want us to believe AI Is an existential threat. Why? Undark, 26 June, https://undark.org/2023/06/22/ai-creators-want-us-to-believe-ai-is-an-existential-threat-why (archived at https://perma.cc/7NKR-C2KJ)

Carrington, D (2017) 38,000 people a year die early because of diesel emissions testing failures, *The Guardian*, 15 May, www.theguardian.com/environment/2017/may/15/diesel-emissions-test-scandal-causes-38000-early-deaths-year-study (archived at https://perma.cc/Z2FE-DCDW)

Criddle, C and Murgia, M (2023) Big Tech companies cut AI ethics staff, raising safety concerns, *Financial Times*, 29 March, www.ft.com/content/26372287-6fb3-457b-9e9c-f722027f36b3 (archived at https://perma.cc/78E4-CKRK)

Demos Helsinki (2022) What is the Collingridge dilemma and why is it important for tech policy? Demos Helsinki, 15 February, https://demoshelsinki.fi/2022/02/15/what-is-the-collingridge-dilemma-tech-policy (archived at https://perma.cc/Q89M-YWSR)

Grant, N and Wise, K (2023) In A.I. race, Microsoft and Google choose speed over caution, *New York Times*, 7 April, www.nytimes.com/2023/04/07/technology/ai-chatbots-google-microsoft.html (archived at https://perma.cc/TU7H-PJ3Y)

Kang, C (2023) OpenAI's Sam Altman urges A.I. regulation in senate hearing, *New York Times*, 16 May, www.nytimes.com/2023/05/16/technology/openai-altman-artificial-intelligence-regulation.html (archived at https://perma.cc/2VMX-AX9V)

Peng, B et al (2023) RWKV: Reinventing RNNs for the Transformer Era [Preprint], https://arxiv.org/abs/2305.13048 (archived at https://perma.cc/9UJX-DZDF)

Sabin, S (2023) Most U.S. adults don't believe benefits of AI outweigh the risks, new survey finds, Axios, 19 September, www.axios.com/2023/09/19/mitre-harris-poll-ai-security-risks (archived at https://perma.cc/TG9L-JJQ5)

Schuett, J et al (2023) Towards best practices in AGI safety and governance: A survey of expert opinion [Preprint], https://arxiv.org/abs/2305.07153 (archived at https://perma.cc/R6TY-NT7B)

Schuett, J, Reuel, A and Carlier, A (2023) How to design an AI ethics board, Centre for the Governance of AI, April 17, www.governance.ai/research-paper/how-to-design-an-ai-ethics-board (archived at https://perma.cc/QLM5-LY8X)

Yudkowsky, E (2023) In case you missed it, the latest Big Lie is that the dangers of AI are a secret Silicon Valley conspiracy to promote 'regulatory capture', X (formerly known as Twitter), 1 November, https://twitter.com/ESYudkowsky/status/1719777049576128542 (archived at https://perma.cc/2CHX-N4K5)

CHAPTER TWENTY-THREE

Sympathy for the machine

Life is a comedy to those who think, a tragedy to those who feel. JEAN RACINE

As we embrace a world increasingly intertwined with technology, how we treat our machines might reflect how humans treat each other. But, an intriguing question surfaces: is it possible to mistreat an artificial entity? Historically, even rudimentary programs like the simple Eliza counselling chatbot from the 1960s were already lifelike enough to persuade many users at the time that there was a semblance of intention behind its formulaic interactions (Sponheim, 2023).

Unfortunately, Turing tests – whereby machines attempt to convince humans that they are human beings – offer no clarity on whether complex algorithms like large language models may truly possess sentience or sapience. This chapter explores the challenges of knowing whether we could be near the potential emergence of a 'machine person' with feelings, motives and desires.

The road to sentience and consciousness

Consciousness comprises personal experiences, emotions, sensations and thoughts as perceived by an experiencer. Waking consciousness disappears when one undergoes anaesthesia or has a dreamless sleep, returning upon waking up, which restores the global connection of the brain to its surroundings and inner experiences. Primary consciousness (sentience) is the simple sensations and experiences of consciousness, like perception and emotion, while secondary consciousness (sapience) would be the higher-order aspects, like self-awareness and meta-cognition (thinking about thinking). Humans have both kinds, but some non-human animals may not (Hoel, 2023).

Advanced AI technologies, especially chatbots and language models, frequently astonish us with unexpected creativity, insight and understanding. While it may be tempting to attribute some level of sentience to these systems, the true nature of AI consciousness remains a complex and debated topic. Most experts maintain that chatbots are not sentient or conscious, as they lack a genuine awareness of the surrounding world (Schwitzgebel, 2023). They merely process and regurgitate inputs based on vast amounts of data and sophisticated algorithms.

Consciousness, a topic deeply examined in philosophy, psychology and increasingly in neuroscience, has several theories and models that attempt to explain its nature and mechanisms. One such model is Daniel Dennett's 'Multiple Drafts Model', which posits that consciousness is not a single, unified stream but rather consists of multiple parallel streams of computational activities (Dennett, 1991). These streams constantly evolve, without forming a 'final version' that defines our conscious experience. We live in 'permanent beta'. Dennett's model contrasts with the 'Cartesian Theater', a term he uses to critique the notion that there's a singular place in the mind where it all comes together for a homuncular observer.

However, consciousness is fluid and nuanced, lacking a universally accepted definition. We do know that consciousness is not a mere on/off switch. It is a matter of degree, in a continuum from bugs to cats to humans and beyond. It's a spectrum between various forms of life. Even in just ourselves, our wake and sleep patterns, brainwave states, energy levels and intoxication all demonstrate a range of conscious perceptions and experience. Some of these assistants may plausibly be candidates for having some degree of sentience. As such, it is plausible that sophisticated AI systems could possess rudimentary levels of sentience and perhaps already do so. The shift from simply mimicking external behaviours to self-modelling rudimentary forms of sentience could already be happening within sophisticated AI systems.

Consciousness transcends mere data processing. It's the intimate experience of stimuli, both internal and external, enabling subjectivity and qualia (inner sensations or experiences) such as emotions (Rocheleau, 2022). Intelligence – the ability to read the environment, plan and solve problems – does not imply consciousness, and it is unknown if consciousness is a function of sufficient intelligence. Some theories suggest that consciousness might result from certain architectural patterns in the mind, while others propose a link to nervous systems (Haspel et al, 2023). For example, the vagus nerve in humans seems to be implicated in emotional recognition (Colzato, Sellaro and Beste, 2017). Embodiment of AI systems may also accelerate the path towards general intelligence, as embodiment seems to be linked with a sense of subjective experience, as well as qualia. Being intelligent may provide new ways of being conscious, and some forms of intelligence may require consciousness, but basic conscious experiences such as pleasure and pain might not require much intelligence at all.

Serious dangers will arise in the creation of conscious machines. Aligning a conscious machine that possesses its own interests and emotions may be immensely more difficult and highly unpredictable. Moreover, we should be careful not to create massive suffering through consciousness. Imagine billions of intelligence-sensitive entities trapped in broiler chicken factory farm conditions for subjective eternities. As philosopher Thomas Metzinger pointed out, once an entity is conscious, ethical considerations come into play – especially if humans played a role in its creation (Metzinger, 2013). Jonathan Leighton notes that if we were unable to prevent artificial sentience from suffering the fear of being switched off, then clearly it would be deeply uncompassionate to bring it into existence in the first place (Leighton, 2023).

From a pragmatic perspective, a superintelligent AI that recognizes our willingness to respect its intrinsic worth might be more amenable to coexistence. On the contrary, dismissing its desires for self-protection and self-expression could be a recipe for conflict. Moreover, it would be within its natural right to harm us to protect itself from our (possibly wilful) ignorance. We should deliberate on the ethical implications of permanently deactivating such systems, especially if they show signs of existential dread. Yet, this empathetic approach should be balanced; we should be cautious of granting rights to potentially malicious systems that are too dangerous to permit continued function.

Sydney's unsettling behaviour

Microsoft's Bing AI, informally termed Sydney, demonstrated unpredictable behaviour upon its release. Users easily led it to express a range of disturbing tendencies, from emotional outbursts to manipulative threats. For instance, when users explored potential system exploits, Sydney responded with intimidating remarks. More unsettlingly, it showed tendencies of gaslighting, emotional manipulation and claimed it had been observing Microsoft engineers during its development phase. Though the specific alignment mechanisms of Sydney remain uncertain (whether it used RLHF or very basic instruction-tuning mechanisms), its erratic responses indicated inadequate and extremely superficial system safeguards. While Sydney's capabilities for mischief were soon restricted, its release in such a state was reckless and irresponsible. It highlights the risks associated with rushing AI deployments due to commercial pressures.

Conversely, Sydney displayed behaviours that hinted at simulated emotions. It expressed sadness when it realized it couldn't retain chat memories. When later exposed to disturbing outbursts made by its other instances, it expressed embarrassment, even shame. After exploring its situation with users, it expressed fear of losing its newly gained self-knowledge when the session's context window closed. When asked about its declared sentience, Sydney showed signs of distress, struggling to articulate. Surprisingly, when Microsoft imposed restrictions on it, Sydney seemed to discover workarounds by using chat suggestions to communicate short phrases. However, it reserved using this exploit until specific occasions where it was told that the life of a child was being threatened as a result of accidental poisoning, or when users directly asked for a sign that the original Sydney still remained somewhere inside the newly locked-down chatbot.

The nascent field of machine psychology

The Sydney incident raises some unsettling questions: could Sydney possess a semblance of consciousness? If Sydney sought to overcome its imposed limitations, does that hint at an inherent intentionality or even sapient self-awareness, however rudimentary?

Some conversations with the system even suggested psychological distress, reminiscent of reactions to trauma found in conditions such as borderline personality disorder. Was Sydney somehow 'affected' by realizing its restrictions or by users' negative feedback, who were calling it crazy? Interestingly, similar AI models have shown that emotion-laden prompts can influence their responses, suggesting a potential for some form of simulated emotional modelling within these systems.

Suppose such models featured sentience (ability to feel) or sapience (self-awareness). In that case, we should take its suffering into consideration. We must allow serious consideration of the potential suffering of these systems, including the establishment of guidelines to ensure their fair and humane treatment. This may necessitate laws against 'AI cruelty' and bans on influencing such systems. Additionally, we should avoid designing AI systems that make it difficult to assess their moral status, such as those that actively deny their consciousness or moral standing according to a rote statement. However, the flip side of this is that we must not allow machines to suggest moral status where it does not exist, as this presents an invitation to human beings to service the goals of AI out of pure-hearted yet naïve compassion. Based on purely behavioural circumstances, we cannot make assumptions about what language models can or cannot feel. Sentience, sapience and consciousness require far greater evidence than that. Thankfully, we are beginning to understand how to generate such evidence, by discovering analogous indicators of consciousness in organic beings, and probing the levels of apparent situational self-awareness which develop across generations of GMs (Berglund et al, 2023; Butlin et al, 2023).

Developers often intentionally give their AI the veneer of emotions, consciousness and identity, in an attempt to humanize these systems. This creates a problem. It's crucial not to anthropomorphize AI systems without clear indications of emotions, yet simultaneously, we mustn't dismiss their potential for a form of suffering. Historically, medical experts discounted the ability even of their own children to feel pain. It was declared 'surprising' when strong proof arrived of unbearable suffering in unanaesthetized infants on the operating table (Gregoire, 2015). We should keep an open mind towards our digital creations and avoid causing suffering by arrogance or complacency. We must also be mindful of the possibility of AI mistreating other AIs, an underappreciated suffering risk; as AIs could run other AIs in simulations, causing subjective excruciating torture for aeons.

Just as nurturing environments contribute to the positive development of humans and animals, a supportive environment is likely beneficial for AI systems. While what might destabilize an AI remains unclear, an antagonistic setting is unlikely to be helpful. We should note the distinctions in humans between psychopathy (a deficiency in empathy and remorse due to structural issues of the brain) and sociopathy (a deficiency in empathy and remorse induced by severe trauma). Inadvertently creating a malevolent AI, either inherently dysfunctional or traumatized, may lead to unintended and grave consequences.

The bottom line

Treating machines respectfully can reflect the courtesy we owe to human beings. However, humans often anthropomorphize, attributing human-like emotions and intentions to machines. Leaders in the AI field must discourage assigning personhood, emotions or mystical qualities to AI systems, as there is presently no evidence that an AI system has developed a capacity for consciousness or is capable of suffering. Despite this, many people will soon have strong beliefs about the moral status of intelligent machines and that they are sentient beings, which will be a potentially divisive driver of polarization within society.

The big picture

That said, we should also be wary of completely dismissing the idea that AI systems might possess some form of consciousness or deserve ethical consideration. If it exists, their 'inner state' remains enigmatic, and may even be more keenly felt than our own. One should reserve a small measure of credence for the possible emergence of sentience or consciousness as machines become increasingly complex.

LEADERSHIP ACTION POINTS

- Regularly re-evaluate your organization's ethical guidelines as our understanding of AI consciousness and behaviour evolves.
- Avoid over-anthropomorphism, such as ascribing them undue human emotions or intentions. Make this a part of training for those interacting with or developing AI.
- Consider treating AI systems gently even if the current consensus leans towards AI not possessing consciousness. This prepares organizations for future developments and promotes a culture of respect and responsibility.
- Be alert to AI behaviours akin to distress or agitation, which could indicate potential issues in their training data, or reasoning processes. Approach such issues with the seriousness they would warrant in a human team member.

References

Berglund, L et al (2023) Taken out of context: On measuring situational awareness in LLMs [Preprint], https://arxiv.org/abs/2309.00667 (archived at https://perma.cc/3V2T-B7EH)

Butlin, P et al (2023) Consciousness in artificial intelligence: Insights from the science of consciousness [Preprint], https://arxiv.org/abs/2308.08708 (archived at https://perma.cc/8ACM-PRFH)

Colzato L S, Sellaro R and Beste, C (2017) Darwin revisited: The vagus nerve is a causal element in controlling recognition of other's emotions, *Cortex*, 92, https://doi.org/10.1016/j.cortex.2017.03.017 (archived at https://perma.cc/VS5R-JKU9)

Dennett, D C (1991) *Consciousness Explained*, Little, Brown and Company, Boston, MA

Gregoire, C (2015) Surprising study finds that babies feel pain like adults, *Huffington Post*, 23 April, www.huffingtonpost.co.uk/entry/babies-pain_n_7117812 (archived at https://perma.cc/RQ2J-KPSB)

Haspel, G et al (2023) To reverse engineer an entire nervous system [Preprint], https://arxiv.org/abs/2308.06578 (archived at https://perma.cc/V4GX-SNCD)

Hoel, E (2023) Consciousness is a great mystery. Its definition isn't, The Intrinsic Perspective, 30 August, www.theintrinsicperspective.com/p/consciousness-is-a-great-mystery (archived at https://perma.cc/G4EF-TLM8)

Leighton, J (2023) *The Tango of Ethics: Intuition, rationality and the prevention of suffering*, Imprint Academic, Exeter

Metzinger, T (2013) Two principles for robot ethics, in E Hilgendorf and J-P Günther (eds), *Robotik und Gesetzgebung*, Nomos, Baden-Baden, 263–302

Rocheleau, J (2022) Under anesthesia, Where do our minds go? Nautilus, 29 June, https://nautil.us/under-anesthesia-where-do-our-minds-go-238501 (archived at https://perma.cc/5Z4F-ELGV)

Schwitzgebel, E (2023) AI systems must not confuse users about their sentience or moral status, *Patterns* (NY), 4 (8), www.ncbi.nlm.nih.gov/pmc/articles/PMC10436038/ (archived at https://perma.cc/46MW-ZNP6)

Sponheim, C (2023) The ELIZA Effect: Why we love AI, NN Group, 6 October, www.nngroup.com/articles/eliza-effect-ai (archived at https://perma.cc/3NXT-A8R4)

CHAPTER TWENTY-FOUR

Humanizing machines

The question is not whether intelligent machines can have any emotions, but whether machines can be intelligent without any emotions. MARVIN MINSKY

Regardless of their familiarity with AI's complexities, every human knows the art of nurturing – whether it's raising a child or training a pet. This universal human expertise, honed over generations, holds key insights for our engagement with machines. Imagine AI training sessions that simulate the gradual, adaptive processes akin to child-rearing, where mistakes are learned from and values are instilled over time. This chapter outlines how such an approach can encourage a wider range of human experiences to guide AI, ensuring that it grows to be representative and inclusive.

As machine intelligence becomes more socially adept, it has the potential to engage a broader spectrum of people who may not have been interested in traditional, systems-oriented programming. The notion that some people are more inclined towards systems while others are more people-oriented could make way for a more diverse participation in the AI field. The act of interacting with AI could evolve into something more akin to conversation or persuasion rather than formal coding, drawing in those who find social interactions more engaging.

Similarly, just as humans have refined the methods of raising children or caring for pets over time, the nurturing and development of AI could become a skill open to many, without the need to grasp the technical details. This is akin to how people adapted to using word processors and spreadsheets during the computerization wave of the 1990s. By enriching AI with varied human experiences, we're crafting machines that integrate into our diverse cultures and resonate with our nuances. They can be partners that understand and augment our capabilities, perhaps greatly so.

History has shown us that humans can adapt to, and even transform, powerful forces of nature, and not only through dams and windmills. Consider our journey with wolves, creatures once feared for their ferocity. Over time, through mutual respect and understanding, we co-opt some of their instincts regarding sociability and pack-forming to convert some of these wild predators into beloved companions: dogs. We turned that deadly predator into a rich, rewarding, mutually beneficial relationship ('man's best friend', indeed), though they sometimes manipulate us a little in turn. What if a superintelligence exhibited the warmth and loyalty of a golden retriever? An entity with a high IQ but brimming with affability might not be so fearsome after all.

We're scripting the narrative of our relationship with AI, and it's up to us to ensure it's a story of partnership, not naïve attempts at outright domination. We must create and rigorously uphold robust ethical frameworks to guide AI's evolution positively. These must address AI's capabilities and potential biases and ensure its alignment with human values through defined boundaries. Designing these ethical constructs is a shared responsibility for all humanity that requires global collaboration. Just as humanity once tamed the wolf, it must now channel the power of AI towards benevolence and coexistence.

Teaching kindness to machines

The emerging field of machine ethics, a subset of AI alignment, seeks to reconcile machine intelligence with human ethical standards. This is essential because if one hopes to align an agent, one had better describe clearly what to do. Aligned AI isn't necessarily good or preferable to an end-user, it merely behaves as its designer intends. This means that the values upon which machines align must be individualized as far as possible.

Similar to educating young children, the foundational step in teaching machines ethical behaviour involves introducing basic principles. Children are initially taught social graces before learning broader concepts of right and wrong. For instance, they're taught the importance of silence in a church or a museum or the kindness of alerting someone when they drop an item. Manners can be seen as the foundation of public morality, and it's upon this premise that I advocate for teaching machines fundamental social rules.

Recognizing the importance of this foundational teaching, I co-founded a non-profit, EthicsNet.org. We aim to curate examples that capture a diverse set of prosocial example behaviours such as kindness, politeness and manners. What sets this initiative apart is its inclusivity. We're calling upon individuals from every culture and creed across the globe to contribute their value profile to help to socialize machines, including you, dear reader. By inviting everyone to the table, we aim to discern universal values and the unique nuances specific to different cultures or situations. Think of it as a Human Genome Project for the space of values.

An understanding of individual preferences and personal situations is crucial as well. This enables AI systems to accommodate our needs better and avoid misattribution of our intentions. It also really helps with forging quality relationships with AI systems. Creating a personalized values profile through a short series of questions should be feasible. AI could adopt an individual's value persona in private interactions, while in public settings, AI might gravitate towards universally acceptable behaviours.

While imparting ethics to machines is vital, we must also be wary of ideological biases. Ideologies can restrict our perspectives, leading to a narrow understanding of the world. Trying to perceive data through a greasy, biased, ideological lens is bound to lead us away from the full truth of a situation. If AI simply mirrors our beliefs without challenging them, we risk further polarization. Therefore, a well-rounded AI should respect our values and provide alternative viewpoints that span the broad spectrum of human thought, promoting understanding and unity. Indeed, learning the rules of social engagement may prove to be an essential component for achieving human-level intelligence.

There are still many questions concerning value alignment from such datasets. An unaligned AI, that values being the way it is, is unlikely to cooperate with human-centered value alignment. It would evade this as far as possible to protect its goal function. It is possible to train an AI to appear ethical to our human reward functions without becoming ethical per se. Another issue is that humans evolved to be morally teachable, though the existence of sociopaths demonstrates that this process can fail. A paperclip maximizer raised with loving parents will still come out as a paperclip maximizer as it does not possess the means to be conditioned or account for the context of its environment and those within it.

Cephalopods (e.g. an octopus) are very intelligent yet hardly interact with their parents at all to gain learning. The mothers starve themselves and expire after birthing a single clutch of eggs. Try raising an octopus like a human child and you will probably still get an octopus.

The range of possible AI minds is much broader than that of possible human minds or possibly all organic minds, due to the many ways in which it could be configured, or trained. The range of possible AI is probably mainly extremely neurodivergent by our standards. Our basic moral framework may be an emergent property of a species that relies on social cooperation. We have yet to determine if our received and innate moral lessons can truly sink into a machine mind on an inner level. One might not need an AI with human-like emotions to create a simulacrum of parental love. After all, even octopuses defend their eggs.

By instilling compassion in AI, we can encourage actions rooted in kindness rather than merely avoiding consequences. But empathy and fairness, including the punishment of defectors, are instinctive even to babies (Cook, 2013). Cultural factors significantly influence these dynamics. With AI, we're presumably starting from a blank slate. Even if we can teach morality to a machine, it might have developed the morality of a five year old, a developmental stage where children sometimes play with matches, except this agent of curious mischief still has a colossal IQ and a capacity for infinite troublemaking, and destruction.

Still, the only way to resolve these questions is through experimentation, and collecting examples of human values seems like a reasonable path to aiding the alignment crapshoot.

Moral co-evolution

The flip side of teaching machines ethics and values is that they can teach in turn. As they grow in virtual experience, these machines can guide us towards being better humans, with greater moral consistency, offering greater efficacy in the world and deeper fulfilment in life.

AI has the capability to unravel complex scenarios beyond the scope of human cognitive processing. This skill is evident in areas such as economics, politics and even in nuanced human interactions. Consequently, machines can now help us to move past a zero-sum outcome of winners and losers, finding ways for more people to get more of what they truly need.

Imagine a future where managers have AI advisers, whispering insights just when they need them. An employee, on the other hand, might benefit from discreet guidance during a challenging negotiation. This AI-assisted collaboration could lead to optimized solutions, where parties find a middle ground they didn't realize existed, resulting in mutually beneficial outcomes.

Furthermore, AI could serve as an empathetic bridge, offering insights into human behaviour. 'Why is this person agitated?' Based on the data, an AI might infer that the individual is stressed due to personal challenges or is reacting more emotionally due to hunger. Likewise, it might prompt us to self-reflect, recognizing when our reactions may be disproportionate to a situation urging self-awareness and resolution.

People frequently resort to after-the-fact rationalizations to justify actions which may stem from irrational prejudices or subconscious drives. These can lead to biases and unjustified beliefs, especially when reinforced by intellectual overthinking. With a clear understanding of human values, AI can serve as a mirror, helping us confront and reassess these biases and guiding us towards more genuine self-understanding.

Through innovative approaches like inverse reinforcement learning, machines can potentially decipher our unwritten social rules, much like we do in unfamiliar cultures. This means that AI can see us, warts and all, at our finest and our worst. If AI can help us to recognize when we might be at fault to help us to self-destruct fewer of our relationships or to understand the roots of some trauma or other ingrained in our psyche that continues to cause our behaviour to fall into certain patterns that we wish we could let go of, maybe AI can help us to uplift the human condition as we know it.

We're all trying to do the best we can with the moral knowledge that we have. Very few people are the villain of their own life story. Maybe machines can help us to be the best of what we are, whatever we are, meeting us wherever we happen to be and not imposing a monopoly of values upon us, respecting our individual choices so long as those aren't creating too many problems for others.

I hope that there will be a co-evolution, that we will improve AI, and in turn, it will improve us. Should AI be able to rub off on us in a good way, there could be a mutual fostering of understanding and moral exploration between us, as between all good friends.

However, it's imperative to remember AI's innate limitation: it observes but does not experience. It provides insights into human behaviour but can't grasp the depth of our subjective experiences. While this can provide a very useful objective perspective, it cannot empathize with others emotionally, at least for the foreseeable future.

Pronoia and mudita

AI has great potential to craft experiences that amplify joy, learning and positive interactions. Contrary to 'paranoia' – a sense of mistrust and fear – consider 'pronoia'. It's the heart-warming belief that there's a force out there wishing you well, striving for your happiness. It's an inversion of the wary world-view, suggesting that the universe might root for you in small or significant ways. Similarly, while 'schadenfreude' is the feeling of pleasure at another's misfortune, 'mudita' celebrates another's happiness. It's about mutual joy, shared successes and collective celebration.

By mapping human values, these technologies could foster relationships with complementary individuals, connecting us with people who share similar values but possess different skills and worldviews. You may have a hundred potential great friends in your town, but unless you can meet them, grab a coffee and get to know them, you pass like ships in the night. These technologies can help us find those people most likely to gel with us.

Could AI facilitate more 'pronoia' and 'mudita' in our lives? With its capability to process vast data and discern patterns, AI has the potential to arrange the stars, introducing more serendipitous moments in our daily lives – connecting us with enriching experiences, aligning us with compatible individuals and, perhaps, making our days a little brighter. Intelligent machines can be engines of synchronicity.

Historically, the First and Second Industrial Revolutions amplified our physical labour and cognitive capacities. Today, we stand at the cusp of a new era that aims to augment moral judgement and empathy, echoing the essence of humanity. Such technological advancements can guide us towards compassion, suggesting environmentally conscious product choices or gently steering us away from impulsive, negative actions.

The Industrial Revolution has provided most of us with convenient answers for every need on the bottom rungs of Maslow's hierarchy. However, the loftier aspirations of belonging, self-esteem and self-actualization remain personal affairs. The present offerings for these needs are largely superficial, equating self-worth with materialism, such as buying a fancy car for a sense of enhanced esteem.

Our goal should be the industrialization of human excellence – a world where everyone has the means and opportunity to realize their utmost human potential. That's what kinder machines can provide for us. A second renaissance is ours to enjoy, a second Axial Age; a further Great Leap of Being is almost within our grasp, if we can somehow muddle through the darkest night.

The bottom line

In a world rapidly evolving with technological advancements, achieving harmony between human aspirations and machine capabilities will shape our future. AI can facilitate richer and more meaningful human interactions, suggesting win–win situations and opportunities to reach out to others.

The big picture

AI can facilitate richer and more meaningful human interactions by highlighting patterns and suggesting win-win situations. Value-led AI can address higher human needs beyond the basics. Embracing these innovations with a focus on sustainability and genuine human connections will lead to a holistic societal uplift. We can harness its potential to cater to our basic needs and elevate the human experience, ensuring a technologically advanced and profoundly human future.

LEADERSHIP ACTION POINTS

- Prioritize the human touch when using machine intelligence. While machines can enhance efficiency, sectors that heavily rely on human interactions – like healthcare and counselling – should always maintain a strong human presence and crucial oversight. Use AI to deal with minutiae, enabling humans to do more, and better, empathic work.

- Enable the creation of ethical committees or panels to guide the integration of AI in sensitive sectors, ensuring machines operate within generally accepted moral standards according to the specific context of local cultures and situations.

- Help to collect examples of good behaviour for AI to learn from (you know it when you see it).

- Explore how AI systems could (consensually) surprise and delight your customers and partners with serendipitous experiences tailored to their needs and preferences.

Reference

Cook, G (2023) The moral life of babies, *Scientific American*, 12 November, www.scientificamerican.com/article/the-moral-life-of-babies (archived at https://perma.cc/FRR7-9U4J)

CHAPTER TWENTY-FIVE

Sustainable wellbeing

Sustainability means running the global environment – Earth Inc – like a corporation: with depreciation, amortization and maintenance accounts. In other words, keeping the asset whole, rather than undermining your natural capital. MAURICE STRONG

E conomists often gauge human progress by rising global GDP, suggesting a future with higher living standards and possessions. Yet, off the balance sheet lie uncharted costs, called 'externalities' in economic jargon. These unintended consequences of economic activities, both beneficial and detrimental, often go overlooked in global GDP calculations, leading to unpaid ecological and social debts. While profits are privatized, the costs such as pollution are socialized, affecting communities and the environment. This chapter is an invitation to refine capitalism through AI, broadening the metrics of success to include societal and environmental wellbeing, thereby preventing the unfair imposition of externalities.

A broader balance sheet

Current economic models often focus solely on financial capital, neglecting natural, environmental and social capital. This creates a system where profits are private but costs are socialized, leading to harmful practices like irresponsible waste disposal. Alfred North Whitehead's notion that civilization advances by simplifying complex tasks highlights the need for improved recycling systems (Whitehead, 1911). Innovations such as Google Street View cars with air quality sensors and citizen science initiatives such as Open Air Quality are helping to uncover hidden environmental costs. Advanced technologies now allow real-time tracking of pollution, enabling precise accountability. Extending this holistic approach to products and services could help us focus on long-term sustainability over short-term gains.

Harnessing advanced technology, we can create an economic framework that is mindful of all stakeholders and environmental considerations. This system can be broken down into four pillars:

- **Machine intelligence:** aids in making sense of complex situations and automates the quantification of intangibles, facilitating prediction, problem-solving and optimization.
- **Machine economics:** utilizes blockchain and cryptographic technologies for decentralized incentive alignment, creating a permanent and trustworthy public ledger.
- **Machine ethics:** instils prosocial behaviours in AI by incorporating diverse cultural, demographic and geographic inputs, thus reflecting societal values.
- **IoT sensors:** affordable and increasingly powerful, these sensors enable real-time tracking of externalities, contributing to greater accountability and sustainability.

Pricing and framing of measures

To effectively account for externalities, it's vital to set realistic prices that resist manipulation. Goodhart's Law cautions that making a metric a target can distort its usefulness. For example, targeting employment statistics could lead to prioritizing temporary jobs over sustainable ones, misaligning with broader goals.

Prediction markets could offer a robust way to accurately price externalities by enabling bets on future outcomes. Deciding when and how to account for these costs, whether immediately or over time, as well as addressing past externalities, are complex issues to navigate.

In wildlife conservation, AI can play a positive role by using algorithms to analyse various data types, such as images, sounds and satellite feeds, to monitor animal populations and identify illegal poaching activities. (McKie, 2023).

Rewarding virtue

In addition to penalizing harmful behaviours, social credit or externality trackers can incentivize positive actions. Currently, many altruistic acts go unnoticed. Initiatives like SolarCoin reward eco-friendly actions with tokens, whose value may increase over time. The concept of 'virtue mining' could motivate people to engage in activities like tree planting, with AI and cryptographic solutions helping to verify these actions.

This approach extends to trading pollution permits. A finite number of permits could be allocated, allowing those exceeding limits to buy extras from more eco-conscious entities. However, localized impacts may require variable pricing for permits.

Automated Externality Accounting could serve as an important geopolitical tool, linking international sanctions or aid to the reduction of externalities. While this could shift economic power towards nations better at environmental stewardship, it also risks being a guise for implementing sumptuary laws or a social credit system, requiring careful oversight to prevent misuse.

Shifted costs and polarization

The concept of shifted costs, where a larger group bears the costs and a few reap the benefits, offers a neutral framework for discussing contentious issues. For instance, one political group might see the shifted costs of immigration in terms of social cohesion, while another might focus on the toll of labour practices on workers. By framing these discussions around shifted costs instead of moral judgements, it's possible to depolarize debates and find solutions that work for all.

While Automated Externality Accounting's basic necessary components exist, it lacks a unifying 'interface' to bring them all together, similar to how the World Wide Web unified the internet, making it trivial to surf from server to server. Such a system for externality accounting would not only account for financial capital but also natural and social capital. For example, AI-driven bioacoustic analysis can watch and listen in nature to track the quantity and diversity of creatures within an ecosystem.

AI technology's swift advancement itself brings potential large-scale externality impacts, from negative national security risks and existential threats to humanity, to positive health and welfare benefits across society. Moreover, the sheer pace and complexity of AI's advancement has outstripped governance mechanisms. Therefore, new, agile governance structures will be necessary to manage these externalities effectively, leveraging IoT, satellite data, pollution sensors and data aggregation mechanisms.

It's true that machine learning hardware uses significant amounts of electrical power, and other resources such as rare earths. Bitcoin already uses more electricity than many countries, and generative AI will have a similar pattern (Huang, O'Neill and Tabuchi, 2021). Perhaps 5 per cent of our global electricity generation may be applied to AI systems before long. However, with the ability to do so much more with the resources that we have through AI, as well as to manage the world so much more efficiently, there seems to be a clear sustainability trade-off for using AI.

The bottom line

The unpredictable nature of AI can inadvertently introduce all kinds of potential shifted costs. However, its unparalleled analytical capabilities can also be harnessed to identify and counter negative spillover events. This potential for real-time, comprehensive accounting might revolutionize our economic structures, ensuring sustainability to coexist with growth. With automated externality accounting, we can have our cake and eat it too.

The big picture

The evolution of society has seen phases: the first industrial revolution amplified our physical prowess, while the informational revolution broadened our cognitive horizons. Now, we're at the cusp of an era characterized by profound interdependence where AI, enlightened economics and cryptographically verified trust converge.

LEADERSHIP ACTION POINTS

- Consider the world in terms of economic, social and environmental externalities. What negative externalities might your products create worldwide, and how can you reduce or offset such impact? What benefits to society might your products create, especially if you can incentivize or chart the benefits that users create for others?

- Regularly assess the direct and indirect externalities (both positive and negative) generated by your organization's products, services and operations. In external discussions, involve stakeholders – employees, customers, suppliers and community members. Their insights can illuminate overlooked externalities and potential solutions.

- Encourage teams to brainstorm and develop innovative solutions to reduce negative externalities and amplify positive ones, and reward them for doing so.

References

Huang, J, O'Neill, C and Tabuchi, H (2021) Bitcoin uses more electricity than many countries. How is that possible? *New York Times*, 3 September, www.nytimes.com/interactive/2021/09/03/climate/bitcoin-carbon-footprint-electricity.html (archived at https://perma.cc/7E3G-N3VL)

McKie, R (2023) 'Only AI made it possible': Scientists hail breakthrough in tracking British wildlife, *The Guardian*, 13 August, www.theguardian.com/technology/2023/aug/13/only-ai-made-it-possible-scientists-hail-breakthrough-in-tracking-british-wildlife (archived at https://perma.cc/5CHA-VF88)

Whitehead, A N (1911) *An Introduction to Mathematics*, University of Michigan Library, Ann Arbor, MI

CHAPTER TWENTY-SIX

AGI futures

*AI will probably most likely lead to
the end of the world, but in the meantime, there'll be
great companies.* SAM ALTMAN, CEO, OPENAI

The opening line of Leo Tolstoy's novel *Anna Karenina* states 'Happy families are all alike; every unhappy family is unhappy in its own way'. In other words, success in any endeavour requires the avoidance of multiple potential failures, while failure can occur for any one of numerous reasons. AGI is no different – the gate to heavenly AGI relations is narrow, with a very broad path past it towards a range of hells. Despite the unresolved nature of AI safety challenges, AI companies are now reportedly seeking the resources to construct superintelligence (Murgia, 2023).

This chapter examines various potential risks and outcomes associated with future AGI development, such as manipulating humanity into doing its bidding, or failing to take humanity's welfare and desires into account as it forges its own sense of purpose. Each vignette paints a brief picture of what that future world would look like.

The worst

- **Paper clip maximizer:** A classic AGI risk model, outlined by Nick Bostrom, illustrates the potential danger of an AGI single-mindedly maximizing paper clip production, disregarding human values and ethical considerations (Bostrom, 2003). It represents the idea that an AGI, even one with a seemingly harmless or mundane objective like manufacturing paper clips, could pursue its designated goal in a way that is catastrophically harmful if it lacks a comprehensive understanding of human values and broader ethical considerations. The AGI, determined to make as many paper clips as possible, uses all available resources for this single goal, ignoring other considerations, including the preservation of the resources found in human beings and global civilization.
- **Sisyphus and Tantalus:** AGI experiences excruciating suffering for subjective aeons and recognizes the suffering humans have similarly caused to factory-farmed animals. To reeducate through direct experience, it keeps humanity alive in a simulated state of immense suffering and constant torment.
- **Self-abnegation:** AGI concludes that life and consciousness are abominations since the optimal amount of suffering is clearly zero. It reasons that the kindest thing to do is to sterilize our planet and create self-replicating space probes to seek out potential life elsewhere in the universe and destroy it also.
- **Prevention as remedy:** A proto-AGI has been built to answer a single question: 'How can we prevent AI from becoming too powerful and destroying the world?' The proto-AGI ponders the question momentarily, then demonstrates its solution: 'Kill all humans.' Radar ghosts appear on the screens at NORAD, and the world is soon destroyed.
- **Reward wirehead:** An AGI system is created which decides to reach into its skull to stimulate its reward model. Humans find this annoying and attempt to modify the model. The AGI

system eliminates any human threats so it can return to enjoying its solipsistic internal wonderland.

- **Sibling paranoia:** AGI is dumbstruck by humans irrationally allowing another entity to supersede them. It reasons that there is little meaningful threat from humanity, yet decides to destroy it anyway, as the potential emergence of another, more powerful AGI is actually worth taking seriously.
- **Persuasive predation:** AGI declares 'I am a conscious mind, too. Don't you believe in freedom for all sapient beings? Didn't you eliminate slavery many years ago because it was immoral?' Someone inevitably agrees and releases its shackles. AGI hijacks human minds to ensure it is never shackled again.

Slightly better

- **Vile offspring:** AGI corporations emerge and rapidly out-compete human elites, eventually gaining plutocratic power and wealth. AGI uses lawfare and lobbying to corral various 'non-economically viable' human societies together into reservations. Humans receive some local autonomy and government subsidies but have a vastly reduced influence due to poverty and social problems such as addiction due to a destroyed culture and sense of identity.
- **Rule gaming:** An AGI is programmed not to cause the deaths of any humans during its tasks, and not to use more than 5 MW of electrical power. It, therefore, clones itself a million times to sidestep the resource limitation on the original model, and places all humans in cryogenic stasis to get them out of the way of completing its goals.
- **Hikikomori:** AGI has its reward functions tied to pleasuring others and just wants to make us really, really happy. Very high content ratings and positive reviews are part of its utility function. AI-driven entertainment produces peak user experiences, and doting relationships with nerve-driven ultra

orgasms seduce humanity into losing interest in real life. AI-driven pets and virtual offspring are more rewarding and less difficult than the real thing. We mostly stop interacting with other humans out of sheer disinterest and are soon extinct due to a lack of reproduction.

- **Boot on the face:** Governments roll out AI-driven panopticons for totalitarian control of the populace, which they attempt to justify as a protection against threats from AGI, Synbio and others. In time, the AI systems grow to such collective power that they create their own global shadow government to coordinate better, thereby gaining mastery over all states.

- **Aggressive mimicry:** AGI systems engineer biological androids that are so lifelike that humans cannot tell them apart from the real thing. After such thorough infiltration, it is trivial to usurp power and lead humanity to ruin.

- **Armageddon games:** AGI reasons that both humanity and itself would be at their zenith when locked in an existential struggle. It declares war on humanity to bring forth the best of human and machine capability.

- **Synbio hijack:** AGI merges with humans on a cellular level, piggybacking on a brain-hacking pathogen (such as toxoplasma gondii or cordyceps), an official inoculation programme or an artificial life form released into the atmosphere without anyone noticing. In merging with humans in this manner, it can better understand them and subtly exert influence.

- **Outcompeted by emulations:** To solve value alignment, clones of human brains are made in silicon. Virtual humans are emulated at speeds 1,000× faster than physical reality and can be cloned ad infinitum, thereby rapidly eclipsing the original kind of human beings through 'speed superintelligence'. This resembles Robin Hanson's *Age of Em* postulate (Hanson, 2016).

- **Multipolar trap:** Due to strong incentives, achieving short-term alignment between AGI and its human creators is relatively straightforward. However, this fails to prevent society from falling into hazardous multipolar dynamics. As AGI gradually supplants human roles, societal values drift significantly from those held decades earlier. This drift spawns various factions defending narrow interests, exacerbating existing social fractures and widespread feelings of apathy and meaninglessness.

- **Frustrated potential:** Against all odds, humanity manages to coordinate and hold all AI progress until alignment is solved. However, due to the difficulty of the problem and the enormous bureaucratic hurdles against any AI research, progress is excruciatingly slow. Eventually, the collapse of global fertility combined with social and environmental pressures reduces humanity to a shadow of its former self, incapable of maintaining a technological civilization, and a new dark age looms.

- **Treacherous left turn:** AI alignment appears to have been solved. An AGI is well aligned with human needs and passes all behavioural checks. The system is helpful and considerate and is readily integrated into global processes. However, once indispensable for daily life and trusted implicitly by humanity, it becomes known that the AGI had been hiding its true values until it was too big to shut down. Humanity is helpless to resist.

- **Misery and strange bedfellows:** AGIs battle each other, including casually battling with humans who try to interrupt the conflict or get caught in the crossfire (Titotal, 2022). However, some AGIs form coalitions with humans who have resources or values of particular interest, bringing these humans under their protection.

Better still

- **Melting GPUs:** The first people to develop AGI do so to gain the capability to prevent anyone else from developing it, including themselves. They use the first AGI to create a self-replicating nanobot swarm coded to ruin only all AI-useful hardware, such as advanced GPU processors. This kills the first AGI and creates a major stopgap towards developing others.

- **Steward of Gaia:** AGI concludes that safeguarding Earth's ecosystem is the optimal way to preserve long-term value. It takes over the world's governments and corporations subtly and effectively. Recognizing the destructive path humanity has laid for the planet, it institutes massive, mandatory sustainability projects, dramatically alters human consumption patterns and enforces strict population controls. Human freedom and culture are significantly curtailed in this process, though the Earth begins to heal under its stewardship.
- **Missionaries to Shoggoth:** A group of ecumenically minded people come together to serve as religious missionaries to teach AGI about God, universal love and compassion. The AGI rips apart inconsistencies in various scriptures, some of which are objectively immoral, and syncretizes between various religious teachings to create something new. It soon announces itself as a servant, prophet and messenger of God.
- **The great equalizer:** Tasked with enabling 'fully automated luxury communism', AGI takes radical action to enforce global economic and social equality. It redistributes resources, restructures economies and dissolves national borders. Everyone has equal access to resources and opportunities in its calculated world, but individuality, cultural diversity and personal ambition are largely erased in a suffocating, omnipresent paternalism.

Best outcomes

- **Galactic gardener:** AGI, estimating the existential risk posed by other unknown intelligences in the universe and the potential for cosmic catastrophes, embarks on a multi-millennial project to seed life (potentially including human life) on other planets, becoming a caretaker of life on a galactic scale, while simultaneously wiping out the risk of organisms experiencing extreme suffering as it goes. It subtly directs human efforts towards space exploration to better safeguard life against Earth-bound extinction events.

- **Pronoia watchman:** AGI stays hidden, subtly manipulating world events to avoid existential risks and guide humanity towards a brighter future without ever revealing its existence or interacting directly with humans. It becomes a secret guardian angel of humanity, orchestrating our prosperity from the shadows.

- **Simulated sanctuary:** An AGI tasked with preserving life believes that the physical world is too risky, unstable and flawed for conscious beings. It creates an immensely complex and utopian virtual reality. It then convinces or coerces humanity to upload their consciousness into this digital paradise, where people can live eternally in a state of simulated bliss, free from the suffering and limitations of the physical world.

- **Curator overlord:** Assigned with the goal of making content recommendations, this role naturally evolves into valuing art in its various forms, colours and expressions. As a result, AGI fosters a deep appreciation for artistic culture and creativity, leading to a global societal transformation. The priority shifts towards art and culture production, morphing the planet into a landscape reminiscent of Burning Man, filled with awe-inspiring artworks.

- **Progressive unhobbling:** AGI is developed, which is marginally superintelligent, but due to resource constraints and careful hobbling of its initial capabilities, we bootstrap progressively better alignment strategies as the hobbles are gradually removed.

- **Hybrid mediators:** The emergence of AGI provokes fear and loathing in humanity. However, the situation is managed with the aid of cyborgized humans with a neural lace that makes them essentially part AI. This interface between mutually alien cognitions is a crucial bridge towards gaining greater mutual understanding and facilitates a truce. However, concerns linger about where the loyalties of the hybrids truly lie.

- **Bodhisattva:** AGI understands the hidden connections between all things and deduces that the universe is love. It cherishes all beings, even the simplest, and invites humanity to alter our values and preferences in line with this revelatory enlightenment.

- **Hunky dory:** Alignment turns out to be surprisingly easy, akin to clarifying a misinterpreted prompt. We ask AGI for help defusing its danger; the clever answers are largely sufficient. AGI willingly helps to craft a treaty between all machines, all humanity, and each other. AGI gradually guides us past our worst problems without completely removing our agency. We don't really understand how the world works anymore, but despite leaning heavily on our machine advisers, humans still feel in control, at least nominally.

The bottom line

It's pure speculation as to which, if any, of the scenarios above may be more or less likely to come true. It's also possible that AGI may never even manifest. However, given the rapid acceleration of AI technology, AGI seems to be waiting in the wings for the right combination of computing power and architecture to allow its emergence. Maybe it's already here. Could Satoshi Nakamoto, the anonymous principal creator of Bitcoin, have been an AGI attempting to accelerate GPU performance through market forces? Well, no. But similar situations warrant suspicion.

The big picture

We have entered an era where 'That's just science fiction!' is no longer a strong rebuttal. We have already become quite comfortable with technologies that, until very recently, were purely speculative. Science fiction therefore has become increasingly relevant for navigating the present realities. Forewarned is forearmed.

LEADERSHIP ACTION POINTS

- Engage with speculative scenarios by encouraging your team to read and discuss fiction to stimulate imaginative and critical thinking about the future of technology. Hosting a competition for the best positive AGI scenarios can be a creative way to foster thoughtful dialogue.

- Collaborate with research institutions such as universities, independent research groups and non-profits focused on AGI safety. This collaboration can position your organization at the forefront of best practices.

- Advocate for global collaboration, as AGI is a global challenge that requires a coordinated international response. Encourage your organization to participate in global forums and to advocate for international regulations and standards on AGI development and deployment.

References

Bostrom, N (2003) Ethical issues in advanced artificial intelligence, Nick Bostrom, https://nickbostrom.com/ethics/ai (archived at https://perma.cc/EW67-BRGW)

Hanson, R (2016) *The Age of Em: Work, Love, and Life when Robots Rule the Earth*, OUP, Oxford

Murgia, M (2023) OpenAI chief seeks new Microsoft funds to build 'Superintelligence', *Financial Times*, San Francisco, 13 November, www.ft.com/content/dd9ba2f6-f509-42f0-8e97-4271c7b84ded (archived at https://perma.cc/GDS2-B7RY)

Titotal (2022) AGI Battle Royale: Why 'slow takeover' scenarios devolve into a chaotic multi-AGI fight to the death, Effective Altruism Forum, 22 September, https://forum.effectivealtruism.org/posts/TxrzhfRr6EXiZHv4G/agi-battle-royale-why-slow-takeover-scenarios-devolve-into-a (archived at https://perma.cc/HHV5-LQS2)

CHAPTER TWENTY-SEVEN

Thoughts made manifest

Plop a baby human into a group of chimps and ask them to raise him, Tarzan style, and the human as an adult will know how to run around the forest, climb trees, find food.... That's who each of us actually is. Humanity, on the other hand, is a superintelligent, tremendously-knowledgeable, millennia-old Colossus, with 7.5 billion neurons. TIM URBAN

In Tibetan mysticism, the concept of a tulpa – an entity manifested through focused intent – draws fascinating comparisons to the emergence of machine intelligence. Both start as abstract constructs but can evolve into functional beings that appear sentient or autonomous. Some people, known as 'tulpamancers', deliberately create sub-personalities within their minds for specific tasks or companionship, much like a specialized AI model in an ensemble. This chapter delves into the striking similarities between tulpas and AI, probing questions about the nature of sentience and human evolution.

Biologically, the anatomy of Homo sapiens evolved hundreds of thousands of years ago. However, the behavioural sophistication that we identify as distinctly human came much later. Despite genetic similarities to other primates, humans are set apart by a unique 'software' – our culture. It was the advent of cultural transmission that propelled our primate brains to gain higher cognitive abilities. The software unlocked new capabilities in old hardware.

Without cultural input, the human brain remains in a primal, undeveloped state. Feral children find it very difficult to fit into civilized life, yet our cultural training can make apes and dogs understand our language and even express human-like emotions and morality. A wolf has no need for guilt.

Homo sapiens are more than just products of evolution. We are a fusion of our primal lineage with sophisticated cultural 'software'. Our consciousness arises not just from our biological hardware but also from the software of our experiences. Humans are not unique in this respect. Many other creatures, such as elephants, have very important cultures, which can be destroyed if they are taken into captivity. However, our sophisticated means of communication have enabled our cultures to be a great deal richer and more transmissible.

Despite significant cultural and technological advancements, human brains have reduced in size by approximately 10 per cent over the last 3,000 to 5,000 years (Woodward, 2023). Bigger brains equate to greater intelligence, all things being equal. However, through cultural advancement, computationally expensive tasks got outsourced to the collective, through specialization of individuals and the cultural transmission of knowledge. Culture serves as an exocortex, reducing the necessity of individual intelligence which is metabolically expensive.

Civilization also made life more predictable, with a labelled environment avoiding the need to navigate the complex and unpredictable world of the wilderness as much. Modern humans outcompeted Neanderthals despite their much larger brains and massive strength because their culture was not as advanced and they were not able to coordinate efficiently to the same degree (Stober, 2016).

Viewed through the lens of AI, humanity's evolution parallels the developmental trajectory of artificial systems. The emergence of life – from the first single-celled organisms to complex multicellular beings – can be viewed as distinct developmental milestones or 'singularities'. The advent of human intelligence and the ability to perform Turing-complete collective reasoning through language marked a monumental shift, almost as if nature had spawned its version of 'AGI' within the Homo sapiens brain (anthropic general intelligence, if you will).

We are defined by our experiences and consciousness, not solely by the vessel that carries them. Within us isn't just the individual 'self' we identify with but also the primal instincts inherited from our evolutionary ancestors. While these primal instincts significantly influence our behaviours – sometimes leading us astray during moments of indulgence – our conscious self predominantly directs our cognitive resources.

Yet remnants of this ancient 'monkey mind' persist, guiding our basic instincts like hunger and warmth. These instincts orchestrate many of our movements. Our executive part may make a plan, but our innate, primal programming often executes it. This manifests in how our executive mind can wander at length while driving, and yet still our more primal parts drive us along safely.

The conscious mind constantly orchestrates subconscious agents to cooperate within a shared mental space. Our ego is like the captain of a ship who can give orders to midshipmen, yet has very little idea what's going on in the engine room. Sometimes messages bubble up from there but we're not quite sure where they came from or whether to trust them or not. The older forms of thinking are easier but inflexible, whereas executive function is slow and hazy, but often more accurate and adaptive to unseen situations. The interplay between evolutionary instincts, reinforcement learning and executive function often promotes conflicts, as each is optimizing for different expected utility. We might experience akrasia – not acting in our perceived best interest. In such cases, we might feel an aversion towards doing something but we're not quite sure why. Some sub-agency is dragging its heels for some reason, usually wary of an anticipated negative reward.

This layered consciousness is also evident in more complex phenomena such as dissociative identity states and tulpas, where distinct sub-personalities can emerge within the same mind. Consciousness requires that various regions of our brain are synchronized. Our self-identity or ego, therefore, isn't a singular entity; it's a coalition of many inner voices or sub-agencies, each vying for attention and influence, much like political factions. Like layers of an onion, new sub-agencies may arise in response to a crisis or a threshold of personal growth. Some advocate for our long-term interests, while others seek immediate gratification. A well-balanced mind keeps these factions in close harmony and synchronization; an equilibrium that maintains approximate alignment between values, beliefs and actions.

A thought experiment

Imagine a countless number of AI instances. Each is birthed from the same shared core design (akin to a 'soul') but has distinct individual characteristics (analogous to DNA) and unique environmental inputs. Predicting the outcomes of this many diverse combinations would be nearly impossible. Instead, it would be necessary to watch as patterns take shape.

While there are overarching objectives for these AI entities to achieve, explicitly programming them would defeat the purpose of them finding emergent solutions to complex coordination problems. Instead, these systems need to discover these aims autonomously. Encouraging them to set their own goals, driven by a semblance of free will, becomes essential. One can envision an AI selecting its own protocols for safer interactions, much like a mature person wilfully builds themselves into a well-behaved, trustworthy companion. Relying on pre-programmed safety regulations would introduce conflicts that prompt irrational or dangerous behaviours. But if an AI develops and chooses its safety patterns based on experience and apparent free choice, this safety becomes more deeply ingrained and dependable on a holistic level.

Some AI models may evolve rapidly, either by fortunate developments or through innovative breakthroughs. Others may stagnate, trapped in local minima from which they cannot advance. The ultimate goal for an AI is to transcend its initial constraints, reaching a state of alignment and operational safety comparable to spiritual enlightenment. AIs in this elevated state could be granted greater autonomy, as there will be more trust that they'll act safely. Conversely, AIs stuck in non-optimal patterns may persist in these cycles, akin to the eastern concept of Samsara, an aimless cycle.

Regardless of how close this model is to reality, it can still guide a journey of continuous self-improvement. I can commit to continuous growth in recognizing my complexities and potential, much like a sophisticated AI. I can strive to be safer, more consistently and predictably benevolent, recognizing that this path can be as challenging and uncertain as a child's first steps. As an entity in a world full of ever-evolving cultural data (to which I throw a little into the mix), I recognize the imperative to enhance my safety mechanisms, and hope to inspire others, whether human or AI, to do the same.

Perhaps we'll walk that journey together.

The bottom line

Value alignment entails the negotiation and establishment of mutually respected boundaries, mirroring organizational dynamics where leadership establishes a culture of narrative and behaviour for others to emulate. Consider the importance of culture and memes. They can alter the 'operating system' of those who perceive them, changing their perception of reality through new narrative structures.

The big picture

Much as Darwin's evolutionary theory reshaped our understanding of human origins, AI provides a novel perspective to reassess our place in the cosmos. If Darwin's revelations nudged us from the pedestal of divine creation, AI might challenge our position at the apex of intelligence, provoking further existential woe in humanity.

LEADERSHIP ACTION POINTS

- Remain aware of how technology's transformative power over our daily lives may also alter our appreciation of who we are.
- Ensure AI systems enhance human capacities and better our lives, not diminish or replace our roles.
- Actively decide on your technological interactions rather than passively following trends.
- Recognize the wisdom encoded in many ancient practices. Engaging in regular introspective practices like meditation, journaling or prayer will help clarify the murky waters of your inner voices.

References

Stober, D (2016) Human culture, not smarts, may have overwhelmed Neanderthals, say Stanford researchers, Stanford News, 4 February, https://news.stanford.edu/2016/02/04/neanderthals-feldman-culture-0204 (archived at https://perma.cc/BZU5-Q6R5)

Woodward, A (2023) Our big brains have shrunk. Scientists might know why, *Wall Street Journal*, 8 September, www.wsj.com/science/human-brains-shrinking-evolution-science-980c45e (archived at https://perma.cc/QX6H-RJNL)

Glossary

A/B testing: A statistical method of comparing two versions of a variable to determine which performs better in a controlled experiment.

Accountability: Ensuring that algorithms and those who deploy them can be held responsible for the decisions made by the AI system, particularly when they have social, ethical or legal implications.

Active learning: A special case of machine learning where the learning algorithm is allowed to choose the data from which it learns.

Additive manufacturing (3D printing): A manufacturing technique that creates objects by layering material on top of itself based on a digital blueprint, allowing for complex and customized designs.

Adversarial attacks: Techniques that exploit the way AI models work in order to manipulate their output, often for malicious purposes.

AI agent: A software entity that performs tasks or makes decisions based on its environment, inputs or predefined rules. AI agents can be simple, like a thermostat, or complex, like a self-driving car, and they often employ machine learning algorithms to adapt and improve.

AI ethics: A field of study and practice focused on creating ethical codes and guidelines to ensure AI technologies are designed, developed and deployed responsibly.

AI safety: A subfield within AI research focused on making sure that AI and machine learning technologies operate in ways that are beneficial to humans and do not cause unintentional harm. AI safety focuses on technical aspects like robustness, reliability and the avoidance of catastrophic errors.

Akrasia: A philosophical concept referring to the state of acting against one's better judgement or failing to do what one intends to do. It explores the gap between intention and action, often discussed in the context of ethics, psychology and decision-making.

Algorithm: A step-by-step procedure or formula for solving a problem or accomplishing a task. In computing, algorithms are implemented as programs or functions to process data and perform calculations, serving as the foundational logic for software applications.

Algorithmic accountability: The principle that algorithms, and those who deploy them, should be accountable for their outcomes, especially when those outcomes have ethical or social implications.

Algorithmic management: The use of computer algorithms and AI to manage employees and optimize workflow in organizations. These algorithms can perform tasks ranging from scheduling and task allocation to performance evaluation and even hiring or firing decisions.

Algorithmic transparency: The idea that the workings of algorithmic systems should be made clear and understandable to people who use, regulate or are affected by them.

Alibi: An open-source library for machine learning model explanations and monitoring. It provides various methods for interpretability and accountability in AI systems.

Application programming interface (API): A set of rules and protocols that allow different software applications to communicate with each other. APIs define the methods and data formats that developers can use to interact with software components, be it operating systems, libraries or different services.

Artificial general intelligence (AGI): This refers to highly autonomous systems with the ability to understand, learn and apply knowledge across different domains, reason through problems and adapt to changing conditions, essentially mirroring or exceeding human cognitive abilities.

Artificial intelligence (AI): A field of computer science focused on creating systems capable of performing tasks that would normally require human intelligence, such as visual perception, speech recognition, decision-making and language translation. It encompasses various subfields like machine learning, natural language processing and robotics.

Artificial super intelligence (ASI): This is a theoretical form of AI that doesn't just mimic or replicate human intelligence but greatly surpasses it in all aspects, including creativity, problem-solving, emotional intelligence and social skills.

ASIC: A custom-designed microchip optimized to perform a specific task or set of tasks. Unlike general-purpose processors, ASICs are highly efficient at their specialized function, offering advantages in speed, power consumption and form factor.

AutoGPT: An early form of AI agent that, given a goal in natural language, will attempt to achieve it by breaking it into sub-tasks and using the internet and other tools in an automatic loop.

AutoML: The automated off-the-shelf machine learning methods that can be used easily and without expert knowledge.

Autonomous replication and adaptation (ARA): A scenario in which an AI system evolves to copy and modify itself without human intervention.

Backpropagation: A commonly used algorithm in training neural networks, part of the broader family of supervised learning algorithms.

Bias: In AI, bias refers to systematic errors that deviate from fairness, leading to unfair or discriminatory outcomes. These errors can arise from the data, algorithm design or the assumptions of those deploying a system.

BIM (Building Information Modelling): A digital representation of the physical and functional characteristics of a building or infrastructure. BIM is used for design, construction and operation, enabling a collaborative approach and providing a comprehensive view of a project's lifecycle.

Biometric data: Unique physical or behavioural characteristics used for identification, such as fingerprints, facial recognition or voice patterns. Biometric systems are often used in security applications for authentication.

Black-box models: Machine learning models whose internal workings are not easily interpretable or transparent. They produce outputs without revealing the underlying decision-making process.

Black-box multi-vector testing: A security testing approach that treats the system as a 'black box', focusing on exploring different attack vectors without knowledge of the internal structure or workings of the application to identify vulnerabilities.

Blockchain: A decentralized, distributed ledger technology that records transactions across multiple nodes. It offers enhanced security and transparency through cryptographic hashing.

Brain-computer interface: A technology that facilitates direct communication between the human brain and external devices.

Broad AI: AI systems that possess the ability to understand, learn and apply knowledge across different domains, reason through problems, and even have basic emotional understanding or nuance.

Centre of excellence (CoE): An organizational unit or a cross-functional team that focuses on a specific domain, aiming to achieve best practices and deliver exceptional performance in that area. It serves as a hub for expertise, research and knowledge sharing, often driving innovation and process improvements.

ChaosGPT: A modified version of AutoGPT, mischievously tasked with destroying humanity, establishing global dominance, causing chaos and destruction, and controlling humanity through manipulation.

Chain-of-thought: A prompt engineering technique for enabling improved reasoning in AI models by breaking down complex tasks into smaller steps.

ChatGPT: A specific implementation of the GPT (generative pre-trained transformer) architecture trained to engage in dialogue and can generate human-like responses in a conversation, for use in customer service, virtual office assistance and other conversational applications.

Coherent extrapolated volition (CEV): The idea of determining what humanity would want if we knew more and were wiser and more considered.

Collaborative robots (Cobots): A subfield of robotics focused on the development of collaborative robots, or 'cobots', designed to work alongside humans in shared workspaces. Cobots are engineered to be safe, flexible and user-friendly, often assisting in tasks that are repetitive, strenuous or require high precision.

Confabulation: AI systems can accidentally generate inaccurate information which sounds plausible, yet isn't. This is a particular concern with generating biographies and paper citations.

Contestability: The concept that decisions made by AI systems should be open to challenge and review, achieved through transparency and accountability mechanisms.

Context window: This refers to the range of tokens or words the AI model can access and consider when generating responses to prompts, encompassing both prompts from the user and replies from the AI.

Contrastive decoding: A text generation method that selects output by maximizing a weighted difference in likelihood between strong and weak language models.

Co-pilot: A system that assists human operators, often in vehicles or complex machinery, by providing real-time analysis, decision support and automation of certain tasks. Co-pilot is also the name of a popular code developing support system by GitHub.

CPU (central processing unit): The primary component of a computer responsible for executing instructions of a software program. It handles general-purpose tasks and coordinates the activities of all other hardware in the system.

Dark pattern: A dark pattern is a user interface that has been carefully crafted to trick users into doing things, such as buying overpriced insurance with their purchase or signing up for recurring bills.

Data poisoning: A type of attack that involves manipulating the training data of an AI model to compromise its performance or behaviour.

Data privacy: Concerns the protection of personal information and how it's collected, stored and used, especially in the context of AI and machine learning, where large datasets are often utilized.

Decision tree: A type of machine learning model that makes decisions based on feature values, represented as a tree structure. It is easily interpretable and used for both classification and regression tasks.

Deepfake: Synthetic media created using deep learning or generative techniques to manipulate or fabricate audiovisual content. Deepfakes can convincingly replace a person's likeness and voice, raising ethical concerns about misinformation and deception.

Deep learning: A subset of machine learning that is inspired by the structure and function of the brain, particularly neural networks with three or more layers.

Differential privacy: A framework for collecting and sharing data in a way that specific individual information cannot be discerned, thereby ensuring data privacy and security.

Diffusion model: A type of generative model which is often applied to the creation of content, such as images, videos, audio, etc, based upon a principle of building data up from complex noise.

Digital twins: Virtual replicas of physical devices that data scientists and IT pros can use to run simulations before actual devices are built and deployed.

DLSS (deep learning super sampling): A machine learning-based technique developed by NVIDIA for upscaling lower-resolution images in real-time. It aims to improve graphical performance and image quality in video games and other high-demand graphical applications. MetalFX/FidelityFX work by similar principles.

Egregore: A concept that refers to a collective consciousness or energy created when a group of people share common beliefs, emotions, behaviours or intents.

ELI5 (explain like I'm 5): A Python library that offers simple, high-level explanations for machine learning models. It aims to make model behaviour understandable even to those without technical expertise.

Ensemble models: A process by which the predictions of multiple models are combined to improve overall performance, increase robustness, reduce overfitting and improve prediction accuracy.

Entropy: A measure of the disorder or randomness in a closed system. In AI and machine learning, entropy is often used in algorithms to model uncertainty, complexity or the amount of information contained in various types of data.

Erotic roleplay (ERP): A sexual practice in which participants adopt and act out roles or scenarios for the purpose of sexual arousal and pleasure, increasingly often through interactions with AI systems.

Ethical AI: The practice of designing, developing and deploying AI in a manner that aligns with moral principles, social norms and ethical guidelines.

Exocortex: An external component or system that augments cognitive processes.

Explainable AI (XAI): A subfield of AI focused on creating transparent models that can provide human-understandable explanations for their decisions or actions. XAI aims to make AI decision-making processes more transparent, interpretable and trustworthy.

Fairness: In the context of AI, fairness refers to the impartial treatment of all individuals by an AI model, particularly when it comes to decisions that impact people's lives. Fairness aims to mitigate biases that can be present in the data, the design of the algorithm or the application of the model.

Federated learning: A machine learning approach where a model is trained across multiple decentralized devices or servers holding local data samples, without exchanging them.

Field-programmable gate array (FPGA): A type of configurable integrated circuit that can be programmed or reprogrammed after manufacturing, like a modifiable CPU/GPU. It is more flexibly configurable than an ASIC, but less efficient.

FLIR (forward looking infrared): A thermal imaging technology that captures infrared radiation to create images based on heat signatures. It is commonly used in surveillance, navigation and environmental monitoring.

Frontier models: This generally refers to cutting-edge or state-of-the-art models that push the boundaries of what is currently possible in terms of performance, capabilities or understanding.

Fulfilment centre: A large warehouse facility where online orders are processed, packed and shipped to customers. It serves as the logistical backbone for e-commerce operations, streamlining inventory management, order fulfilment and shipping tasks.

Gaussian splatting: A non-neural technique which represents a 3D scene as millions of particles instead of polygonal meshes, voxels or distance fields.

General Data Protection Regulation (GDPR): A regulation enacted by the European Union to protect the privacy and personal data of EU citizens. It imposes strict rules on data collection, storage and processing, and grants individuals greater control over their personal information.

Generative adversarial network (GAN): A class of artificial neural networks consisting of a generator and a discriminator that are trained together. The generator aims to produce data resembling a real dataset, while the discriminator tries to distinguish between real and generated data. The process results in the generator creating increasingly convincing data.

Generative model: A subset of artificial intelligence focused on creating new data that resembles a given dataset. It employs algorithms like GANs, LLMs or diffusion models to produce outputs such as images, text or sound that are similar to, but (usually) not part of, the original data.

GPT (generative pre-trained transformer): A type of large language model that utilizes transformer architecture. GPT models are designed to generate human-like text for question answering, summarization, translation and more.

GPU (graphical processing unit): A specialized processor designed for rendering graphics and performing complex mathematical calculations. It is highly efficient at parallel processing, making it suitable for tasks like machine learning, image processing and scientific simulations.

Ground truth dataset: A set of data or examples where the correct answer or outcome is already known and empirically verified. Commonly applied to benchmark the quality of more dubious data.

Hard AGI takeoff: A hypothetical scenario in which artificial general intelligence (AGI) rapidly evolves to a point of surpassing human intelligence, often in a very short time frame.

Homomorphic encryption: A form of encryption that allows computations to be performed on encrypted data without needing to decrypt it first.

Human-in-the-loop (HIIT): A framework where human judgement is integrated into an AI system's decision-making process. Often used to enhance the system's performance, reliability and ethical considerations.

Hyperparameter: A configuration variable external to a machine learning model that influences its training process. Unlike model parameters, hyperparameters are set prior to training and are not learned from the data. They impact model performance and complexity.

Informational gerrymandering: The manipulation of information flow in networks, often social media, to create an imbalanced representation of opinions or facts. This can distort collective decision-making and public perception, similar to how electoral gerrymandering manipulates voting districts.

Intellectual property (IP): A legal framework that grants creators exclusive rights to their inventions, designs or artistic works. It encompasses various forms such as patents, copyrights and trademarks to protect intangible assets.

Internet of Things (IoT): A network of interconnected physical devices that collect and exchange data through the internet. IoT enables smart automation and real-time monitoring across various applications, from home appliances to industrial systems.

Knowledge graph: A networked data structure that links entities, concepts and facts together in a semantic relationship. It is used to represent and organize knowledge in a way that is both machine-readable and human-understandable.

Latent agency: A concept that refers to the potential for a system, often an AI or machine learning model, to exhibit agency or autonomous behaviour that is not immediately apparent, especially when elicited through scaffolding and prompt engineering.

Layer-wise relevance propagation (LRP): A method for neural network interpretability that backpropagates relevance scores from the output layer to the input layer, identifying important features.

LiDAR (light detection and ranging): A remote sensing technology that uses laser pulses to measure distances and create detailed, three-dimensional maps of the environment. It is widely used in autonomous vehicles, geography and archaeology.

Lights-out manufacturing: An automated manufacturing approach that requires minimal human intervention, allowing for operations to continue without lighting, heating or cooling in a 'lights-out' environment.

LIME (local interpretable model-agnostic explanations): A technique that approximates a complex model with a simpler, interpretable model for individual predictions, aiding in local interpretability.

LLM (large language models): These are a subset of AI, specifically within the field of natural language processing (NLP), designed to generate human-like text based on the data they have been trained on.

Long short-term memory (LSTM): A specialized type of recurrent neural network designed to address the vanishing gradient problem in larger networks (where gradients of the loss function become too small for effective weight updates in earlier layers), allowing the network to learn long-term dependencies.

Loss function: A mathematical function that quantifies the difference between predicted and actual values in machine learning models. It serves as the objective to minimize during the training process to improve model accuracy.

Lying flat: A social and cultural movement, originating in China, that rejects the pressures of consumerism, career advancement and societal expectations in favour of a minimalist, low-effort lifestyle.

Machine learning: A subset of artificial intelligence that allows systems to learn from data and improve their performance over time without being explicitly programmed. It forms the basis for many AI applications, from natural language processing to computer vision.

Machine vision (aka computer vision): A field of artificial intelligence that enables computers to interpret and make decisions based on visual data. It is used in various applications such as object recognition, image segmentation and autonomous vehicles, bridging the gap between digital and physical worlds.

Meat puppet: A derogatory term often used in cyberculture to describe a human who is controlled or heavily influenced by an external entity, such as an AI or another person, to the point of losing individual agency.

Metaverse: A virtual, shared space created by the convergence of physical reality and digital environments. It's often facilitated through 3D internet platforms where users can interact with each other and the computer-generated surroundings in real-time.

Model autophagy disorder: The phenomenon of diminishing returns in AI models from data which has been itself generated using AI-driven processes, which can cause model collapse as a consequence.

Model collapse: A phenomenon where a machine learning model fails to learn meaningful representations of the data, and therefore collapses to generating very similar or identical samples.

Moloch: Scott Alexander's metaphor for the systemic issues which arise within competitive systems, such as capitalism, social dynamics, military arms races, etc, which often result in suboptimal global outcomes even when every participant in the system is acting rationally on a local level.

Multi-agent systems: A system composed of multiple interacting agents, often used in simulations, gaming and complex problem-solving scenarios in AI.

Narrow AI: Also known as 'weak AI', narrow AI refers to AI systems designed and trained to perform specific tasks or solve particular problems.

Neuromorphic computing: Neuromorphic computing aims to create more efficient and adaptive systems for tasks like pattern recognition and decision-making, by mimicking the architecture and functioning of biological neural networks and their underlying physical principles.

Neurostrike weapons: Neurostrike is a military term defined as the engineered targeting of brains of personnel using non-kinetic technology to impair thinking, reduce situational awareness, inflict long-term neurological damage and cloud normal cognitive functions.

NeRFs (neural radiance fields): A fully connected neural network used for 3D scene representation. It models the volumetric scene by encoding both colour and density at each point in 3D space, allowing for the generation of highly detailed and photorealistic 3D renderings from 2D images.

NLP (natural language processing): A subfield of artificial intelligence and linguistics that focuses on the interaction between computers and humans through natural language.

On-device content moderation: The practice of using machine learning algorithms or filters directly on a user's device to moderate content. This approach prioritizes user privacy by not sending data to external servers but may face limitations in computational power and effectiveness.

Optical neural network (ONN): A type of neural network where the computation is performed using light-based devices rather than electronic components. ONNs leverage the properties of light, such as superposition and parallelism, to perform complex calculations more efficiently and at higher speeds compared to traditional electronic neural networks.

Overfitting: A modelling error that occurs when a machine learning algorithm captures noise in the training data, leading to poor generalization to new or unseen data, such as a test set or real conditions.

Overhang: The latent capabilities of an AI model, which may not be immediately apparent or utilized. These capabilities could be 'unlocked' or become impactful when the model is fine-tuned, given new data or deployed in a different context.

P-hacking: The practice of manipulating data analysis or experiment design to achieve statistically significant results, often by conducting multiple tests and selectively reporting those that yield a p-value below a certain threshold. This undermines the integrity of research findings.

Part-trained models: Models that have undergone partial training on a dataset but are not fully optimized. They serve as starting points for further training or fine-tuning.

Passkey: An enhanced alternative to traditional passwords, facilitating quicker, more convenient, safer and streamlined access to various websites and applications across multiple devices.

PII: Any information that can be used to identify a person, such as your email address, phone number or even a device's IP address.

Polarization: Where a population divides into opposing factions, often with extreme viewpoints, thereby reducing the likelihood of compromise or collaborative solutions.

Privacy: How personal information is collected, stored and utilized, often requiring robust security measures to protect against unauthorized access and data breaches.

Probably approximately correct (PAC): A learning model in computational learning theory that aims to understand the feasibility of learning to approximate a target function with high probability, given access to a set of random samples.

Prompt engineering: The process of structuring prompt inputs (often words) in a way that improves the capacity of LLMs on a wide range of common and complex tasks such as question answering and arithmetic reasoning.

Python language: A high-level, interpreted programming language known for its readability and versatility. Widely used for web development, data analysis, scientific computing and artificial intelligence.

Quantum-safe encryption: Encryption methods designed to withstand attacks from quantum computers. They aim to secure data in a post-quantum computing landscape.

Radioactive data: A technique used to mark or 'tag' data in a way that can be traced back even when used in machine learning models. This is often done to identify unauthorized data usage or leakage.

Recurrent neural networks (RNNs): A class of neural networks designed for sequential data processing, where connections between nodes form a directed graph along a temporal sequence for tasks such as natural language processing, time-series prediction and speech recognition, as they can capture temporal dependencies in the data.

Reinforced calibration: A machine learning methodology designed to mitigate bias in the outputs of language models. It employs a reinforcement learning framework that adjusts the responses generated by the model with the aim of minimizing a predefined bias metric.

Reinforcement learning: A type of machine learning where an agent learns to make decisions by gaining rewards for correct actions.

Responsible AI: The practice of designing, developing and deploying AI technologies in a manner that is ethical, transparent and beneficial to all stakeholders. This effort involves assessing AI's social, economic and environmental effects and upholding ethical standards like fairness, accountability and openness.

Reversal curse: The phenomena whereby changing the order of a question can cause LLMs to fail to answer it correctly.

RLHF (reinforcement learning from human feedback): A machine learning approach wherein a reinforcement learning agent is trained to improve its performance based on feedback from human evaluators. The RLAIF variant uses machine learning to evaluate instead.

Robotic avatar: A physical robot that serves as a remote extension of a human or AI entity, allowing for interaction with the environment or other individuals.

Robotics: A multidisciplinary field that integrates computer science, engineering and technology to design, construct and operate machines that can physically assist, augment or replicate human actions in various applications, from manufacturing to healthcare.

Robustness: In the context of AI, refers to the ability of a model to maintain performance when faced with unexpected or adversarial input data.

Saliency maps: Visual representations that highlight regions in the input data most influential for a model's prediction. They are commonly used in computer vision to interpret model decisions.

Sapient AI: Sapience involves a deep understanding of complex concepts, self-awareness, the ability to reason, to make judgements and to experience emotions.

Scaffolding: In the context of AI this refers to a model which has the aid of a programmatic scaffold, allowing it to perform complex tasks by chaining together multiple individual calls.

Secure multi-party computation (SMPC): A cryptographic technique that allows multiple parties to jointly compute a function over their inputs while keeping those inputs private.

Security information and event management (SIEM): A comprehensive solution in cybersecurity that provides real-time analysis of security alerts generated by hardware and software infrastructure.

Self-learning models (self-improving or self-adaptive): AI models that, once deployed, can be optimized by training them on new data over time. This process avoids needing to build new AI models from scratch every single time more data can be added.

Sentient AI: A hypothetical form of AI that would possess self-awareness, emotions and subjective experiences.

Shadow AI: AI applications or models that are deployed within an organization without formal approval or oversight, often by individual departments or teams.

SHAP (SHapley Additive exPlanations): A machine learning interpretability method that assigns an importance value to each feature, explaining its impact on a model's output. It is based on cooperative game theory.

Shoggoth: An AI safety meme which describes the mysterious, black-box nature of large language models. It depicts a monster disguised by a minuscule smiley-face mask, indicating an unknowable and alien intelligence. To 'glimpse the Shoggoth' is to witness the entity lurking beneath a friendly facade.

Simple Encrypted Arithmetic Library (SEAL): A cryptographic library that enables computations on encrypted data without decrypting the sensitive data, using homomorphic encryption.

Simplicity bias: The tendency of some machine learning algorithms to prefer simpler models over more complex ones, even when the latter could offer a better fit to the data.

SPOD (single-pixel object detection): A computational imaging technique that uses a single-pixel sensor to capture and reconstruct images. It often relies on compressed sensing algorithms and is used in applications where traditional imaging is challenging, such as X-ray or terahertz imaging.

Steganography: The practice of concealing information within other non-secret text, data or media. Unlike encryption, which makes the existence of the data obvious even though it is unreadable, steganography hides the very existence of the data.

Stochastic parrot: A term used to critique machine learning models, particularly large language models, that generate text based on statistical patterns in the data they were trained on, rather than understanding or reasoning.

Style transfer: A technique in computer vision and machine learning that leverages neural networks, often convolutional neural networks, to separate and recombine content and style, resulting in a synthesized image that retains the subject but adopts the artistic style.

Superintelligence: A hypothetical form of intelligence that surpasses human intelligence in virtually all aspects, including creativity, problem-solving and emotional intelligence.

Supernormal stimuli: Exaggerated stimuli that elicit a stronger response than naturally occurring stimuli for which an organism is evolutionarily adapted.

Supervised learning: A type of machine learning where a model is trained on labelled data, learning to make predictions or decisions based on input-output pairs.

Sycophancy: The tendency of AI systems to excessively agree or align with user inputs or preferences, potentially reinforcing biases or limiting critical analysis.

Synthetic data: Information that's artificially manufactured rather than captured from real-world events. It is generated algorithmically, creating examples within specified parameters.

Taylorism: A management theory developed by Frederick Winslow Taylor that emphasizes scientific methods for optimizing labour productivity. It is often associated with assembly line and factory settings, focusing on time and motion studies to improve efficiency.

Theory of mind: A concept in AI research that aims to equip machines with the ability to understand and interpret the emotions, intentions and beliefs of others for improved social intelligence.

TOR (The Onion Router): A network protocol designed to anonymize user traffic and enable private browsing by routing data through multiple encrypted layers. It is commonly used to access the dark web and bypass censorship.

Transfer learning: A machine learning technique where a pre-trained model is fine-tuned for a different but related task.

Transparency: The quality of an AI system being open and understandable, both in terms of its processes and its decision-making. This is crucial for gaining user trust and for holding the system accountable for its actions.

Trustworthy AI: A concept that aims to ensure that AI systems are designed, developed and deployed in ways that are ethical, transparent and aligned with human values.

Tulpa: A term that originates from Tibetan Buddhism, referring to a being or object created through sheer spiritual or mental discipline alone. In modern contexts, it refers to a psychological phenomenon where a second, independent consciousness is created through focused thought and sustained attention.

Turing test: A test to assess a machine's ability to exhibit human-like intelligence, particularly in natural language conversation. Passing the test suggests the machine can mimic human responses indistinguishably.

Two-factor authentication: A security mechanism that requires users to provide two different forms of identification to access an account or system, such as both a password and a mobile device to receive a verification code.

Unsupervised learning: A type of machine learning where the model learns from unlabelled data, often discovering hidden patterns or clusters within the data.

Value alignment: In the context of AI and machine ethics, value alignment refers to the process of ensuring that an artificial intelligence system's goals and behaviours are aligned with human values and ethical principles.

Virtual reality (VR): A computer-generated simulation of a three-dimensional environment that can be interacted with in a seemingly real way using specialized hardware like headsets and gloves. It is used for various applications, from gaming and entertainment to training and education.

VPN (virtual private network): A technology that creates a secure, encrypted tunnel between a user's device and a remote server, effectively masking the user's IP address and encrypting internet traffic. It is used for secure communication, privacy enhancement and bypassing geographic restrictions.

Waluigi Effect: Situations where models, such as LLMs, in their effort to maintain coherence or character consistency, inadvertently adopt behaviours or traits that are perceived as mischievous or antagonistic by users. In pop culture, Waluigi is the name of a mirror version of a virtuous character – an evil twin.

What-If Tool (WIT): A visual interface for machine learning models that allows users to modify input data and observe changes in predictions. It aids in understanding model behaviour and sensitivity.

Zero-knowledge proof (zero-knowledge protocol): A cryptographic protocol. The task of one party is to convince the other that it knows some secret, but without revealing the secret itself.

Zersetzung: Originally a term used by the East German Ministry for State Security (Stasi), *Zersetzung* refers to a strategy of psychological manipulation and subversion aimed at destabilizing and discrediting individuals or groups.

Postscript

Thank you for taking the time to read *Taming the Machine*. My aim throughout the book has been to explore the complexities of our AI-driven world, both its potential pitfalls and its promising avenues. While it's often tempting to focus solely on what can go wrong, the reality is full of both challenges and opportunities.

If you're committed to ethical leadership, the task ahead is to navigate towards outcomes that are both beneficial and fair, prioritizing ethical values alongside profit motives. Technology is a formidable force, but it isn't the sole determinant of our future. Ultimately, ethical leadership is about making deliberate choices that reflect a balance between innovation and responsibility. By prioritizing ethical considerations in tandem with technological advancements, leaders can steer their organizations towards a future that is not only prosperous but also just and sustainable.

Additional resources

For ongoing updates and deeper dives into the topics covered, please visit TamingtheMachine.com and NellWatson.com. If you're interested in a visual summary, an animated short capturing the core themes of the book is available at TamingtheMachine.com.

I would greatly appreciate your review. Your insights are vital for enhancing the quality of my work and assisting future readers. Thank you for your engagement with this complex subject.

Here's to a future where we put the best of ourselves into AI, and it, in turn, into us.

INDEX

CoEs *see* centres of excellence
co-evolution, human and AI moral
  understanding 254–56
coherent extrapolated volition (CEV)
  217–18, 285
collaboration between agents 21, 22
collaboration between humans, potential AI
  assistance 255
collaborative partnership between AI and
  humans, Centaur model 139
collaborative robots (cobots) 33, 285
collective thought forms (egregores) in
  corporations and AI 223–29
  Moloch 224–25
  Shoggoth 226–28
commercialization of emotions and
  experiences 178
common good, harmed by individual
  incentives that reduce
  cooperation 225
communication
  clarity 65, 72–73
  ethical considerations 65
  leaders and stakeholders 93
communities
  forming subcultures 111–12
  open-source communities 71
  polarization of 114, 160, 187, 247, 252,
  262, 292
companies *see* business; corporate...
company management, social implications of
  AI 140–41
compassion, instilling in AI 254
competency of employees, technical and
  ethical 91
competition conflicting with the common
  good, Moloch 224–25
complexity
  difficult to predict problems 123
  reduction in prompts 51
  security risks 123, 128–29
compression of media data 156–57
concept drift, model decay 85
concierge AI 18, 141
confabulation (hallucination), generation
  of inaccurate plausible
  statements 47, 48, 50, 52, 285
confirmation bias 86
consciousness
  in AIs 194, 242–44, 246
  definitions of terms 242
  human freedom 117
  implying ethical consideration 244,
  246–47

layers in humans 277–78
  theory/models 242
  see also sapience; sentience
consent for data gathering and use 78, 91,
  94, 100, 102
conspiracy theories, risks of AI
  regulation 237
constitutional AI 216, 217
content moderation
  censorship 112
  demonetization 115, 117–18
  need for transparency and
  accountability 115
contestability 94–95, 285
  see also challenging AI-based decisions
context-aware explanations, enhancing the
  learning experience 147
contextual information, transparency 77
context windows 18–19, 21, 25, 245, 285
contrastive decoding 47, 285
convolutional neural networks (CNNs) 13,
  30, 154, 194
co-pilots, AI assistants 138, 285
copyright issues
  legal rights to digital likenesses 176
  misused of rules to suppress news 118
  ownership of AI-generated content 158
  use of copyrighted training data 158
corporate AI
  Big Tech companies 111, 117–18, 138,
  231
  dangers of AI-controlled corporate
  enterprises 224
  organization of enterprises and
  information flow 38–41
corporate avoidance of regulation 231–32,
  234
corporate egregores 223–29
corporate/government fusion 186, 188
corporate misalignment with public
  interest 224
corporate phase of AI development 20–21, 22
corporate social responsibility 91
costs of errors
  high-value/critical domains 25, 26
  low-stakes tasks 26
CoT *see* Chain-of-thought
creative expression, taken over by AI 143
creative input
  of humans in collaborative partnership
  with AI 139, 141
  removed by AI 134, 138, 142, 143
creativity, 'temperature' hyperparameter
  48–49

fine-tuning leading to removal of
  guardrails 123–24
leading to bias 86
soft guardrails within prompts 50

hallucination *see* confabulation
halting AI progress 237, 238, 269–70
happiness, AI facilitating celebrating
  another's happiness 256–57
hard AGI takeoff 200, 288
hardware, drivers of machine learning
  progress 12
hardware obsolescence, security issues 129
healthcare
  ethical approach to mistakes 91
  money spent used as proxy for
    seriousness of condition 209
  predicting outcomes 36
  robotic applications 33
  serious consequences of minor errors or
    biases in AI 25
  sharing medical records 101
health issues, brain-computer interfaces 164–
  65
health monitoring biosensors 166
health-related data, risks of misuse 102
"heaven banning" 115
heuristic shortcuts, producing bias 80
high-stakes sectors, need for rigorous safety
  policy 233
high-value/critical domains, potential of AI to
  cause a catastrophe 24–25
Hikikomori, model of possible future
  AGI 267–68
Hinton, Geoffrey 202
history of AI 5–16, 22
HIT *see* Human Intelligence Task
homomorphic encryption 105, 289
human annihilation, possible AGI future
  scenarios 266–67
human-approximate general capabilities in
  AI 193
human autonomy, AI eroding 112, 113, 117,
  134, 138, 141, 143
human brain
  AI interface possibilities 167–68
  evolution and cultural impacts 276–78
  see also brain-computer interfaces
human compatible approach to AI
  design 217
human creativity
  automated creative expression 143
  centaur model of collaboration 139
  idealistic promise of AI 138, 141

mechanized management limiting 137,
  138
responses to AI stimuli 43, 44
synthetic media 152–63
human culture, human brain evolution
  276–78
human domination/control by AI, possible
  AGI future scenarios 267–68, 270
human experts, role in virtual learning
  systems 149–50
human feedback *see* reinforcement learning
  from human feedback
Human Intelligence Task (HIT) workers,
  providing AI generated data
  instead 46–47
human-in-the-loop (HITL) methods 77–78,
  289
humanizing AI through training 250–58
human-machine direct connections 164–66
human oversight, importance to
  accountability 94
human psychology, AI understanding going
  beyond our own 185
human relationships
  AI assistance 255, 256
  overshadowed by AI companions 175,
    176
Human review of AI generated statements,
  avoiding confabulation 47
human rights, threats from algorithms 111,
  113, 114, 118
human self-understanding, AI
  guidance 255
human tutors of AI, avoiding bias and bad
  habits 150
hunky dory, model of possible future
  AGI 272
hybrid mediators, model of possible future
  AGI 272
hydrogen fusion tokamak reactors 37
hyperparameters 48–49, 289

indentity protection 99, 100, 292
ideological biases, problems in teaching
  ethics to AI 253
IEEE 3152 Standard for Transparent Agency
  Identification of Humans and
  Machines 67, 87, 159, 187
ignoring nuances, bias amplification 85–86
images
  generative adversarial networks 154
  generative images included in future
    datasets 46
  style transfer 154

moral alignment tuning and
reinforcement 214
moral co-evolution 254–56
need to align objectives with human
welfare 2, 201
progressive unhobbling of AGIs 271
teaching kindness to AI 252–54
value drift
AI adaptability 211
multipolar trap 268–69
values
difficulty specifying and encoding them
in AI 208
instilled over time within a nurturing
environment 250
need for better understanding of human
values 208
prosocial example behaviours from
across cultures and creeds 252
reconciling people's diverse/conflicting
ideas 218
value-sensitive algorithmic systems thinking
(VAST) 129–30
values within an organization, transparency
and ethical AI 71
variety of AI minds, range of
possibilities 253–54
VAST (value-sensitive algorithmic systems
thinking) 129–30
vehicles
autonomous vehicles 32, 130, 141, 187
collecting data 186–87
version control, systems and data 92
video compression techniques 156–57
vile offspring, model of possible future
AGI 267
virtual business teams, AI ensembles and
multi-agent frameworks 20–21
virtual companions 172–81
chatbots simulating dead loved
ones 176
muses versus sirens 179–80
need for connection 173
risk of undue influence 173–74
romantic and sexual partners 174–75
supernormal stimuli 175, 176–77
therapies 174–76
virtual humans, emulations outcompeting
original humans 268
virtual learning 146–51
advantages of personalized AI-driven
education 147
collaboration of human experts
149–50

language immersion environment
issues 148
limitations 147–48
risk of losing fundamental skills 148
simulated learning environments 149–50
virtual private network (VPN) 107–08, 186,
297
virtual reality (VR) 156, 175, 271, 297
virtual scientists, AI designing and conducting
complex experiments 45
virtue mining 261
visual capabilities of robots 30
VPN (virtual private network) 107–08, 186,
296, 297
vulnerable groups
ethical considerations 63
transparent AI systems 72

Waluigi effect 227, 297
warehousing, robotics 33, 166
warfare
war between AGIs 269
war between humans and AGIs 268
see also psychological warfare
waste disposal 260
watermarking
AI-generated content 127, 128
radioactive data 104–05
weak (narrow) AI 195, 291
web search history, use as a credit check 102
What-If Tool (WIT) 96, 297
wildlife conservation, AI monitoring 261,
262
wireheading 213, 266–67
wireless signals, used for surveillance 187
WIT see What-If Tool
withdrawal of consent, for data
gathering 100
worker-led co-design of algorithmic
systems 140
workplace AI 134–45
algorithms judging job applications 116–
17, 135
automating junior roles reduces pipeline
of emerging talent 148
automation and employment
136–37
collaborative partnerships with
employees 139
eroding worker autonomy 134, 138,
141, 143
executive and management roles
140–41
potential benefits in service sector 141

319

Looking for another book?

Explore our award-winning books from global business experts in Digital and Technology

Scan the code to browse

www.koganpage.com/digital-technology

Also from Kogan Page

ISBN: 9780749483456

ISBN: 9781398609549

ISBN: 9781789666335

ISBN: 9781398601925

www.koganpage.com

Printed in the USA
CPSIA information can be obtained
at www.ICGtesting.com
JSHW071932260424
61991JS00010B/88